MENNONITE FOODS & FOLKWAYS FROM SOUTH RUSSIA

VOLUME II

For Thelma

Norma Jost Voth

MENNONITE FOODS & FOLKWAYS FROM SOUTH RUSSIA

VOLUME II

Norma Jost Voth

Good Books

Intercourse, PA

This book is affectionately dedicated to
my husband, Alden,
and to my daughter, Susan, who gave the gift
of life, a kidney, to her brother, Tom.

Credits and Acknowledgments

Color photography on front and back cover by Mark Wiens. Color photographs taken at Kauffman Museum, North Newton, Kansas. All black and white photographs from the Peter Gerhard Rempel collection.

The following publishers have generously given permission to use material from copyrighted works. Pages 20–21, 52, 234, 252, from *Singing Mennonite, Low German Songs among the Mennonites* by Doreen Helen Klassen. Copyright 1988 by University of Manitoba Press, Winnipeg, Manitoba. Reprinted by permission of the publisher. Pages 9 and 22, from *Mennonite Heritage Village Brochure.* Used by permission of Mennonite Heritage Village (Canada) Inc. Pages 73–74, lyrics for the song *Faspa.* Used by permission of Ray Plett, Locusts and Wild Honey.

Scripture quotations on pages 56 and 180 from the Holy Bible, New International Version. Copyright 1973, 1978, 1984 by International Bible Society. All other Scripture quotations from the King James Version.

Please see Volume I Acknowledgments for the enumeration of all those to whom I owe much appreciation for their advice and help!

Design by Dawn J. Ranck
Cover Design by Cheryl A. Benner
Mennonite Foods and Folkways from South Russia, Volume II
© 1991 by Good Books, Intercourse, PA 17534
First published in 1991. New Paperback edition published in 1994.
International Standard Book Number: 1-56148-137-8
Library of Congress: 90-81731

Library of Congress Cataloging-in-Publication Data
(Revised for vol. 2)

Voth, Norma Jost.
    Mennonite foods & folkways from South Russia.
    Vol. 2 has title: Mennonite foods and folkways from South Russia.
    Includes bibliographical references and index.
    1. Cookery, Mennonite. 2. Cookery, Russian. 3. Mennonites — Soviet Union, Southern — Social life and customs. I. Title. II. Title: Mennonite foods and folkways from South Russia.
TX715.V82   1990   641.5947   90-81731

Table of Contents

6   Introduction

7   The Mennonite House
16   The Russian Mennonite Oven
33   *Plautdietsch* — Our Low German Language
38   Early Russian Mennonite Education
56   The Mennonite Church
62   The Festive Sabbath
77   Celebrations among Russian Mennonites
138   Russian Mennonite Wedding Customs
159   The Seasons
180   Wheat Harvest from the Steppes to the Plains
201   The Celebration of Butchering
212   Busy Days
231   Orchards and Gardens
244   Food Preservation
255   Russian Mennonite Menus
272   Handwritten Cookbooks

276   Notes
282   Readings and Sources
284   Index
288   About the Author

Introduction

Much has been written about the Mennonite sojourn in Russia. From scholarly works to colloquial stories of human experience most agree that especially for those people who stayed in Russia through the 1920s it was a particularly painful chapter in Mennonite history. Some Mennonites, feeling the winds of change, decided to leave as early as the 1870s (while other Mennonites were still emigrating from Prussia). They braved the hardships and challenges of pioneer life on the prairies of both western Canada and the United States. Those Mennonites who stayed in Russia found themselves in the thick of the Bolshevik Revolution during the 1920s. Because the battles between the Red and White armies raged over Mennonite farmsteads, many thousands more Mennonites eventually fled the lands of south Russia for Canada, the United States and Paraguay. Many of them were women and children whose husbands and fathers had been either killed or deported. In Volume II of *Mennonite Foods and Folkways from South Russia* are stories of life in Russia during both the "golden years" prior to the Revolution and the dark years following the Revolution, of life on the North American prairies and of life in the jungles of Paraguay.

Wherever they went, these people made a garden out of a wilderness with bone-hard work and ingenuity learned from their tradition. Whether in south Russia, the American prairies or the Paraguayan Chaco, they formed a culture all their own; they developed a distinguishable society. In so doing they strengthened their identity.

A distinctive way of living encircled these Mennonites, from housing styles to their own language to an educational system to the routine of their work week. Through it all ran the pleasure of eating — for necessity, of course, but also filling out all social occasions. Their food tradition flourished, and so, eventually, did they.

Often told from the woman's point of view, the stories in this collection offer an unusual window into Russian Mennonite life. So it is that Anna Reimer Dyck spent little time philosophizing about the political events which shaped the Revolution. Instead she remembered the good food and good times on a large Mennonite estate in the Kuban. Tina Harder Peters did not express opinions about the many problems faced by the Russian Mennonite church which led to various factions through the years. Instead she told a story about helping her mother build a Russian-style brick oven for baking in their new home in Manitoba. Tales of carving a life out of the jungle in South America say little about how it came to be that Mennonites were allowed to settle the area known as the Chaco. Instead they included one woman's account of converting giant ant hills into outdoor bake ovens and making thousands of mud bricks by hand.

These women, our mothers and grandmothers, were persons of great courage, stamina and faith. Even against overwhelming hardship, they determined to make life as normal and bearable as they could for their families. They continued to serve *Borscht, Zwieback, Varenikje* and *Mooss.* They had babies and did their utmost to protect them. They had funerals and picnics and weddings and watermelon feasts. They were survivors who passed their legacy on to us, their daughters and granddaughters. Let us not forget.

— *Norma Jost Voth*

The Mennonite House

Our house had a dirt floor. Hammered and wet and hammered again. We were very rich and very blessed when after a wonderful wheat harvest in 1915 we got a wooden floor. *Daut wea oba waut grootet.* [That was something very special.]
— *Helen Harder Peterson*

The Mennonite House

Great-Grandfather Peter Jost's adobe house and all the houses of the tiny Alexanderfeld village near Hillsboro, Kansas, had a unique style and plan. Quite unlike other wood frame or sod houses of the Kansas prairie of 1875, the history and background of this "Mennonite house" goes back to the Vistula Delta some three hundred years prior to the arrival of the 1874 immigrants in America.

When the first Dutch Anabaptist refugees escaped Holland's severe religious persecution, they found refuge in the free cities of Danzig and Elbing (West Prussia) in the 1530s.

Upon their arrival in the Delta, they found their Prussian neighbors settled in compact, closed village patterns, established by the Teutonic knights. They built house, barn and shed separately. The Mennonites brought a new architectural style to the entire Delta area.

Because the Mennonite land lay in very low areas, it was necessary to build with flood control in mind. To elevate the building site, dirt was hauled from considerable distances. Most homes were built along rivers or dikes. In the lower villages dirt embankments were erected around the houses to prevent spring flooding. To accommodate the small, elevated area and to save space, these Dutch farmers built their houses and barns under the same roof. Probably an old Frisian style of architecture, these buildings were called "row houses."[1]

When additional farmland became available, and they could enlarge their dwellings, they set the barn and shed at right angles (L-formation) or in a triangle or cross (*Kreuzhof*) shape so the farmyard was located inside the angle. The house was always built in one story with two entrances, one in front and one in back. There was a *Vorderhaus* and a *Hinterhaus* (fore-house and rear-house). A fireproof wall separated the barn from the house. A hall flanked the entire length of the barn with stalls to the right and left for cattle. The shed for storage and implements was next to the barn. Mennonite farmsteads were also easily identified by the tall trees surrounding the buildings and the immaculate gardens filled with flowers.[2] In Polish Prussia Mennonites lived on individual homesteads rather than settling in villages as they would later in Russia.

This house, barn and shed architectural style followed the Mennonites to Russia in 1789. In the Ukraine they settled in compact villages as a "protection against the world around them." This near isolation led to a "cultural Mennonitism" where people often thought of them as a racial or cultural group rather than a religious group.[3]

In Russia Johann Cornies (1789–1848), chairman of the Agricultural Association, introduced rigid rules for the layout of the villages, exact location of each building, building construction, planting of shade trees and orchards, location of the school and church and, even, maintenance of the village street.

Mennonites who joined the 1874 migration to North America brought the Prussian style house and Russian village pattern with them. Great-Grandfather Peter Jost's house had this identical plan. The Mennonite house continued to be built in Russia until World War II when all village life came to an end.

Room Layout Plan

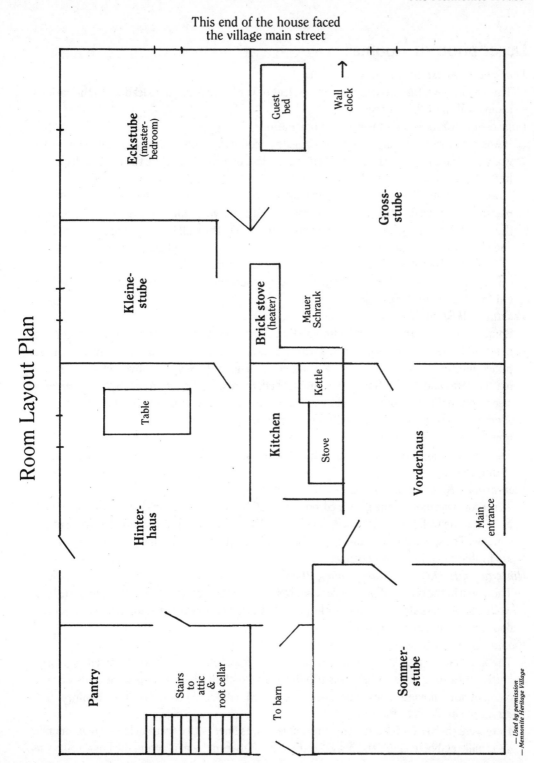

This end of the house faced
the village main street

Eckstube (master-bedroom)

Guest bed

Wall clock

Kleine-stube

Gross-stube

Brick stove (heater)

Mauer Schrauk

Table

Kettle

Kitchen

Stove

Hinter-haus

Vorderhaus

Main entrance

Pantry

Stairs to attic & root cellar

To barn

Sommer-stube

Description of Rooms

Vorderhaus, Fäastow - Front Room Entry

This small room, the entryway from the street or yard, had four doors leading to the various rooms and the village street.

Grossestube, Grootestow - Living Room or Parlor

It was here that the family entertained guests or company. Children were not allowed. There was a built-in cabinet with drawers below and glass doors on top. Here the mother displayed her china showpieces — perhaps wedding gifts of fancy cream pitchers, gilt-edged plates, flowered teapots. There was a guest bed (folded) with extra bedding. There was often a large, massive wardrobe for clothing, a small cradle for guests with babies. There were shelves with the family Bible, song books and a few other books. On the wall hung a large Kroeger clock and photos of the emperor and empress. There were upholstered chairs, a table in the middle.

In winter the room was gently warmed by the large glazed tile oven which extended to the ceiling. There was an *Ofenbank* (*Owebenkj*), a bench next to the tile stove, a good place for old folks to warm their backs.

Eckstube, Akjstow - The Corner Room

Sometimes called the winter bedroom, this room was also the master bedroom for the parents. There was a big wooden bed with a drawer (similar to a trundle bed) which could be pulled out for the night. It was filled with corn husks or barley straw over which a feather mattress was laid. In addition to the parents' bed, there were *Schlafbänke* (*Schlopbenkje*) or sleeping benches for younger children. There was a table with chairs in front of the bed. The room was used for daytime activities such as sewing and needlework.

Sommerstube, Sommastow - Summer Room

This was the boys' bedroom. It also had a small stove or oven and was used as a daytime sitting room.

Kleinestube, Kjleenestow - Little Room

This room was used as the girls' bedroom. Sometimes it had a *Himmelbett* (four poster bed) built into the wall with curtains. A small table, chair or a clothes chest stood in front of the window. The girls, and sometimes a Russian maid, slept on the sleeping benches. The family ate in this room in the wintertime.

Hinterhaus, Hinjahüs, Ätstow - Dining Room

This room in the center of the house served as the dining room. In summer the family ate here while the workers ate in the summer kitchen. It was the entryway to the kitchen, pantry, back door and a passage to the barn.

Küche, Kjäak - Kitchen

The kitchen was a small room which had a stove for cooking and baking as well as a large kettle for heating water. There was usually a table with benches. Between the halls was the chimney for smoking hams. The stove was heated with straw, wood or dried manure.

Speisekammer, Koma - Pantry

Here were shelves for food storage. In summer it was lined with dozens of large bowls of milk, sour milk, clabbered milk and heavy sour cream. Between the pantry and the boys' room was a passageway leading to the barn. A thick fire wall of brick separated the buildings. A door led to the barn from the hallway. Steps led to the basement.

Fenstre - Windows

All windows were shuttered. Closed in summer, they kept out the heat and in winter the cold. They offered protection from burglary as well.

Dachstube, Bowabän - Attic

The long upstairs room was used to store the grain sacks (wheat, oats, barley) and feed for the stock in winter. There were also smoked hams in barrels of ashes and sausages, as well as sacks of dried apples and cherries stored there. "It was an altogether interesting place up there, but no children were allowed to nose around in the loft," says Helen Siemens.

Stahl, Staul - Barn

In the Mennonite house plan the barn, much larger than the house, was always attached to the house, away from the street. One side was for horses, the other for the cows. The well was either in the barn or near the door. Mary Dirks Janzen says, "My memories would not be complete without mentioning our horses and cows, even our calves. These animals were almost as close to us as our family members. In the cold Ukrainian winter, all our animals were in our barn, which was next to the house. In fact, there was only an iron door between the house and barn."

Scheune, Schien - Barn Annex

From the barn one entered directly into a large shed where hay, chaff, wagons and machinery were stored. The threshing machine was in a separate storage room. Because churches were not large enough to accommodate large groups, a family wedding ceremony and reception might be held there. It was thoroughly cleaned out and decorated with flowers and garlands of greenery.

Hoff - The Yard

Every house was surrounded by large trees, an orchard and well-kept flower and vegetable gardens. The predominance of large tulip beds was evidence of the Dutch Mennonite background.

Before the Mennonite House

When the first settlers came from Prussia to Russia in 1789, they made the long trek in wagons drawn by horses. Some of the women and children walked alongside on foot. The early years in the Chortitza settlement were extremely difficult. Lumber was scarce and expensive. For a while these Mennonites lived in tent camps, then in two-room dwellings made of beaten clay.

Anna Rempel Dyck describes her own ancestors' later arrival in the Molotschna Colony (1804). "The first huts they built were called *Semlin* and looked like molehills. In the beginning there was poverty and struggle to make ends meet. But in time these mud huts were transformed into one beautiful village after another. It was a pleasure to see the ornate and proud white-limed peasant houses with their thatched or even tiled roofs, the polished and shining window panes, the clean-swept courtyards encircled by the proud shadows of trees."

The primitive *Semlin* were also built in 1874 on the plains of Kansas and Manitoba following the first Mennonite migration from Russia to America. In Manitoba it was especially urgent that shelter be found before winter set in. Once more they used native soil, sod and grass. Simple and unadorned, these houses kept out the cold, wind and rain until more substantial shelters could be built.

The Other House—The Estate Manse

During the "golden era" of Mennonite life in Russia, there were those who broke away from the confines of the small native villages. Ambitious and enterprising young men bought land elsewhere and established themselves independently. It was, perhaps, inevitable that the Mennonite virtues of diligence, thrift, hard work and good farming methods would pay off. Coupled with this came a period of expanded agricultural opportunities as well as a growing market for Russian wheat.

Some of these men became fabulously wealthy and established large estates. Pictures of that era show big houses with formal gardens. They became the "farm nobility" employing large staffs of household servants and farm workers. Before World War I there were 384 Mennonite estate owners owning an average of 283 acres each. One very wealthy landowner had a 50,000 acre estate.[4] All of this came to an end following World War I when the Russian Revolution turned the Mennonite world upside down. Estates were plundered and families were separated or sent to work camps in the far north. The "golden era" was over.

New Life on the Prairies

The early days of providing shelter in a new land were exceedingly difficult as these firsthand stories indicate.

Peter Barkman: Our first dwelling [in Kleefeld] consisted of a sod house dug two feet into the ground, eighteen feet wide and forty-eight feet long. The walls of the building were made of thin tree trunks, having the interstices between the trunks filled with clay. The roof was likewise made of thin logs covered with mud. Thirty feet of the building was used as a dwelling and the remaining eighteen feet as a barn for the livestock.

Maria Klassen: And so began our life as Canadians. Logs were hauled to make the frame for a grass hut *[Semlin]*. The knee-high grass was cut with scythes that we had brought from Russia. Enough grass was also cut to cover the sloping roof of the hut, which was our first home. Till then the open sky had been our only shelter where we slept, cooked and ate. The house was finished in time for winter.

Louise Kornelsen: We were very poor when we arrived on the barren prairie of Saskatchewan in the 1920s. At that time my mother was eight months pregnant but still helped to dig the foundation of our log house. I, her fifth child, was born in November.

Johan W. Dueck: After we had completed it to the extent that it was more or less habitable, we moved into one end of the house. Here we had made ourselves two rooms with boards. We had put the cattle into the other end. But, it seems that we had hardly believed that a Canadian winter could be so frightfully cold, as it was hardly possible to keep the two rooms warm enough with the cookstove.[5]

The story was the same in Kansas. In the villages of Gnadenau, Huffnungstal and Alexanderfeld, where our great-grandparents settled, the first dwellings were called *saraj* (Russian) or pronounced *Serrei* in Low German. Jacob Wiebe, pastor of the Gnadenau congregation, described them as extremely crude A-shaped huts, sides held up by poles thatched with reed grass. "An adobe chimney projected above the grass roof some twelve inches — a constant fire hazard. The one end contained a brick stove and quartered the family, the other end a few head of livestock."

Eventually they built more substantial dwellings in both Canada and the United States, although many of these were also plain and simple. In time and despite the difficulties, many of the settlers came to love the prairie wilderness with its vast unobstructed view, fleecy white clouds driven by the constant wind and splendidly colorful sunsets.

*   *   *

My husband's great-great grandparents, the Johannes Fasts and his great-grandparents, the Heinrich Flamings, arrived in Kansas in the fall of 1873. They spent the first winter at Marion Center, Kansas. Their first temporary home was a small wooden house which Fast described in a letter to his children in Russia who were to follow in the summer of 1874. Schoolteacher Fast wrote:

> You, dear son, asked about housing. The farm houses here are all built small. The house we are living in is one of the best ones. It is 12×18 feet. We and the Flamings have two rooms, one for each. You will have space with us in our room. The floor is roomy for sleeping 20 or more persons and we have already calculated that we each want to add a tent for eating and sleeping purposes. Regarding the kitchen, that will work out. You will not want to stay here long, but will want to go on to the land to work as soon as possible.

> We can get lumber for building in Florence [Kansas]. The construction here is very different from what we are used to, mostly of wood; and then the construction is not for eternity. Buildings are also made of stone and brick, but the latter I recall seeing in the cities. One also sees much made from stone.

> We thank God cordially for preparing a place of refuge for us; and one then forgets about the many things one has to do without.

An Invitation to a Canadian House Raising

Following is a letter translated from the German inviting neighbors to help Heinrich Harder rebuild his house. The letter of invitation was in the pattern and style of a wedding or funeral invitation. Such letters were passed from one family to the next. It was the sacred duty of the recipient to forward the letter immediately to the next named person on the list. According to J.G. Toews, "To do this might require a person to stop his own work forthwith and deliver the letter promptly, and if need be, as far as the next village."

Esteemed Friends!

In as much as God the Lord, in times past, said to Noah, "While the earth remaineth, seedtime and harvest, and cold and heat, and summer and winter, and day and night, shall not cease;" under which we may also understand what Solomon says; "To everything there is a season, a time to build and a time to plant," and we may add, a time to build up and a time to tear down, etc. and so we have arrived at the point where we want to rebuild the torn-down part of the house with the help of others, if it pleases God and we shall live, tomorrow the 26th day of May, and hence we invite the below-named friends with their spouses and families to our home for 12 o'clock noon on the above stated day, to assist us, with the help of God, to accomplish our project; and this to follow by a simple meal in recognition of the goodwill and love for us, for which we are at all times appreciative.

Your friends,
Heinrich Harders

Bergthal, the 25th of May, 1883
The friends will be pleased to deliver this letter, one to another, in the sequence of the names below.

— Peter Wiebe
— Boernhard Wiebe
— Aron Schultz[6]

The Mennonite House Today

The chapter is closing on the familiar Mennonite house-barn combination. Siegfried Rosenberg, chronicler of Vistula Delta history, indicates that prior to 1940, when he wrote his book, there were still Mennonite settlements (*Holländerdörfer*) identifiable in the Delta area.[7] In his 1989 book, *A Homeland for Strangers*, Peter J. Klassen also mentioned that some of the large Delta Mennonite houses still stand today. Today there are no Mennonite people living in Poland.

Little of these buildings, if anything, remains after the massive destruction in Russia. However, Dr. Helmut T. Huebert in his book, *Hierschau, an Example of Russian Mennonite Life,* includes a photo of the only remaining house-barn in the village of his grandparents.[8] A few other Mennonite houses still stand deteriorated and forlorn in appearance scattered in former village sites. Photos of several of these houses appear in Volume I.

Southern Manitoba has fine examples of Mennonite architecture. Some old-style houses are currently occupied, neatly lining old streets in small Mennonite villages.

Two museums — The Mennonite Village Museum in Steinbach, Manitoba, and the Pioneer Adobe House Museum in Hillsboro, Kansas — have preserved on their grounds examples of this distinctive Mennonite architectural style.

House Building In Paraguay

Mennonites from Russia found their way not only to the United States and Canada, but also to Paraguay. Although the government was friendly and welcomed newcomers, the unfriendly, inhospitable environment of the Chaco jungle brought difficulties which were almost insurmountable. Newcomers built with great difficulty. After World War II many of the Mennonites arriving in Paraguay were single women whose husbands had disappeared or were killed in Russia. Their stories have been recorded in numerous books.

In 1930 Anna Siemens and her family came to Paraguay from Russia. She related her story to Mariam Penner Schmidt, who with her husband, Dr. Herbert A. Schmidt, lived and worked in one of the Chaco colonies.

Mariam Penner Schmidt: The Siemens family came to Paraguay from Russia in 1930. They were given a tent in which the family lived in the jungle with tall grass all around. Snakes, scorpions, spiders — all manner of insects abounded near them.

For a month they slept on the dirt floor until they could make some beds out of jungle trees. Each one had a blanket from the ship on which they arrived. They also had a few blankets and clothes they had brought along. From the Mennonite Central Committee each had a cup and some silverware. They spent seven months in the tent.

Soon after arrival they started making bricks with a wooden form. Mud was mixed with lime and bitter grass. It was "kneaded" or worked with the feet in a small hole in which there was a little water. When it was all mixed, Mrs. Siemens put the mixture into this form where it was allowed to dry. "I made thousands of these bricks," she says, "15 mm. × 40 mm." They first made the walls of this brick and then pulled the tent over the top until they could saw logs or beams in the jungle to make the roof.

After the rafters were up, they gathered bitter grass, long strands of it which were dipped in mud and lime, and laid the lattice work over the rafters. That was their roof.

Marie Wiens: In the early years there was no money for wood or tile floors. The Mennonites made a mixture of sand and fresh cow dung which made a nice, smooth floor, quite practical. And no, it did not smell!

Frieda Siemens Kaethler: Who could forget sleeping on the grass under a tent? One night rain was pouring down as it does in the tropics. Father was a teacher in a faraway village, and mother was alone with us four girls. Soon water collected in our tent, which was standing in a low place.

Mother was trying to put our few belongings on some blocks as we children awoke crying. There was a blinding light and a deafening noise. Lightning had struck our tent. The carefully made adobes at the end of the tent fell over. Our parents thanked God that they fell to the outside so that no one was hurt.

I can still see my mother at the mud hole. Because Daddy was away teaching, she had to make bricks with us girls. In those days the adobe bricks were made with straw. The mass was not mixed electrically or by an animal-drawn mixer as later. No, we mixed it with our bare feet and legs. When the mass was mixed, Mother filled the large forms and carried them into the sun for drying. Mother was pregnant at the time.

The Russian Mennonite Oven

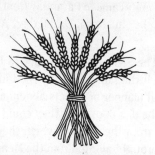

Dee weet nijch fäl;
Dee es blooss hinj'rem
Owe oppjewosse.

He doesn't know much;
He grew up behind the oven.
— *Old Low German Saying*

T'hüss es T'hüss,
Enn hinj'rem Owe
Es tweemol T'hüss.

Home is home and behind
the stove is twice at home.
— *Old Low German Saying*

The Mennonite Grassburner Oven

Skillets of potatoes browned on the front firehole. Pots of *Borscht* simmered gently on the back burner. At suppertime waffle batter bubbled in a cast-iron waffle iron that fit into a special opening. Women baked huge batches of *Zwieback* and seven loaves of *Bulkje* (white bread) or rye bread at one time. Big pans filled edge to edge with apple *Plauts* browned to perfection.

Such was the large, brick, grassburning oven which was built into every Mennonite house in the villages in Russia. Here the women did all their cooking. In a special built-in compartment was a chimney chamber where hams, bacon and sausages hung for several weeks after butchering day, smoking to the perfect flavor. The oven had a small warming compartment built into the *Kljeenestow* (little room) which kept food warm for a long time.

This central heating system served a three-fold purpose. It heated the entire house. It provided a place for cooking, baking and smoking. It was incredibly economical for it burned prairie or steppe grass. Built into the center of the house, the big oven was fired twice a day with bundles of grass or other fuels, depending on what was available.

In the living room the stove's surface was covered with smooth, glazed tiles, making a comfortable, cozy place to lean against. Sometimes there was a backless bench in front of the oven. Grandparents loved sitting on a nearby couch. Here the family spent long, winter evenings.

Most houses had a summer kitchen with a smaller stove which saved firing up the huge oven during the warmer months. All cooking during the summer was done in the summer kitchen.

So great were the advantages of this versatile, multi-purpose heating system with its extraordinarily cheap fuel, that immigrants from the Mennonite colonies in South Russia copied its design for their homes in the United States and Canada. These old grassburning ovens may be found in some of the original houses which still stand in the villages of southern Manitoba.

Bakehouse—Vistula Delta

When Mennonites lived in the Vistula Delta of West Prussia, most every farmstead had a bakehouse outdoors. This was a small, sheltered house with a built-in oven or just a simple roof built over the outdoor oven to provide protection from the rain. A kiln in this bakehouse was used for drying fruits, mainly plums. During plum season neighbors gathered, young and old alike, to help prepare the large quantities of fruit for the drying kiln.

The Russian *Pietsch*

It is completely spring now. The big oven isn't heated any more. The inner living rooms lie deserted.[1]
—*Arnold Dyck*

With the coming of warmer spring days, the large oven in the big house was no longer heated. This called for cooking and baking in another place. Mennonites found the Russian outdoor clay oven, called a *Pietsch,* very practical. It too burned straw, kept the house cool and did a superb job of baking. Sometimes the *Pietsch* stood under a shady tree a little distance from the summer kitchen. Sometimes it was built into one end of this small building so it could be kindled from the inside when it rained.

A woman had to be something of a genius or magician to gauge the oven temperature. She seemed to know by "feeling the heat," by holding her hand in it on a quick count to ten or by judging the color of the ashes. Sometimes she threw in a little new flour which blackened without catching fire. (Old flour did not work for this test.) Lubow Wolynetz, curator of the Ukrainian Museum, New York City, says her mother used to cool the outdoor *Pietsch* with a branch or switch wet with water. She knew by feel when the oven was ready. She also knew exactly how many bundles of fuel it took to heat the oven to the proper temperature.

Practice made perfect. The women knew their ovens, how to feed them, what fuel worked best. They became skilled, not always by choice, but out of necessity, baking day after day. Many perfected bread baking to a delicate art.

Stories of bread baked in the outdoor clay ovens are legendary. My own grandmother, Bertha Golbek Jost, baked in such an oven in the early years of her marriage to Martin Jost. They lived in the original Jost family adobe house which had an outdoor *Pietsch* in the Alexanderfeld village near Hillsboro, Kansas.

The older uncles in the Jost family insist there has never been bread so high and crusty, fragrant, soft and flavorful. It was their task as young boys to gather the kindling and build the fire. This required quantities of straw and frequent tending to get the temperature up to 500°F where the walls and floor were hot with a steady, evenly diffused heat. They waited patiently while the bread baked. Each time there would be a treat — a small loaf which Grandmother made from dough scraped together from the sides of the dough trough. This little loaf they called *Toopschropsel* (scraped together).

There is good reason why we cannot duplicate the fragrance and texture of this delicious bread. It was baked in a very different oven than we use today.

Alan Scott, who builds clay brick ovens professionally in Tomales, California, explains some of the mechanics of these outdoor ovens.

The three-way heat of these ovens radiates off the walls and penetrates everything inside. The heat is conducted rapidly and directly off the hearth straight into the loaves that sit on a tripod or directly on the brick floor. Heat is further convected by the movement of fragrant steam escaping from the cooking bread dough. All this adds up to a final loaf of unbelievable splendor. This all-pervasive heat bakes the largest loaves (four-pound whole grain, for example) in about half the time of a gas or electric oven.

These clay or brick ovens also guarantee the maximum spring from any loaf because the atmosphere in a tightly sealed oven is kept steamy from the very beginning. This keeps the crust pliable and the loaf expanding well into the bake. That fragrant steam coming directly out of the fermented dough gradually bakes itself into the crust and gives the bread its unique flavor and, finally, that all-important same steam also accounts for the sheen on the deep rich brown crusts so characteristic of brick oven-baked breads.

*   *   *

A Russian outdoor oven is used at the Mennonite Village Museum in Steinbach, Manitoba. Another historical farm complex, located near the Bethel College campus in North Newton, Kansas, also has a brick outdoor oven where women occasionally bake *Zwieback* for special events.

Pioneer Women Build Ovens

"Women built the outdoor ovens in the early pioneering days in Canada," says Tina Harder Peters. "The men helped only to provide and haul the materials." It was in the early 1920s, after her family had come from Russia, that Tina helped her mother build an outdoor oven. Because of this experience and knowledge, Tina was appointed to build an oven for the first Pioneer Day celebration at the Mennonite Village Museum in 1969. "There were no plans, no written instructions telling how to build an outdoor oven. Instead, I had to rely entirely on my memory of having helped my mother almost fifty years earlier."

With the help of her husband, Jake, and a neighbor, she set to work and built an oven "that stole the show that day. It proved to be the main attraction." This oven is now used regularly to bake fresh bread, *Zwieback* and *Schnetje*, which are served to museum guests. Jake and Tina Peters have been stalwart contributors to the preservation of Mennonite pioneering history in Canada. Following is the story of building this oven.

How to Build a Brick Oven *by Tina Harder Peters*

In the early days we seldom used new bricks for these ovens, but much preferred used bricks from the chimney of a house torn down or destroyed by fire. White bricks were more desirable than red bricks because they seemed to absorb and retain the heat much longer.

In our area mortar to hold the bricks together came from a special type of sandy loam or clay, which had been marked or identified by someone while digging ditches or basements. These particular spots became well-known sources and served everyone in the surrounding area.

The clay was then mixed with a binding agent—chaff and/or finely chopped flax straw to keep the clay from cracking during the drying process and after the oven was heated. Water was added to the clay, straw and chaff and thoroughly mixed to a smooth, creamy consistency.

We prepared our clay in a shallow, wooden trough, using a garden hoe to push the thick, dark mass back and forth until it was smooth. My grandmother always insisted that good clay mortar could only be produced when the mixture was thoroughly mixed with one's bare feet. I became convinced of this when I watched some women—recently returned to Canada from Paraguay—mixing mortar with their feet. They were proficient not only in mixing the clay, but also in making their own "adobe" bricks.

For our oven at the museum we built a wooden platform strong enough to bear the weight of the brick and clay about two feet above the ground. The bricks were mortared together on the platform, smooth side up and joints alternating. The sides and back of the oven were built in the same way, smooth side of the bricks to the inside.

We built the front end of the oven around a framed 18″ × 18″ metal door, especially made for us at the local machine shop. The opening was large enough to allow space for the *Dree Foot*—the three-legged iron foot on which the large homemade bread pans were set during the baking process.

When we had completed the walls, we tackled the top. We laid narrow strips of metal or scrap iron across the top, using only enough metal to support the bricks and mortar until they were thoroughly dry. Too much metal creates an uneven baking temperature. A short length of stovepipe with a damper was mortared in at the rear of the oven.

Two or three inches of clay around the outside of the oven were necessary to retain the heat the bricks had absorbed during the firing. It is this heat which bakes the bread—not the fire or the remaining glowing embers, as is sometimes mistakenly believed. The last clay covering was put on in separate layers, allowing each layer to dry in between.

To protect the oven from outside weather, it was common to cover the top and sides with burlap secured with a homemade flour and water paste. When all was thoroughly dry, the outside was whitewashed, making the bake oven an attractive as well as functional part of the household.

Heating or firing the oven was quite an art in itself. The type of fuel used, and expertise in firing came with personal experience. Flax straw, when available, seemed to be the most popular fuel. When fed into the fire in small amounts, it kept a steady, flaming fire burning and produced the proper baking temperature in quite a short time—twenty or thirty minutes.

To know when the baking temperature was just right, one kept watch until the blackened bricks turned white (the soot turned to ash, as it were). The oven was now ready to bake a huge pan of bread—six or more loaves—in about an hour and a half, depending on loaf size and kind of bread being baked.

Backe, Kuaktjes, backe (Baking, Cookies, Baking)

woa wie am be - gro - wen? Hin - ja onn - sen Back - o - wen. Daut

spoken

Näs-tje ess met Ausch be-sto-wen. Schoaw auf,[2] schoaw auf, schoaw auf.

Translation
Baking, cookies, baking.
The flour is in the sack,
The egg is in the basket,
The cuckoo has died.
Where will we look for him?
Behind our oaks.
Where will we bury him?
Behind our outdoor oven.
The nose has been powdered with ashes.

Spoken
Wipe/shove off, wipe off, wipe off.

The Paraguayan Oven

Russian ovens were built by Mennonite immigrants arriving in Paraguay after World War II. There in the Chaco, the new settlers chopped their way into the bush and built little shed-homes with leaves and straw. They devised ingenious ways to do their cooking and baking.

"Some of the first ovens were made from giant anthills," says Marie Wiens, a former Mennonite Central Committee worker. "They were huge and hard and probably reminded the people of the outdoor ovens in Russia." The women burned the ants from their nests, then hollowed out the shell and made an opening big enough for baking sheets to pass through. Sometimes they erected a shelter over this anthill turned oven.

Mariam Penner Schmidt recalls that Anna Siemens made her first oven by digging a hole in the ground, then building a fire and laying a flattened tin can across it, leaving room for air to circulate. "There she baked her coarse, *kafir* bread."

"While the Mennonite immigrants still lived together in large buildings," writes C.A. DeFehr in *Memories of My Life,* "there stood a whole row of stoves, built of sod in the shade of the trees." The women even understood how to build the top stove with mud, forming two round holes on which they placed cooking pots. When dried by the fire and burned, the sod became strong and durable. An eighty-year-old grandmother showed C.A. DeFehr an oven she had built by herself.

"My cousin and I built our own outdoor oven and also an oven for inside the house," recalls

Maria Guenter of her first days in Paraguay. "We were surrounded by bush, yet with hardly anything to burn. So we dried manioc trunks and used them for firewood."

These women, especially those who had lost their husbands and come with little children, possessed enormous courage. To begin anew under such difficult circumstances, after having known plenty and prosperity, required great poise and strength. No doubt they often quoted the Bible verse, "I can do all things through Him who strengthens me."

The *Spoaheat* (Hearth)

The big house ovens and cookstoves which proved so warm and cozy during the winter became unbearable for continuous cooking in summer. An alternative (to avoid heating the house) was a brick oven built into the outdoor summer kitchen or into the summer room in the big house. The *Spoaheat* was used throughout the hot months for family and company cooking and, especially, for the enormous meals cooked during the time of summer harvest and threshing.

The *Spoaheat* had two fireboxes, one on top for cooking, baking waffles or deep fat frying. The other in the oven below baked long (18" × 48") pans of bread and *Zwieback*. Sometimes this oven was large enough to accommodate four such pans at one time.

The *Spoaheat* used flax, hay and kindling as well as straw for heat. An eight-inch tripod or frame raised baking pans over the glowing embers.

In Low German *Spoa* means spare and *heat* (pronounced hate) means heat.

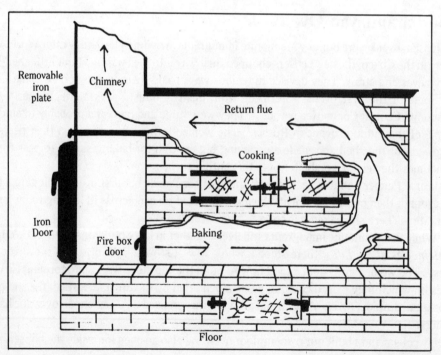

— Used by permission, Mennonite Heritage Village

The *Miagrope* (Copper Cauldron)

A *Miagrope* is a rendering kettle or cauldron. In Mennonite homes the *Miagrope* was bricked into a corner of the basement or the outdoor summer kitchen. With a small front door that closed off the firebox, the kettle could be heated quickly with only a minimum of fuel.

On washdays it was used to heat large quantities of water; often white clothes were boiled in it as well. Large batches of tallow and lye were cooked in it to make snowy-white homemade soap. At Easter, in Russia, the women used it as a large soup kettle, cooking great batches of *Salankje* (mutton soup) for dinner. Its generous size made it the perfect place to boil large hams or cook gallons of *Plümemooss* for family reunions or weddings.

On butchering day it was in use from sunrise to sunset. Water for scalding the hog was heated in it. Later it was used for rendering the lard, cooking cracklings and frying the spareribs. When the lard had been dipped into pans to cool, the *Miagrope* was filled again with water for cooking the liver sausage.

This large kettle was one of the most useful items in the Mennonite home.

The Old Wood Stove

During the late 1800s the wood burning cookstove came into use, replacing the large built-in Russian oven in the early settlers' homes in both the United States and Canada.

There was something cozy and comfortable about the big wood burning kitchen range in Grandmother's kitchen. As children we played in front of it, Grandmother cooked on it, mittens and socks dried on top and shivering children, who had slept in cold, unheated rooms, huddled together and dressed in front of it. It was the center of the house on cold mornings.

The wood burning range was black and stood on four legs. To the right was a firebox, to the left a hot water box. A shelf with insulated doors, called a warming closet, was at the rear of the range.

In winter the stove was "banked" every night — to keep a little warmth in the kitchen, but also so the cook would not have to start a fire from scratch the next morning. A roaring fire could be built quickly with paper and wood kindling. Sometimes kerosene was poured on the wood for a quick start.

Getting the fire going early was a necessity. Breakfast required boiling water, perking coffee, baking biscuits and cooking oatmeal. By the time children came downstairs, the kitchen, at least near the stove, was warm.

Managing the stove took a lot of skill. The amount and kind of wood used along with opening and closing the flue with the damper control were important considerations. The wise cook had many little ways of adjusting the heat; leaving the oven door slightly ajar for a few minutes or setting the stove lids off center to cut down the draft. She tested the heat by putting her hand briefly into the oven or by laying a piece of white paper on the rack. How fast the paper turned brown determined the degree of heat. Sometimes she put a spoonful of flour in a pie tin and set it in the oven. If the flour browned in sixty seconds, the heat was right for bread.

With a roaring fire, water boiled easily on the back middle burner of the stove while tea and sauces were kept warm on the front. Sad irons were kept at the back for heating beds at night. Sometimes cereal simmered overnight at the back. All the baking was done in the oven. Sometimes the oven was also used to warm cold feet.

One of the most useful features was the warming oven. It kept food warm without further cooking. Mothers kept leftovers warm for children coming home from school. It was a fine place to warm plates, raise bread, clabber milk and dry wet socks, mittens and caps.

Ashes, a byproduct of the wood fire, could be used to clean the hearth, absorb spilled grease and as a source of lye for homemade soap. They were also good for the garden mulch pile.

The stove also had many other uses. Says Bertha Harder, "Dad sometimes needed the stove for some of his business. Very early in spring the mother hogs started to have little pigs. Sometimes when a baby pig wasn't doing so well, or was cold, my dad would put them into a straw-lined basket (We used those baskets for everything!) and bring them into the house and set the basket beside the stove. All of a sudden those little pigs would start coming to life — getting all frisky and squealy. When I think about it, my mother sometimes had to be very patient and understanding."

In spring the warmth of the range often provided a good place for newly hatched chicks. A sick baby calf or newborn spring lamb might be allowed to stay behind the stove overnight. Sometimes such a calf was found roaming the kitchen in the morning.

My uncle Dan Jost remembered a sudden spring storm that caught them one day when they were returning home in their buggy. "When we got home, the storm had subsided. But we found the chicks. They had tried to find shelter, huddled together in piles. We quickly ran for baskets. We took about fifty that looked as though they had had it, fired up the kitchen stove, warmed them and lost only a few. When they came to, there were live chicks all over the kitchen."

Dr. Rhinehart Friesen tells the story of triplets being born to a Mennonite immigrant mother in a very humble house in southern Manitoba in the mid-1920s. The doctor had the three very tiny (incubator-size) babies wrapped in blankets and placed in the warming oven above the old kitchen stove. All three babies and their mother survived.

Cheap Fuel

When Mennonites came to the Molotschna in the Ukraine, there were no trees or shrubs, only tall grass covering the vast steppes. Steppe grass was fed to the horses and cattle and was used to cover settlers' huts when they first arrived. It also became a cheap source of fuel for their stoves.

Later, when they planted and grew wheat, wheat straw was used, along with corn and sunflower stalks. Straw and grass were both plentiful and cheap. Wheat was cut low so there would be ample straw.

During the early years in Kansas the pioneers used hay for burning, twisting it into little bundles. Every night a big pile of hay was brought to the door. Evenings were spent twisting hay into bundles for fuel. The tighter the twist, the longer it burned.

Still another source of fuel was the *Mesthüpe* (manure pile). "The top layer was used for fertilizer," says Mary Dirks Janzen, "and the bottom layer was kneaded and then smoothed out and cut into squares and dried and used as fuel. It was dried and stacked. Dung cakes were highly valued to burn in the cookstove, too, for they held the heat much better than straw which was the main source of heat in Russia."

John Block, who grew up in the early 1900s in Kansas, remembers having to pick up cobs from the pig pen as a boy. "We'd throw corn ears into the pen for the hogs. After they were chewed clean, we would get the cobs for the cookstove fuel."

Bertha Fast Harder says her mother liked to burn corncobs. "After the hogs had eaten the corn off, the cobs would lie on the cement floor and dry for a while. Then my mother would send us out with a bushel basket, and we would gather those cobs. When she really wanted to do good baking — she always liked her baked things crispy brown, like *Zwieback* — then my dad would say, '*Dee senn et!*' ['Those are the ones.'] She always claimed that corncobs made the best kind of heat — a kind of sharp, intense heat which she liked for her baked goods."

Later, during the era of the wood burning range, a woodpile was part of every household. Large pieces of wood had to be split with an ax into stove-sized pieces. The pieces were split not only for size, but also for drying. After the wood was stacked, the area around the block was covered with wood chips. Anyone going by the woodpile was expected to pick up chips and carry them indoors. Grandma frequently would stop on a hurried trip outdoors, make a sack by holding up the corners of her apron and fill it with chips. These chips were placed on the floor under the stove, not in the woodbox. Wood chips gave the fire an extra boost of sharp heat, just right for browning *Zwieback, Schnetje* and baking powder biscuits.

*B*AZAAR *ROGGEBROOT*

Anna Lohrenz, who lives at Bethel Place, a retirement center in Winnipeg, Manitoba, still bakes her special bread for fund-raising activities. Her bread is usually spoken for before the sale begins.

Mrs. Lohrenz says her family always ate rye bread with chicken noodle soup while the white bread accompanied a meal of *Borscht.*

2 Tbsp. active dry yeast	1 Tbsp. salt
½ cup lukewarm water	1 egg
1 tsp. sugar	9 cups white unbleached all-purpose
4 cups lukewarm water (part potato	or bread flour
water)	3 cups Canadian (or other) rye meal

Sprinkle yeast and sugar over ½ cup water and stir briskly. Allow to become foamy. In large mixing bowl combine yeast mixture, 4 cups water, salt and beaten egg.

Gradually add half the white flour. Add the rye flour and mix. Gradually add remaining white flour.

Turn dough out onto floured board and knead until smooth and elastic, about 8–10 minutes, or finish with dough hook, 5–7 minutes until gluten has developed.

Place in greased bowl, turning to grease top of dough. Cover with plastic wrap and set in warm place until doubled in bulk. Punch dough down. Divide into 5 pieces and form into loaves. Place in greased loaf pans.

Cover lightly with clean kitchen towel and set in warm place until doubled in size. Brush lightly with oil or butter.

Bake at 375°F. for 35 minutes or until bread is hollow sounding when thumped on bottom. Remove from pans and cool on racks. Makes 5 loaves.

—Anna Lohrenz

$\mathscr{W}$HOLE WHEAT BREAD

When whole wheat flour and white flour are combined as they are in this recipe, the resulting bread has more gluten. Because of the gluten in the white flour, the dough will rise more actively and the loaves will be airier and lighter and slice more easily than 100 percent whole grain wheat bread.

2 Tbsp. active dry yeast	1 Tbsp. salt
1 Tbsp. sugar	3 cups whole grain wheat flour
2 cups lukewarm water	3 cups white unbleached all-purpose
1 cup lukewarm potato water	or bread flour

In a mixing bowl combine 1 cup of the lukewarm water, sugar and yeast and stir briskly. When yeast is bubbly, add remaining liquid, salt and whole grain wheat flour. Let this mixture stand for about 45 minutes.

Now gradually add the white flour, ½ cup at a time. Turn out onto floured surface and knead until smooth and elastic, about 8–10 minutes. If using dough hook, knead 5–7 minutes.

Grease sides of bowl, turning to grease top of dough. Cover with plastic wrap and set in warm place until doubled in bulk. Punch dough down. Divide into two equal pieces, shape into balls, flatten slightly and place in greased bread pans.

Cover lightly and set in warm place until doubled in size. Bake at 375°F. for about 45 minutes or until bread is hollow sounding when thumped on bottom of crust. Cool on racks. Makes two loaves.

OATMEAL CRACKED WHEAT BREAD

Minnie Jost Krause: Mother baked almost every other day, at least three times a week, and generally six loaves at a time. She had a big mixing pan, aluminum with a lid. She'd make the starter in the evening, and the next morning she baked bread. She did all the kneading by hand. The loaves were great big. Of course with eight or ten at the table a loaf didn't go very far. Often we had milk soup and bread and butter in the evening.

3 cups lukewarm water	2 Tbsp. yeast
1 cup buttermilk	1 tsp. sugar
2 cups old-fashioned oatmeal	½ cup warm water
1 cup cracked wheat	5 Tbsp. shortening or vegetable oil
½ cup molasses	9 – 10 cups bread flour*
1 Tbsp. salt	

* ½ cup wheat germ may be added, if desired, in place of part of the flour.

Heat water and buttermilk and bring to boiling. Pour over oatmeal, cracked wheat, molasses and salt. Mix well and allow to cool. Sprinkle yeast over warm water with 1 tsp. sugar. Stir and allow to become bubbly. Combine oatmeal mixture, yeast and shortening.

Gradually add half the white flour and mix 5 minutes with electric mixer. Gradually add remaining flour.

Turn out onto floured board and knead until smooth and elastic (8 – 10 minutes) or finish kneading with bread hook. Place in greased bowl and cover with plastic wrap. Set in warm place and let rise until double in bulk. Punch down and let rise a second time. Punch down. Shape into six balls and form into loaves.

Place in greased bread pans. Cover with clean kitchen towel and let rise until doubled in size.

Bake at 375°F. 40 – 45 minutes or until bread is hollow sounding when thumped on the bottom. Cool on racks. Makes 6 loaves.

— Minnie Jost Krause

BULKJE

Sponge	Dough
1 cup lukewarm water	½ cup scalded milk cooled to
3 tsp. sugar	lukewarm
1 Tbsp. active dry yeast	3 Tbsp. shortening or margarine
Flour – unbleached all-purpose or	1 Tbsp. salt
bread	3 cups lukewarm potato water
	3 cups bread or unbleached all-purpose flour
	10 – 10½ cups additional bread flour

To make sponge sprinkle sugar and yeast over water in small bowl. Add enough flour and stir or mix until the dough becomes gummy and glossy. Cover bowl with plastic wrap and set in warm place until it is bubbly and has risen to double in bulk.

To make dough scald milk and add shortening and salt. Stir until dissolved. Cool to lukewarm. In mixing bowl combine milk and lukewarm potato water. Gradually add 3 cups flour and beat well.

Stir down sponge. Pour it into a small area of the dough. With a spoon stir down again.

Continue to add flour, ½ cup at a time, always stirring the dough mixture. You will need enough flour to make it firm but not dry. Continue kneading on a floured surface, 8 – 10 minutes until dough becomes smooth and glossy.

Place in greased bowl, turning to grease top of dough. Cover with plastic wrap and set in warm place to double in bulk. Punch down. Divide into 3 or 4 pieces of dough. Shape into balls and place on large baking sheet. (For round peasant loaves you may also use cake pans or casserole dishes.) Flatten top of balls slightly. Cover with clean kitchen towel and let rise until doubled in size.

Bake at 400°F. for 15 minutes. Reduce heat to 375°F. and continue baking for about 30 minutes. Bread is done if it has hollow sound when thumped on bottom of loaf. Makes 3 or 4 loaves.

—Bertha Fast Harder

Kneading bread is a relaxing, therapeutic exercise. You need not baby the bread dough; kneading is not a gentle art. You may punch the dough rhythmically, occasionally throwing the ball of dough down hard against the kneading surface. Slap it. Wham! Don't be gentle with it.

ℛAISIN BREAD
(*Rasienenstretsel*)

Striezel (High German) or *Stretsel* (Low German) is simply white bread made with fine white flour and raisins. It was common among Mennonites in West Prussia.

Luise Schroeder: In Danzig until World War II, *Striezel war immer da.* [Raisin bread was always there.] In our *Gebäck* [baking] we had *Butterstriezel,* which was white bread made with a lot of butter; *Milchstriezel,* which was white bread made with flour, milk and no butter (this took the place of *Zwieback*); and *Rosinenstriezel,* a white bread made with raisins. Sometimes this was made with buttermilk and it was not quite so sweet.

Katherina Jantzen Prieb: Stretsel was sometimes made from *Zwieback* dough during the big baking on Saturdays. Other times it was a white bread dough with raisins added. For special occasions eggs, more butter and sugar were added along with the raisins. *Stretsel* has been served at weddings. I remember my mother making it for Easter.

2 cups milk	3 eggs
½ cup margarine	Rind of 1 lemon, grated
½ cup sugar	1 tsp. cinnamon
1 tsp. salt	6 – 7½ cups unbleached all-purpose
2 Tbsp. active dry yeast	or bread flour
1 tsp. sugar	3 cups raisins
½ cup lukewarm water	

Over medium heat combine milk, margarine, sugar and salt and heat until very warm. Cool to lukewarm. Sprinkle yeast and sugar over lukewarm water and stir briskly. Allow to stand until bubbly.

In a large mixing bowl beat eggs. Add cooled milk and yeast mixtures, lemon rind and cinnamon. Gradually add half the flour and beat 5 minutes with electric mixer. Gradually add remaining flour and turn onto floured board. Knead until smooth and elastic, about 8 – 10 minutes. If using dough hook, knead 5 – 7 minutes. Add more flour if dough is sticky. Work in raisins and distribute evenly.

Place in greased bowl, turning to grease top of dough. Cover with plastic wrap and set in warm place until doubled in bulk. Punch dough down and divide dough into two or three balls. Shape loaves and place in greased 9″ cake or bread pans. Cover with kitchen towel and allow to rise until doubled in size.

Bake at 350°F. for about 45 minutes. Cool on racks. Cover with a soft towel if you wish a soft crust. Makes 2 or 3 loaves.

Kringel—Russian *Bubliki*

Called *bubliki* by the Russians and *Kjrinjel* (Low German) by the Mennonites, these are actually bagels. Boiled until puffy, then baked to a golden finish in the oven, they evoke nostalgic memories.

Johan W. Dueck: I was sometimes able to go along with Father to market [in Nikopol]. The streets were filled with street walkers and vendors who offered all sorts of articles for sale. For a pair of *kopeken* one could have a whole cluster of grapes and other fruit. If one then added a pair of Russian *Kringel* to the grapes, one had a glorious repast.

Margaret Klassen Sawatsky: Kjrinjel were sold by the dozen. They were about a finger-width thickness and were eaten almost like a pretzel. We kept them in a drawer.

Mary Dirks Janzen: They looked like bagels and were a little dry like pretzels. They were cooked in water and then baked. We bought them in a market. *Kjrinjel* are also cookies as well as bagels by name.

KJRINJEL/KRINGEL
(Russian *Bubliki*)

Kjrinjel or bagels, as the Mennonites remember them from the Russian markets, were donut-shaped dumplings poached, then baked. The tops were brown and shiny.

1½ cups lukewarm milk	1 tsp. sugar
⅓ cup butter or margarine	9 cups unbleached all-purpose or
2 Tbsp. active dry yeast	bread flour
1 tsp. sugar	2 quarts water
1 cup lukewarm water	½ tsp. salt
3 eggs	1 egg, beaten
2 tsp. salt	1 tsp. water

Combine milk and butter in saucepan over medium heat until butter melts. Cool to lukewarm. Sprinkle yeast and sugar over warm water and stir briskly. Combine milk and yeast mixtures in mixing bowl. Add eggs and beat thoroughly. Add salt and sugar.

Gradually add ½ of the flour and, if your mixer is sturdy enough, beat 5 minutes to develop the gluten in the flour. Gradually add enough remaining flour to make a very stiff dough.

Turn out onto floured board and knead until smooth and elastic, about 8–10 minutes, or finish kneading with a dough hook. Place dough in greased bowl, turning to grease top of dough. Cover with plastic wrap and set in warm place until doubled in bulk. Punch down. Methods for shaping *Kjrinjel* follow this recipe.

While the *Kjrinjel* rise, bring 2 quarts water and ½ tsp. salt to a boil. Preheat oven to 450°F. Drop *Kjrinjel* two or three at a time into gently boiling water and boil each side about 1–2 minutes. Remove from water with slotted spoon. Drain and arrange on greased baking sheet. Brush tops with 1 egg beaten with 1 tsp. water.

When baking sheet is filled, bake at 450°F. for 15–20 minutes or until tops are shiny. To test for doneness, break one *Kjrinjel* open.

Method #1

Cut off small pieces of dough about 4 ozs. each in size. Roll each piece into an 8-inch strip about ½ inch wide. Form each into a circle. Pinch ends together securely. Place on greased baking sheet. Cover and let rise 15–20 minutes.

Method #2

Divide dough into 3½–4 dozen pieces. Cover with towel. Shape each piece into a ball, then flatten to about 2½ inches in diameter. Flour your index finger and push a hole into the center. Twirl it around your finger to stretch the hole. Plump and evenly smooth the roll. Let rest for 20 minutes.

Method #3

Tester Phyllis Reimer suggests rolling out a rectangle of dough 8 inches long and ½ inch thick. Cut into ½-inch strips. Roll each strip with palms of hands to round edges. Wet the ends with water and pinch together. Place on greased baking sheet. Cover and let rise for 20 minutes.

Holländisches Brot

Danzig, during the era of early Mennonite settlement, was a bustling port city which ranked in prestige with London, Paris, Antwerp and Rome. It was an "open city." Dutch settlers coming to the Vistula Delta brought with them their own Dutch specialties, one of which was *"holländisches Brot"*(Dutch bread). In spite of being in competition with some of the bakers' guilds, Paul von Wachten (1577), a Dutchman, baked this bread which caught on quickly and became very popular with the resident Danzigers.

Langfuhr Brot

One of the specialties of Dutch and Mennonite bakers (1800s) in the Langfuhr area outside Danzig was a delicious white bread. An enthusiastic visitor to that area reported: "There is a first-rate white bread, *the Gonesse of Danzig.* A good French bread is baked here, which is also very nice, but it fades into the background in comparison with Langfuhr bread. It is so white and fine, so light and tender, that Parisians cannot bake better bread."

Franzoli, the Chortitza Bakery Bread

Gerhard Lohrenz: Franzoli was a kind of French bread sold in the market place. It was a good tasting white bread, sometimes baked at home as well.

Nick (N.J.) Kroeker: Another savory product of the bakery (in our Chortitza village) were the small loaves of white bread named *Franzoli*. They too were sold rapidly and so was the small brown rye bread. However, the biggest treats were the large white loaves of bread called *Boolka* to be served with Russian red *Borscht*. The crust of these loaves was brown and probably brushed with egg white to present an unforgettable treat.

Winter in the village of Rosenthal, Chortitza Colony.

A young Russian Mennonite woman in a formal parlor, 1912.

Plautdietsch—Our Low German Language

Plautdietsch by Jacob H. Janzen

Maunjch eena kaun kjeen Plautdietsch mea	Hardly anyone can speak Low German anymore
Onn schämt sikj nijch enmol.	And isn't even ashamed of it.
Em Jääjendeel; hee meent sikj sea	On the contrary, he thinks he's something
Met siene hüage School.	With his advanced education.
Rät Hüagdietsch, Englisch, Rusch . . . so fäl	He speaks High German, English, Russian; so much
Daut eenem dieslijch woat.	That one gets dizzy.
Weat es dee gaunsse Kjlätamäl	This whole business isn't even worth
Nijch eene Schinkjeschwoat.	A single bacon rind.
Au(l)s ekj noch kjleen wea,	When I was still young
Saut ekj oft aunt Mutta oppe Schoot;	I often sat on Mother's lap.
Enn Plautdietsch sä see — o soo oft,	How often in Low German, she said to me,
"Mien Jung, ekj sie die goot."	"My boy, I love you."
Waut Mutta too mie Plautdietsch säd,	What Mother said to me in Low German,
Daut klunk soo woam onn trü,	Sounded so warm and true,
Daut ekj daut niemols mea fejät,	That I shall never forget it,
Bott too dee latste Rü.[1]	Until I find my final rest.

The Story of Mennonite *Plautdietsch*

Low German was the language spoken in my father's boyhood home in Kansas. When the older Jost children entered West School — the white, frame, one-room rural school near their farm in the early 1900s — they spoke only *Plautdietsch*. Lessons were usually recited to the teacher in accented English, which many children learned after starting school. Some of the teachers forbad anyone to speak Low German in school. That was the rule. Whenever possible, the children ignored the warning and slipped back into the comfortable, familiar Low German when playing at recess or when whispering behind the teacher's back while she was busy at the blackboard.

One of the West School teachers, Sarah Goertz, tried to squelch the offenders and levied a penalty. "She had a Low German card," remembers one of my uncles, "which was passed around. The last one caught speaking *Plautdietsch* toward the end of the last recess was stuck with the card and the penalty of staying after school. You can imagine what a rumpus that caused."

Like my grandparents most other Russian Mennonites who came from the steppes of the Ukraine to the plains of Kansas in 1874 spoke *Plautdietsch*. This was not a dialect of High German, but of Low German which is a separate language. To discover why Russian Mennonites speak it, we must go back to the origin of the Mennonite church in The Netherlands.

This church began in the provinces of West Friesland, Groningen and East Friesland.[2] The entire northern fringe of Holland, northwest Germany from Bruegge to the Eider and as far as Jutland was the larger area from which the Mennonites who migrated to Prussia came.

The first Mennonites to arrive in West Prussia were mostly Flemish tradesmen, merchants and sailors who settled in the Baltic city of Danzig, because their work had previously brought them in contact with that city. They were from The Netherlands and other Low German areas.

The next group to arrive were farmers of Frisian stock who settled in the Delta (Grosses Werder) at the mouth of the Vistula River. It was they who drained swamps and turned the marshy lowlands into arable land. They first settled on large estates, but rapidly built homes and villages for themselves.

These Mennonites from The Netherlands and other Low German-speaking areas brought with them to Prussia a dialect of the Lower Saxon branch of Low German or "Low Saxon *Plattdeutsch*, spoken in Ostfriesland" (East Friestland) from which the majority of settlers came.[3] According to Reuben Epp, "The original Low German of the Netherlandic Mennonites of Groningen and East Friesland is still spoken there by Mennonites and descendents of Mennonites who did not make that trek to West Prussia or who were among those who returned."[4] The worship services — sermons, Scripture, singing — were in Dutch.

Low German is not a dialect of High German, as some may think, but is a language with several dialects, *Plautdietsch* being one of them. The Low German language does not exist in a standardized form, but in numerous dialects.[5] Several of these dialects are represented in quotations and sayings in this book.

The History of *Plautdietsch*

To better understand our Mennonite *Plautdietsch,* it is helpful to take a brief look at the history of the language. The historical development of Low German can be divided into three periods: (1) Old Low German or Old Saxon (a period before the Anglo Saxon invasion of the British Isles until 1050 A.D.). "Old Low German appears to have developed among the Angles, Jutes and Saxons in the northern part of central Europe, the Saxons having been centered in the area currently known as Holstein from whence they spread southward and westward on the continent as far as Normandy, and from whence they eventually crossed the English Channel to the British Isles."[6] This accounts for the kinship between Low German and English. Unfortunately, there are few remnants of the literature of this period.

(2) Middle Low German (early 1200s until the decline of the Hanseatic League, 16th-17th centuries). During this time Low German flourished as the language of commerce and "was spoken in the highest circles from Bruegge to Memel and from Bergen to Novgorod."[7] It was the language of administration, of business, recorded history and religious devotion. When the Hanseatic League disappeared in the 17th century, Low German lost its significance and was dropped as a written language. It was replaced by the High German used by pastors and teachers, trained in the south, who filled positions in the north. High German gradually became the written language of the north as well as the south.

Low German Mennonites will find it interesting that Menno Simons wrote in several local dialects after his departure from West Friesland in 1536.[8] According to the Dutch Mennonites, his writings were influenced by languages "east of Holland." In about 1554 he began writing in the local Schleswig-Holstein dialect which he used until his death in 1561.[9]

(3) Eventually Low German went into a period of decline. However, it continued as the spoken language of the common people. Many centuries later people began writing in Low German again. The new Low German period is considered to be the era from the 1850s to the present time. In the twentieth century there has been a resurgence of literature in Low German dialects.

Plautdietsch Migrates from West Prussia to the Americas

When the Dutch Mennonites arrived in the Vistula Delta of West Prussia, the area was under Polish domination and the population spoke a dialect of Low German called West Prussian *Plattdeutsch.* Siegfried Rosenberg called it *Werder Platt.*[10] This language was somewhat different from the Nether-Saxon *Platt* of Groningen and East Friesland, but similar enough that the new Dutch arrivals could easily understand the local people. While High German was the language of business and commerce, West Prussian *Platt* was the language of the Delta home.

Mennonites gradually assimilated West Prussian *Platt.* However, some of their own Netherlandic Low German (Low Saxon) words (and words from other dialects) were introduced into this language.[11] Or, as Henry D. Dyck says, "Traces of Saxon remained in their speech."[12] This new mixture became the language of the Mennonite home, what we now call *Plautdietsch.*

In church these Mennonites had always used Dutch. They clung to it as the formal language of the elders' sermons and the written word until the middle of the 18th century. For many people the switch to High German for church services was a difficult and painful process.

According to Dr. Walter Mitzka the earliest attempt to introduce High German into a Prussian Mennonite church was made in 1757 when a teacher named Buehler of the Grosses Werder began to preach in High German. The congregation refused to go along with this. In 1762 a similar attempt was made at the Danzig Mennonite church. In 1767 a guest preacher finally gave the first German sermon in that church. The first songbook in High German appeared in Koenigsberg in 1767. Mitzka states that "Dutch was used alongside High German among the Mennonites until 1800." According to Siegfried Rosenberg, "In old records and Bibles you find notations in both languages.[13]

When the first group of Mennonites, mainly from the Danzig area, left West Prussia and settled the Chortitza Colony in 1789, they brought with them three languages — High German, Dutch and *Plautdietsch*.

In the fall of 1803 a second and larger wave of Mennonite immigrants arrived in Russia and wintered in the Chortitza settlement. These were farmers from the Marienberg-Elbing area, wealthier than their Chortitza brethren had been. In the spring of 1804 they settled along the Molotschnaya River and founded the Molotschna Colony. More followed. These settlers brought with them the Low German of the Marienberg-Elbing region, "a sub-dialect with variations," which was different from that spoken by the Chortitza or Old Colony Mennonites.[14] There were even variations in the Molotschna dialect because of the distance between Marienberg and Elbing. Henry D. Dyck says the explanation for the Chortitza-Molotschna difference is to be found in the fact that "toward the end of the eighteenth century a tendency toward an *Allgemeinsprache* amongst the wealthier population of the Vistula lowland became noticeable. The Molotschna settlers, leaving for Russia after 1800, and coming from a higher social level, showed this influence in their Low German."[15]

Our Mennonite *Plautdietsch* is a language rich in color and expression. "It is a robust language without adornment, handed down by our Werder forefathers," comments Rosenberg of the Werder *Platt*. It is an everyday language used in the family, the farm, the kitchen and the village.

It was the language of my grandparents' home, but interestingly was left behind on Sunday mornings when they went to church. My Uncle John Toevs spoke to his mother in Low German, but when he was away at school, she wrote to him in High German. Grandfather Toevs read from the Bible and prayed in High German.

There is little doubt that Low German is at the heart of our experience and culture in a way High German never was and English never can be. "High German was a language picked up along the way, made their own; as a people they knew little of Germany's history for they had never been part of it," comments Victor Carl Friesen.[16] Arnold Dyck referred to Low German "as the soul and sinew of our way of life, as the very essence of Mennonite identity."[17] Bertha Fast Harder recently commented, after visiting with Mennonite *Umsiedler* (Mennonites from Russia) who live in Western Germany, "It is amazing, this common bond which we have with Mennonites of different countries. Through Low German we can still feel a kinship with each other."

While English has become the primary language of most North American Russian Mennonites, *Plautdietsch* remains strong in some parts of Canada and is even used as the language of business and of the home. We heard it spoken on a public bus and in a department store in Winnipeg. In Steinbach, Manitoba, it was spoken among customers in a restaurant as well as in the bank. While driving one night along the Trans Canada Highway, to our surprise and amazement, we heard a Low German sermon on the radio. Among some younger Canadian Mennonites there is renewed appreciation for Low German. Several Winnipeg groups perform original music and comedy in Low German, playing to capacity audiences in the United States and Canada. There is a nostalgic hunger for such entertainment among those of us who understand the language, but as many people say, "Our grandchildren understand very little."

For many years Mennonite *Plautdietsch* was without formal grammar, syntax and spelling. Siegfried Rosenberg, in attempting to write down expressions and stories in Werder *Platt,* found it extremely difficult because of the many differences and colorful variations in each of the sub-dialects within the Vistula Delta.

In Winnipeg, Manitoba, a committee of linguistic specialists under the direction of Al Reimer of the University of Winnipeg, devised a rationalized orthography for *Plautdietsch* in 1982. The first formal system to receive a degree of acceptance is outlined in Reimer's book, *A Sackful of Plautdietsch.* Herman Rempel from Morden, Manitoba, and Jack Thiessen from Winnipeg have each compiled Low German dictionaries. The Rempel book, *Kjenn Jie Noch Plautdietsch?,* is the basis for spelling of Low German words in *Mennonite Foods and Folkways from South Russia.*

"Since the middle of the nineteenth century, Low German literature in Europe has resurged in an atmosphere of increasing tolerance and greater appreciation of its worth. The *Institut fuer Niederdeutsche Sprache* in Bremen annually lists new publications in or about Low German which number several hundred annually," says Reuben Epp.[18] Four northern German universities now have chairs for Low German studies. Many north German cities have Low German theater groups and radio broadcasts. A 1984 survey in northern West Germany found that some 35 percent of the population spoke good to very good Low German. But is there anyone there who still speaks the Mennonite *Platt?* "There is a small group of about 100 people living in the Danzig Bay area (now Gdansk) who speak a *Plattdeutsch* identical to that which the Old Colony Mennonites spoke in Russia," says Henry D. Dyck.[19]

While Mennonite *Plautdietsch* is an endangered language, especially in the United States, the *Mennonite Mirror,* March 1988, estimates that there are 80,000 Mennonites worldwide who still speak *Plautdietsch.*[20] It is interesting to note that a group of Mennonites from Russia, visiting Kansas in 1989, found it easy to communicate with their American hosts in *Plautdietsch.*

Let this now be a call to those of us who still love and appreciate *Plautdietsch.* Let us fan the embers and rekindle the flame of enthusiasm for this language of our heritage. Let us be willing to learn to read, speak and write it. Let us set aside a little time and patience to teach it to our children and grandchildren.

Early Russian Mennonite Education

Low German ABC Rhyme

Obraum,	Abraham,
Beant,	Bernhard,
Kjnals onn Derkj,	Cornelius and Dietrich,
Eefkje onn Fraunz,	Eva and Franz,
Jeat onn Hauns,	George and Hans (John),
Ietje onn Klos,	Ida (or Edith) and Klaus,
Leenkje onn Mitschkje,	Lena (Helen), Marie,
Neetje, Oomkje Peeta	Neeta (Aganetha), Uncle
Qwiarinj,	Peter Quiring,
Reimasch Saunkje	Reimer's Susan,
Teewse Ultritj,	Toews' Ulrich,
Wrucke wull'a nijch.	Turnips he didn't want,
Aulsoo bleef's hungrijch.	So he remained hungry.

The Village School in Russia

When Mennonites first arrived in Russia and settled the Chortitza Colony, the village or *Dorf Schule* filled simple, basic needs — learning to read, write, and live in the Mennonite tradition, to speak Low German, but also to adjust to the High German, and what was most important — to get the rudiments of their forefathers' faith.[1]

—N.J. Kroeker

Each village in the Mennonite colonies in Russia had its own schoolhouse, centrally located, which provided seven years of schooling for all the children of the village. These Mennonites believed it was the duty of parents to provide for the elementary education of their children, as they had done in the Vistula Delta. When they decided to move to Russia, they made sure that the Russian government would allow them to educate their own children.

The first schools in the Chortitza were held in private homes in the teacher's *Grootestow* (living room). There was little to make learning appealing to children. The teacher might be a farmer too old for farm work, one who could find time to "teach."

"Early schools were austere places where pupils were put at the mercy of the teacher," comments N.J. Kroeker. Classrooms were sparse and primitive.

Two years were spent memorizing passages from the Bible or a hymn book, followed by an introduction to a German primer. Arithmetic lessons and the alphabet were learned by rote and chanted in unison, repeating after the teacher. Eventually, catechism lessons were added. Almost all lessons were committed to memory.

Young children, who did nothing except observe for the first half of the year, exhibited much patience, sitting through long periods of recitations with only occasional breaks when they might be allowed to join in singing or reciting.

In the early years schools were under the jurisdiction of the church. In 1843, however, the entire school system of the Molotschna Colony was revamped and reorganized under the leadership of Johann Cornies, head of the Agricultural Association. Cornies required teacher candidates to pass examinations. He established rules and regulations for teaching subject matter and for disciplining pupils. He introduced a "monitor system" using uniform textbooks and required compulsory pupil attendance. He established teacher training and vocational schools.

Basic instruction in reading, writing, arithmetic and religion were given in German with a continuing heavy emphasis on memory work. Some progressive teachers introduced Russian as a second language as early as the 1830s. Cornies now prescribed the teaching of Russian to all pupils since that was the national language.

The plain early village schools were replaced by attractive buildings of good design and solid construction. Each building had one or two classrooms which were spacious and bright. Living quarters for the teacher's family were usually provided in the same building. Frequently, community functions and even church services took place in the largest classroom.

The school term lasted from six to eight months. Summer was the time for farm work.

This system lasted approximately forty years (1840–1880) until all school administration came directly under the supervision of the Russian government. Only German, Bible and music remained under local authority. This Russification program was the reason many Mennonites immigrated to North America in 1874.

Translation

Let Us Sing With Heart and Soul

Lord, let your kindness and your trust
Be renewed in us each day.
Oh Lord, my God, do not abandon me
When I face this misery and death.
Let me see your wondrous glory,
Your wonders and your loving grace
For now and all eternity.

—From a *Choralbuch* printed in Leipzig in 1865, used in Russian Mennonite village schools and brought to North America by a Mennonite immigrant.

—English translation by Herman Rempel.

Number Recitations

Among the many Low German nursery rhymes are several which have to do with learning numbers. Nursery rhymes were probably the first exposure Mennonite children had to folklore. No doubt some of these rhymes were used playfully while counting fingers and toes.

Old Vistula Delta Counting Game
(In High German)

1, 2 *du bist frei;*
3, 4 *eine Flasche Bier;*
5, 6 *alte Hex;*
7, 8 *gute Nacht;*
9,10 *schlafen gehn;*
11,12 *Gott helf;*
13,14 *Ich muss sitzen;*
15,16 *Ich muss hexen;*
17,18 *Ich muss waschen;*
19,20 *Ich muss reisen bis Danzig.*

1, 2 you are free,
3, 4 a bottle of beer,
5, 6 an old witch,
7, 8 good night,
9,10 go to bed,
11,12 God helps,
13,14 I must sit,
15,16 I must practice magic,
17,18 I must wash,
19,20 I must travel to Danzig.

Another Old Counting Game in Werder *Platt*

Oah, wie leewe Gaenskjes,
  wi lieden groote Noot;
Wi weeren uonser twelwkjes,
  on elwen send all dood;

Fief soen gefraden,
  sess soend gebroaden,
Oah, oeck oarme eene,
  oeck schwemm hier ganz aleene!

A Mennonite *Plautdietsch* Translation

O wie leewe Janskjes,
  wie liede groote Noot;
Wie ware onsa twalw,
  onn alw seen nü aul doot.

Fiew senn (opp) jefräte,
  sass senn jebrode,
O, ekj oama,
  ekj schwam hia gaunss auleen!

An English Translation

Oh we dear little goslings,
  we suffer such great need;
We were twelve,
  but eleven now are dead;

Five were eaten,
  six were fried;
Oh, poor little me—
  I swim here all alone.

Schönschreiben und Frakturmalen, A Specialty of the Village Schools

The typical village school day opened with morning hymns and prayer. Then came solid study—reading, writing, arithmetic, Bible memory work, spelling and, in later years, the learning of the Russian language along with German.

In addition to the basics, however, Mennonite children learned the fine art of *Schönschreiben* and *Frakturmalen.* These were compositions written in beautiful, near-perfect script and embellished with colorful flourishings and drawings of flowers, angels, animals and geometric designs. In some instances the children produced their own arithmetic texts (some 200–400 handwritten pages), geography texts and grammar books, all with colorful illustrations.

Every Christmas children prepared beautifully written and hand-decorated Christmas poems and essays which they presented to their parents on Christmas morning. These were written with a quill pen on rag paper using ink made from lamp-black and delicate colors from natural sources such as grape skins, walnuts and other vegetable materials.

Unfortunately, these arts rapidly deteriorated in quality in the village schools after 1820. Mennonites coming to America brought a remnant of this art with them, but it was no longer practiced in the pioneer village schools by the year 1900. A few hand-sewn composition books brought from Russia are reminders of this artistic era. These have been recorded and photographed in the book, *Frakturmalen und Schönschreiben* by Ethel Ewert Abrahams.

Higher Schooling in Russia

In 1920 there were approximately 450 elementary schools with about 16,000 pupils in the Mennonite colonies in Russia. Elementary schools offered a seven-year course. Some of these schools had as many as sixty students with only one teacher. However, most schools with fifty or more pupils had two teachers.

Following elementary school many of the boys and a few girls attended one of the twenty-five *Zentralschulen.* These four-year schools were comparable to the Russian "higher elementary schools." Nineteen of these institutions were for boys, four were for girls and two were coeducational.

Among the Mennonite colonies there were several other educational options. An eight-year girls' *Gymnasium* offered equal exposure to both the Russian and German language, teaching most subjects in both languages. A school of commerce also offered French and English. There were two business schools. There were also two three-year teacher training schools. The most advanced Mennonite school was an eight-year business school for boys located at Halbstadt. Graduates from either the teacher training or business schools could be admitted to the state universities.[2]

Memories from a Chortitza Village School 1840–1848

Kornelius Hildebrand: I carried my catechism book with me to school. My father being a church elder had much paper work, so that it was easy for me to get extra sheets from him. For writing pens we used goose feathers. One day I got a feather from an eagle about 21 inches long and I was very proud when I guided it across the paper except the teacher cut it off.

We began with a morning hymn, then prayed. After that there was reading, writing, and arithmetic. We practiced opening the song book to see who was quickest when the teacher called a number. We became very efficient. With a new teacher, Jacob Epp, we were given some practice in spelling. But we also learned the Russian language. This teacher gave me opportunity to draw pictures which filled me with enthusiasm. My father bought me a paint box and this was the only one in the whole school. Generally there were few reprimands. I will never forget how this teacher prayed.[3]

*   *   *

During the years when Kornelius Hildebrand was in school the Bible was used as a reader. This continued up until the 1870s. Classes were divided into the *Fibler* (lower) who used the primer, the *Testamentler* (middle) who studied the New Testament and the catechism, and the *Bibler* (upper) who used the Bible.

The *Dorf Schule* was the largest building in the village, with one classroom where boys and girls sat separately on long benches. It was not difficult to see who the best scholars were for they were seated according to scholastic achievement. All classes were taught in High German. A pupil who did well was promoted to a higher rank. There was no question about order and discipline. They were taken for granted.

"When children address the teacher, they rise, stand erect, and answer the question. When a question is posed to the whole class, those who think they know the answers raise their hands, elbows remaining on their desks, fingers pointing toward the ceiling. The straighter the finger, the surer he (the pupil) is of his answer," wrote Arnold Dyck. Good parents gave the teacher solid backing. Children could expect double punishment if word of bad behavior got to their parents.

School Days in the Molotschna

Anna Rempel Dyck grew up in the village of Gnadenfeld in the Molotschna. In 1934 she wrote of her childhood days in Russia, including some memories of the village school.

Anna Rempel Dyck: We entered the famous Alliance School, much feared because of its strictness and the severity of Teacher Franz. Since my power of comprehension was better than that of most of my fellow students, I did not have to suffer so much under his strictness and severity. It often was terrible when Teacher Franz was flying into his violent temper, forgetting the bad influence it had on the innocent children. There was no permission to complain at home. However, the students learned much and he was able to impart knowledge even if with the help of the rod.

*   *   *

Mary Dirks Janzen grew up in the same Molotschna village, some forty-five years later. In a journal written for her grandchildren she shares memories of her school days in Gnadenfeld.

Mary Dirks Janzen: September first grade school opened. At home our family spoke Low German. To the hired boys and girls we spoke in Russian; in school we learned High German. We learned Bible stories in High German. We did not learn arithmetic in German, no, never. It was learned in Russian. We learned grammar in both languages. Sang songs in both languages.

Our teacher, Abraham Braun, had also been my father's teacher years before. He possessed much self-assurance, was an excellent teacher, song director and Bible teacher. Blessed were the children who understood the lesson and completed their assignments, but woe to those who either were unable to comprehend the lesson, were slow to grasp or forgot to have the lesson ready, or worst of all, had badly infected eyes and were unable to read properly. In any of these cases Mr. Braun would feel the need for punishment. When Mr. Braun asked a question we did not know, he became stern, so that we shook in our boots.

Our school had two large classrooms, with first through third grades in one room and fourth through seventh in the other. As we entered the first room, which held the lower grades, we would pass the teacher's desk and chair. Pupils' desks would reach from one side of the classroom to the other, leaving an aisle at each side of the room. Each of us owned a slate. If we were in a hurry we would use our hands to wipe it.

At recess we played "Drop the Handkerchief," "Hide and Seek," "Last Couple Out" and "Jacob, Where are You?" In the fall we would build houses from fallen leaves and form walls for the rooms in our house. In winter we skated on the ice patch in hand-knitted wool stockings and socks and warm dresses with an apron over the dress. Sometimes I went home at recess to embroider.

After seventh grade the students were accepted in the two high schools, which consisted of four grades. Most boys went on, but only a limited number of girls went further than the seventh grade. The more progressive went still further on, but this number was small. Education was controlled from the county. A uniformed, slick, handsome inspector came to Gnadenfeld to conduct exams, in cooperation with our schoolmaster, Mr. Abraham Braun. The students were relieved when this examination had been passed with high grades so they were able to continue their schooling if they wished.[4]

The School Year and Celebrations

Whole villages celebrated the coming of spring. School was dismissed. Parents and families came by *Droshka,* wagon or bicycle to a nearby woods, quiet meadow or river where the end-of-school-year festivities took place.

For the children there were ball games, folk songs, activities and free time for exploring in the woods. Older folk sat under the trees listening to the music and watching the children play. At noon everyone spread blankets in the shade of the big trees to enjoy the lunch. Following is a typical menu from a village in the Molotschna Colony, around the year 1910.

All-School May Festival
Picnic Menu
Zwieback
Zuckertorten (Cake)
Cookies
Kjrinjel
Marzipan
Fresh Cherries
Coffee
Milk cooled in the spring
Kvass

Mary Dirks Janzen: One of the highlights of the school year was an outing, or *Spazier-gang* when the whole school would go on an afternoon walk, either to the meadow, which was two miles out of the village, or to the forest, which really was a windbreak, consisting of four to six rows of old poplars, oaks, elms and maples with flowers here and there. A delight for little girls' hearts.

These outings were rare and, therefore, highly prized. The meadow grass was thyme, which had a rare fragrance. Then there were flowers. Once at the destination, we could break off from the usual two by two marching form and play for an hour or so. When we were ready to return home, we would get in line and march two by two back to the village, each child carrying his precious bouquet of flowers home. This had been a rich day, since we had gone beyond the borders of our village, and seen the blue sky, the soft white clouds and the large meadow, which held a treasure of lovely things which God had created.[5]

Anna Reimer Dyck: Another day we liked to celebrate (in the Kuban) was May 6, the birthday of our Czar. On this occasion, the whole village joined in the festivities. On the morning of that day the imperial flag could be seen flying proudly from every home in the village, for this was a great day of celebration, when all of us honored our rulers. We went to school in the morning, sang the national anthem, prayed for the Czar and his family, heard a short address, then rushed home to get ready for an excursion into the woods.

All our families joined this excursion. We would ride our comfortable wagons well fitted with springs. Groups of friends would gather under tall trees and eat their lunches. Here and there one could see a sheep roasted on a skewer, and samovars set up to provide hot water. The young people sang songs and played, or went for walks in the woods. Now in May the May flowers were blooming in such profusion that the whole atmosphere was filled with their aroma. Then, in the evening, we returned with huge bouquets.[6]

N.J. Kroeker: In May it was the custom for the schools to have an outing. We went by hayrack, with much happy laughter and talking along the way. This was the day to spend in the lovely Dnieper valley, a day of singing and talking. The older girls filled the samovar with water and the boys gathered branches to stoke the fire. We played games, went exploring, and perhaps had time for a boat ride. There was also the spring outing — when we went looking for crocuses in the meadow and hunting for violets by the stream Chortitza. There was also a spring concert and a play.[7]

The Village School Christmas Program

For a few minutes let us imagine we have traveled back in time. It is December 24th. This is the evening of the school program. For weeks the students have practiced their parts: singing, reciting poems and rehearsing parts for their skits.

At home the chores are done early. Everyone is scrubbed clean from late afternoon baths. Supper is served early tonight. Dusk settles slowly over the village. Soon the streets are full of people. Stooped grandmothers and gray-haired-grandfathers, young mothers and fathers carrying little children — all are walking with quick steps toward the schoolhouse in the middle of the village.

In the large school room the lights are dim. There is a special fragrance in the room — the smell of pine boughs. It is the Christmas tree which sets the mood for the evening.

People enter, find their places along the benches; women sit on one side, men on the other. Where the students wait to perform, there is hard-to-contain excitement, a little jostling and quiet scuffling among the boys.

Finally the teacher walks to the front of the room, welcoming parents and visitors. The program begins with prayer and singing. An older child recites the familiar Christmas Scripture. Children stand in front with shiny eyes and joyful faces. How eager they are to speak their lines, to take part in the songs, poems and plays!

When each has finished, the room becomes hushed. Everyone waits for this beautiful moment. Two stalwart men, school board members, bring long sticks with lighted candles to the front of the room. Candle by candle, the tree begins to glow. Surely this is the loveliest tree ever. In the gentle, flickering light all the children join and sing softly, "Silent Night, Holy Night."

There is still one final pleasure. The teacher comes forward with a large laundry basket filled with sacks of sweets and nuts — his treat to his students. Older girls help him pass the sacks to the children.

Snow is falling as the families return home. By the warmth of the large brick stoves there is talk of the program, remembering each child and each part. Yes, it has been a good evening. Tomorrow is Christmas.

* * *

After the Russian Revolution, times were not so tranquil and peaceful. Celebrating took place at considerable risk.

Kaethe Kasdorf Warkentin: When my mother went to school in the little village of Blumenfeld, they didn't have a church building, so they celebrated Christmas Eve not as a school but as a village function. They had a Christmas tree and the children learned little poems from what they called *Stille Bilder* (Silent Pictures).

When I grew up, during the Communist times, there was nothing. In school there were no celebrations except the approved functions.

Christmas Eve was celebrated in church as a village but under a lot of stress. We were forbidden by the government to go. And until 1933, when they closed the church, we just sneaked to the services, not really with the old enjoyment and always under the threat of being shipped to Siberia, if discovered. Our fathers were all taken away.

Early Education Among the 1874 Pioneers

Schools in rural America were not concerned at all about occupational studies. Children went to school when they were not required to work in the fields. And they learned to plow straight furrows, to butcher hogs, to sew straight and dainty seams, to make butter, to dig a well, to repair fences — as they worked alongside their parents. They expected to live out their lives much like their parents.[8]
—*O.L. Davis, Jr.*

For the 1874 immigrants settling on the prairies of Kansas, Manitoba and Nebraska meant giving up many of the comforts of a well-established community. However, formal education remained a high priority with the newcomers, and they immediately established private schools for their children so they might continue the education begun in Russia.

Paying for private schooling was not always easy. Most families were still improving home-steads or paying for land purchased from the railroads. Many early farm families found it hard to pay school taxes. Sometimes they were forced to balance educational goals with their ability to afford schooling. In bad weather pupils often studied their lessons at home with the aid of other family members.[9]

In Marion County, Kansas, three schools opened in the Alexanderwohl village near Goessel the year the immigrants arrived. Other private church-sponsored schools opened shortly there-after. Often students ranged in age from five to twenty years. They were placed not according to age, but according to level of achievement. When the public schools began to compete with church schools, some Mennonite pupils attended public schools during the winter months and church schools during vacation period. In Goessel, Kansas (1901), the school pattern was to have English school before Christmas and German school the rest of the year, according to O.B. Reimer. In 1874 Kansas law required "that a child between the ages of eight and fourteen should be under competent instruction" for at least twelve weeks of the year. My grandfather Martin Jost probably continued his schooling in the nearby home of Heinrich Wiebe who opened a school in his living room in the Alexanderfeld village near Hillsboro, Kansas.

In the early days of the Manitoba settlement, private schools stressed the three *Rs* and Bible studies. A typical timetable for a week of classes consisted of eight hours of arithmetic, three hours of Bible stories, one hour of geography, two hours of grammar, ten hours of reading and five hours of writing. On Friday afternoons Bible catechisms were recited. All instruction was in the German language.[10]

Johan W. Dueck recalls, "The school children were not taught as many subjects as today in the district school. Testament and Bible were our only subjects and textbooks. There was no geography. One learned the rudiments of reading, writing and the first four rules of arithmetic and fractions. But we studied catechism, Bible stories and other edifying materials.[11]

In the little village of Reinland, Manitoba, the school was patterned much like those in Russia. Children were divided into groups as they had been in Russia, studying the primer, catechism, New Testament and the Bible. Village schools such as this one on the Canadian prairies taught skills that served the pupils well in their rural setting. Upon leaving school most were proficient in arithmetic. Many were avid readers of German language newspapers and periodicals. Many learned to write in an artful manner or at least well enough to correspond with relatives and friends during the pioneer years when even short distances were barriers. To a large degree the pioneer village school was successful.[12]

*　　*　　*

In the midwestern United States the private elementary schools gave way to public education. In my father's family the children attended a branch of Hillsboro's District #82. In the following account my uncle describes this country school as he remembers it from 1904 to 1912.

West School *by Dan G. Jost*

All of the children in the Martin Jost family attended West School at one time or another. The school, located one mile west of the old Hillsboro depot on the south side of the railroad tracks, was a wooden frame structure approximately 30′ × 50′, facing east.

The inside walls had a wainscoting of grooved ceiling wood. The upper part was plastered and large blackboards covered the west wall. The wooden floor, running east and west, was oiled several times during the school season to keep it smooth. The school yard had two out buildings to the west and a coal shed in the center for storage.

When a strong cold south wind blew in winter, the old pot-bellied stove was fired red hot. To protect those of us who sat close to the blazing stove from this intense heat, it was partially surrounded with a tin plate. The old stove was a good place to dry water-soaked gloves or other wet clothing.

School attendance varied from fifteen to thirty pupils ranging in ages from six to fourteen years. There were many reasons for absences. Whenever a family had a butchering bee (and everyone butchered), the older children stayed home to help. Other farm work and home chores at times interfered with class attendance. When corn husking season was on or the time when molasses was pressed, the older members of the family stayed home to help. You can well imagine what that did to the teacher who at least at some time had to teach the eight grades. If the teacher got behind in her schedule, she called on the older pupils to help with the teaching.

Our main subjects were arithmetic, spelling, penmanship (writing), geography and grammar. What more did you need? We did not have computers to help solve our arithmetic problems. The multiplication tables were learned so well that when we multiplied we knew that 12 times 12 was 144 without hesitating.

Discipline was sometimes a problem. There were some teachers who were strict; others lost classroom control. Because the school board had financial problems, salary frequently took precedence over the quality of teaching.

The door of the schoolhouse was always open and it often became a gathering place for young folk in the evening. An uncle of mine once shot some snowbirds while hunting. He dressed them, cooked them over the big stove and had dinner there at the school. The school-yard was also a good place for movers to stop or for horse traders to graze their horses.

We sometimes wonder how the teacher could do justice to teaching so many grades with so many pupils. However, we all learned to read, write and spell. We memorized the multiplication tables and a good bit of poetry as well.

Country Schools and the Weather

Winter weather often posed a threat to both teachers and pupils in rural areas. But there were times when neither snow nor ice daunted the spirits of the pioneers. Often ruggedness and courage were displayed by their children as well. In the late 1920s a group of Mennonites fleeing famine and the Bolshevik Revolution in Russia settled in Reesor, Ontario, Canada. One of the school teachers, John Enns, tells the following story.

John H. Enns: My pupils trudged over those long, often barely passable forest paths without incurring any unduly adverse records of belatedness. Two boys of a family had to leave their home by the light of a lantern during the short days of mid-winter. They would leave the lantern at the home of a settler who lived along their path in the bush and would make the rest of the way by the growing light of dawn.

In spite of all these difficulties I have never had better attendance than this pioneer school at Reesor. One example of the high sense of duty in these children was furnished by an eight-year-old boy. He had to walk a full two miles along the railway tracks before he could turn into the "school road" to do another mile and a quarter on it. One day a dangerous snowstorm was blowing along the railway, one that the boy would have to face in going to school. On a sheltered forest path the storm would have been of no account, but the two miles against the blowing sleet on the tracks! Thus the parents told this boy to stay home that day. He protested, but the parents did not change their decision. This pupil appeared in school that day, late, but early in the forenoon. I happened to hear later that he had run away from home in order not to miss school. I felt I had to reprimand the boy for disobeying his parents, but I could have bussed him in admiration for his loyalty.[13]

Mountain Lake, Minnesota

Bertha Fast Harder: In winter we would use a "Santa Claus sleigh" and the other farm kids just loved it if we picked them up along the way. Very often along those three miles we packed as many kids as we could into the sled and they rode along with us. When we would get to school, we put the horses into the barn and fed them hay. In the evening we hitched them back onto the sled.

Sometimes we would walk. We liked it especially on the very blizzardy, cold days. I don't think there were many days when we didn't go to school in that cold Minnesota weather. We could walk as long as it was not dangerous.

On some days there would be only a few in school—just my sisters and me and a few others. The teacher already had the fire going in the big pot-bellied stove. We wouldn't have class. We were allowed to sit around this big old stove with our feet up and read and read and read. We would go home early. We just loved that.

Western Kansas

Before the days of school buses, children walked to school, rode horses or came by sleigh or buggy. Marie Loewen Franz occasionally rode a horse to school on the western Kansas prairie.

Marie Loewen Franz: One day in spring when I was on my way home from school, the horse stumbled and fell by stepping into a hole. My feet stayed stuck in the stirrups which Dad had fashioned for my short legs. When my horse got up, my feet stuck. Both feet were on the left side of my pony as I got up. There I was, hanging head down. This spooked the horse and she took off at a fast gallop. My face was in a cloud of dust. I saw the hooves just missing my face with every running step. I was completely helpless. The next thing I remember, I found myself lying in the grass and half a mile ahead was my steed contentedly grazing away. I knew then that I had passed out. My feet finally came loose and I fell and sprained my back. It healed quickly and I kept right on riding.[14]

The Best Part of the Day—Recess

Dan G. Jost: We played a lot of baseball at recess. The first one to say "Striker" would be the batter. The pitcher would be next. The catcher about third and then fielders came last. We had a little rubber ball about the size of a good-sized walnut and a great big, heavy bat.

The big boys would be batters most of the time and we young kids had to chase that ball. The ball would fly when it was hit hard. And they would run around and continue to be batters all recess. That's how the older boys took care of us. Fights were prevalent during recess and there was always rivalry about certain things.

Helen Peters Epp: There were forty-eight students in our one-room school, Hillsboro West. We played "Charades," "Andy Over," "Crack the Whip" and in winter "Fox and Geese."

Martha Letkeman Funk: We would play jump rope mostly. Sometimes we played "Pump, Pump, Pullaway" and "Crack the Whip." There was a park east of the school (in town) with lots of trees. When the leaves fell, we girls would go over there and play and fix houses out of leaves. The boys played baseball.

Minnie Jost Krause: Our school was near our pond. We'd go skating at recess and never hear the bell. The teacher would ring and ring the bell. Finally, our consciences would bother us. She'd be crying because it was probably an hour later.

School Lunches

Du best bedocht aus Bleiwboat
Dee wosch ea hee eet.
You are as resourceful as Bluebeard.
He washed before he ate.
                    —*Low German Saying*

Conveniences and accommodations were not hallmarks of the old country school. It is unlikely that many hands were washed before digging into student lunch pails. Whatever food the children ate at noon came from home and was frequently packed in a syrup bucket. O.B. Reimer, who attended school near Goessel, Kansas, around 1900, remembered a tin pail he used in which the bottom contained food and the upper part held milk or coffee. However, in winter, the lunches lined up in the unheated cloakroom might be frozen.

Frieda Pankratz Suderman remembers well the days before children were served in a school cafeteria. "School lunches were monotonous and sometimes rather unappetizing. They were survival kits rather than balanced meals, so the children liked to get them over with so they could get out to their noon play.

"A few of them ate with a left arm protectively around the bucket so that no one could see what they had. At that, they kept no secrets. Smells of boiled eggs, canned peaches and fried ham cannot be mistaken. Lunches were packed without convenience foods, plastic wraps or thermoses. There were no potato chips or Hostess cupcakes."[15]

Helen Peters Epp: For school lunch we took anything that was leftover. Baked sweet potatoes, bread and butter, bread and molasses, ham or sausage. We had dried apple pie a lot. We didn't have thermoses for hot or cold like we do now. We didn't know about disease germs then. Everybody used the same cup. One for all.

Dan G. Jost: Coming from a big family, there wasn't always the best of food to go around. Rabbits were prevalent and cheap, and we boys liked to go hunting. Generally Mother saved the back leg or the backbone of the rabbits for us to take to school, and we would have that or a piece of fried sausage. She'd cut a pretty good slice of sausage and send it with rye bread, *Jreeweschmolt* (crackling lard) or molasses. Perhaps an apple. We carried our lunches in tin syrup pails with lids.

Katharina Jantzen Prieb: Our school lunches were rye bread with molasses. Sometimes a little chicken. Apples were scarce. Anxiously we looked at the children with apples. We followed the girls with apples, hoping to eat their apple cores. We were hungry for apples and meat.

Bertha Fast Harder: I remember that the big stove in our country school had a big, black tin jacket around it so we wouldn't burn ourselves and it would heat the room better this way. The top of that big casing around the stove was like a moat with water in it and of course the water would get hot from the heat. Sometimes we would carry our lunch of green bean soup in a quart jar and put it in that water and by noon it would be nice and hot.

Otherwise our lunch would be homemade bread, maybe a chunk of homemade sausage or a piece of cold ham. There were those years when sometimes we didn't have meat. There were also those children who were not Russian Mennonite. They were Scandinavian and they always had boughten bread sandwiches. That looked so good. And they would have bananas, and that looked so good. We hardly ever had bananas in winter. Sometimes they would trade their bananas for something my mother had made.

Nellie Lehn: At home we had a box of apples for the winter. I took a half an apple in my lunch. No one else had apples. Sometimes I had syrup sandwiches, a half an apple and a cookie, all packed in a Roger's Golden Syrup pail.

Miene Mame ess mie goot (My Mother Loves Me)

Mie-ne Ma-me ess mie goot, Jeft mie schee-net Ä-ten,

Schin-kje-fleesch en Bot-ta-broot, Daut woa'k nie fe-jä-ten.

Translation

My mother loves me,   Ham and butered bread,
Gives me good food,   I'll never forget that!

School Clothes

Anna Epp Entz: We had only two dresses and one that was from last year was worn after school. We always changed immediately after school and church.

Frieda Pankratz Suderman: Our dresses came in three classifications. Sunday clothes were only for church and for extra special occasions. Semi-good dresses were for visiting, for school or for Sunday afternoon wear. They might be last year's best. We liked the everyday dresses best because in them you could do what you liked.

Bertha Fast Harder: My mother always made us wear long underwear because we had to walk three miles to country school. When we got a little older, we tried to tuck the long underwear into long stockings. No matter how neat we tried to do it, with the bottom cuff over to the inside, it always bulged. Some of our friends who were not Russian Mennonite didn't have to wear long underwear, so I remember when we were away from home and our mother wouldn't be able to see us any more, we stopped and rolled it way above our knees and pulled our stockings up again so that long underwear wouldn't show. But all day we worried that the long underwear would roll down.

Herbert Neufeld: Poverty enveloped us. Every material aspect of our life was shabby, but most noticeable was our clothing, as any snapshot of the time will show. Bib overalls ($1.50 at the general store) were universal and therefore not a stigma. The problem was I never had a pair that fit me.[16]

The Country School—A Community Center

Not only was the little country schoolhouse a place of learning for children, but it also served as a community center. Here the children presented their long-practiced Christmas programs. Here parents and friends gathered for Literary Club, an evening of drama, recitations or music. Entire communities turned out for box suppers, cake walks and spelling bees. The school sometimes served as a center for political gatherings with candidates giving speeches. In some instances the school building served as a church on Sundays. The memories of those events are very pleasant.

Literary Programs

Marion County, Kansas, February 22, 1878: A "school exhibition" took place at the Gnadenau (Krimmer Mennonite Brethren) school near Hillsboro, Kansas, at the "close of the winter term." According to the Marion reporter who braved the muddy roads for the event, there was a full house of "miscellaneous Russians, Germans, Africans and Americans."[17] The Gnadenau School had combined with neighboring district schools to present a program with music "furnished by two violins, several humorous plantation songs by several small colored urchins and music made by a choir of German boys with flute accompaniment. Songs were all rendered in their native tongue, many declamations were spoken as well as dialogues." There was also a patriotic address by Marion's author and poet laureate, John Madden, Jr., on "America and Americans." The audience felt amply repaid for being present.

Minnie Jost Krause: On the evenings of the literary programs at West School [Hillsboro, Kansas] the room was crowded. There were plays and pantomimes, recitations and poems. Once one of the girls sang "Annie Laurie" while my sister played the violin and I pantomimed it. I had a glittering crown on my head and a white sheet for a gown.

Dan G. Jost: I was quite interested in learning and reciting poetry and readings. When Miss Harms was our teacher at West School, I learned a recitation about a half mile long for the evening literary program. A little melodramatic, but it kept the audience interested.

Bertha Fast Harder: In that two-room schoolhouse in Mountain Lake, Minnesota, we really gave some very good programs. One time we harmonized "Beautiful Dreamer." There were Christmas plays. We had a little stage in the front of that room where we had our programs. We would string up a wire and hang a curtain. However, we were absolutely unaware that the curtain was thin, and everyone could actually see us back there getting the stage set up for our play.

Spelling Bees

Friday afternoons, after the last recess, there was often a spelling match. Two of the higher grades were asked to be on each side of the school. According to Dan Jost, the teacher at the West School would open her book to a certain page. The side which guessed a number closest to the number of her page got to go first.

In some schools an entire evening program consisted of a spelling bee. These gatherings were moved around from school to school. The spelling bees were replaced by basket socials sometime after 1900.

Basket Socials

Bertha Fast Harder: We had basket socials in which the girls would pack boxes and decorate them with tissue paper. We would dream up ideas and usually two girls would go together. There would be two men who would buy our lunch.

The night before the social my friend would come to my house. We bought paper and had decided ahead of time how to decorate the basket. Perhaps we would make a flower with white paper and we would frill green leaves and frill all kinds of shades of blue and purple to make a great big blossom on top of the box. Some girls might decorate their box like a schoolhouse.

The night of the social, the auctioneer held up the boxes, "Here, gentlemen, look at this beautiful box!" It was my box. My heart would be pounding to see who would buy it. Sometimes we were disappointed, other times just delighted. Sometimes a young man had to pay dearly for a certain basket. Then we would sit and eat our lunch together. To this day I think this is so romantic.

Cake Walks

Dan G. Jost: We had cake walks at West School. A date was set for the walk and advertised by word of mouth. My sisters and other young women of the community baked cakes, wrapped them in beautiful boxes and brought them to school. There were musicians and a place for couples to "walk" or march to the music. Young men who "won" a cake had the privilege of eating the cake with the girl who baked it as did those who bought a box lunch. This was a kind of money-making "beau-catching" scheme. Young men often asked the girls for a date later. Folk games were played outdoors after the social.

Graduation

Upon completion of the eighth grade, the graduating students from all over the county drove to Marion, the county seat, for graduation exercises. In the old Jost family album is a beautiful sepiatone studio photo of the three graduates of West School and their teacher. Uncle Dan Jost vividly remembers the buggy ride to Marion with his sister Ann. His parents did not attend.

Some graduates went on to local public high schools. A number of Mennonite young people enrolled in nearby church related preparatory schools such as the Hillsboro Bible Academy for further study.

The Mennonite Church

Enter his gates with thanksgiving
and his courts with praise;
give thanks to him and praise his name.
For the Lord is good and his love
endures forever;
his faithfulness continues
through all generations.

—Psalm 100:4-5

The Mennonite Church

I was glad when they said unto me,
Let us go into the house of the Lord.
— *Psalm 122:1*

At the beginning of the Anabaptist movement in Holland (1530-1570) the new converts to the faith did not gather in meetinghouses because of severe religious persecution but worshiped outdoors, in attics, cellars, barns or granaries. When the persecution ended, they were able to assemble in homes and rented warehouses. The oldest Dutch Anabaptist church, Singel Mennonite Church in Amsterdam, dates back to 1609.

The situation in Prussia (1550s-1720s) was much the same. There, too, the Dutch Mennonites sought to be unobtrusive. By 1550 a large Anabaptist congregation had been established outside the city walls of Danzig.[1] Mennonites formed congregations but were restricted from building meetinghouses for almost two centuries, although the Elbing congregation erected its first structure in 1590.[2] Records indicate the first rural church buildings were not built until the 1700s.[3] These Prussian churches were typically simple wooden structures, square or rectangular in shape, buildings which did not look like churches. Anna Rempel Dyck states in her autobiographical sketches that the first missionary festival in Polish Prussia at the end of the eighteenth century was celebrated in Coldowa (near Marienburg) in her grandfather Dietrich Rempel's big barn.[4]

The first Mennonite meetinghouses had no pews or chairs, only benches with no backs. Women sat on the main floor; men occupied the balcony. The pulpit, located on a platform in the center front of the church, confirmed the centrality of preaching in Mennonite worship. Dutch remained the language of the Prussian churches until shortly before their migration to Russia in 1789.

Mennonite churches in Russia, for the most part, bore a striking resemblance to those in Prussia. These plain, wooden buildings (at first unpainted) with no ornamentation were located in the center of the village. This architectural pattern continued on into the prairie states and provinces of the United States and Canada.

Worship services were simple and almost austere. Ministers were usually unpaid laymen, chosen by secret ballot as were other elders and deacons. Being untrained, the minister customarily read his sermon, frequently in a singsong fashion, sitting on an elevated chair. His sermon might last two hours and the service up to three. Mary Dirks Janzen remembers long sermons from her childhood home in Gnadenfeld in the Molotschna. "Sometimes, when the windows were open in summer, one or two barn swallows joined the service, a most welcome diversion when the sermon was long and my eyelids started to droop."

The office of chorister or *Vorsänger* originated in Holland. This man, who was seated on the platform beside the preacher, led the congregation in long hymns without accompaniment. His position was held in high esteem throughout the historical migrations and on into the United

States and Canada. Tina Friesen Klassen often recalled with pride the fact that her father had been the *Vorsänger* (*Fäasenja* in Low German) in their church in Hillsboro, Kansas. Eventually, the *Vorsänger* was replaced by choirs and instruments.

Originally there were no organs or pianos in the churches because musical instruments were banned. The first organ was installed in the Neugarten church in Prussia in 1778.[5] It was not until the last decades before World War I that musical instruments were introduced into the Russian churches. Early hymns were sung in unison; musical harmony was also frowned upon in the beginning. In later years strong four-part singing became common and is still enjoyed and practiced in many Mennonite churches.

In the middle of the nineteenth century a new and more spontaneous pattern of worship developed in the Russian churches under the influence of the Pietists and Baptists. Edward Wuest was an evangelistic Lutheran Pietist preacher assigned to a village within a few hours driving distance of Gnadenfeld.

Anna Rempel Dyck writes of his work in her autobiography. "The Lord used Pastor Wuest to bring new spiritual life into our quiet native village. Missionary festivals [Lutheran] were celebrated in which the Stuttgart and Prischib [German] colonial settlers participated with enthusiasm. Classes were also offered. Whenever Pastor Wuest, with his church members from Stuttgart, was on his way to a festival in Prischib, they stopped in Gnadenfeld to spend the night due to the long distance between the two towns. Unexpectedly, it once so happened that several wagons loaded with guests drove singing into our yard. Mother rushed into the kitchen to prepare the evening meal. I still see her standing by the stove, hands folded, eyes looking upward through the open chimney, praying that God would be kind enough to bless the bread and apple soup, that all the dear guests would have enough to eat. After the evening meal the guests sang songs of thanks and Pastor Wuest said a powerful prayer."[6]

Wuest had a profound evangelical influence upon neighboring Molotschna Mennonites, among whom a newly-formed organization, the Mennonite Brethren Church (1860), grew out of this time of spiritual awakening. This church promoted lighter hymns (Gospel songs), evangelism, missions, prayer meetings, Bible studies and extemporaneous preaching. A strong pioneer in this new spiritual movement was Bernhard Harder who preached warm evangelistic, spontaneous and original sermons. Teacher, poet and preacher, he was a great admirer of Edward Wuest.[7]

Mary Dirks Janzen wrote a brief description of her own more spiritually progressive Gnadenfeld church. "Ours was a one-story structure with doors and a porch with steps on three sides and large, arched windows. We had four local ministers. The pulpit from which they preached was quite elevated and there were seats on either side for the deacons and visiting speakers.

"We had Bible study meetings in the grammar school building. I had never heard of revival meetings until I was twelve years old. A group of our church members organized a new movement which included this practice. Our pipe organ, located in the women's balcony, was pumped manually. Our choir sang a cappella and our music books were written with numbers instead of notes. All our music was copied by hand, which was a great chore. On one occasion we took part in a music festival in another village. This was rare for us because we hardly ever left our own village. We enjoyed it beyond measure."

The Prairie Churches

When the Mennonites arrived in Canada and the United States in 1874, they continued to build wooden churches along simple lines with plain windows and often austere interiors. The first white frame church in Hillsboro, where my grandfather Martin Jost was one of the founding members, was just such a small, plain building. Built in 1884 it resembled a country school-house more than a church. The pulpit was in the middle at the front end of the church so the sermon could be heard by all. The men and women sat segregated on opposite sides of the church with an aisle in between. This was "to foster complete concentration on the sermon."

Ministers were usually laymen and in the first years read lengthy German sermons. By the late nineteenth and early twentieth centuries most congregations were permitting their ministers to preach without notes. The worship services of the various groups strongly resembled those from their past in Russia.

The Language Change from German to English

A major change took place when churches switched from German to the English language. German services were still part of my own early church experience at First Mennonite Church in Hillsboro, Kansas. Some of the older people strongly resisted the change and came to church only for "German preaching Sunday." Frieda Pankratz Suderman remembers, "My grand-mother almost took it as a personal insult when she miscounted and went to church on an English Sunday. She did not stay." In a diary kept by my grandmother Bertha Golbek Jost, she carefully noted the German sermons and her personal satisfaction when there was German preaching on a second holiday. She penned many hymns into this diary, all in German.

In my husband's home church, Tabor Mennonite, near Goessel, Kansas, an experiment with ten-minute English meditations in addition to the German began in 1923. English found its way into Sunday schools earlier to accommodate the young. Women's and girls' mission programs were added at this time. Christian Endeavor, a Bible study conducted in English, met on Sunday nights.

*   *   *

"If we lose the German language, then we lose much more than a language."
—*A Mennonite Prophet's Warning*

In the western provinces of Canada, the switch to English came as late as the 1950s. In an article in the *Mennonite Mirror,* March, 1990, H.W. Friesen explored his feelings about that change. Here is part of that article.

"When we switched to English more than a language was lost. For most people it was making a simple switch to English, a matter of continuing in English what had been done in German, most thought.

"Few conceived language as a conveyor of more than words. Words can readily be translated into another language and inevitably something is lost in translation. The concepts, the history, the theology, the ideas of a people known as Mennonites had over many years been refined in German words; these are easily replaced by other concepts during the language transition.

"The German language insulated Mennonites from the theological extremes that periodically swept across North America.

"The German language bonded Mennonites to the theological cues from the more established centres of Europe, and by the time they reached Canada, they had been tested, refined and assessed. With the protective barrier of the German language gone, the churches have been buffeted by various winds whose velocity and direction are seldom tested.

"A 'prophet,' warning of this change, saw churches which could not make the language change and at the same time ensure that the essence of our forefathers' understanding of scripture was not only maintained but also communicated."

Mennonites and Music

"Our church life was full and satisfying," says Marie Harms Berg. "We always looked forward to Sunday; singing the gospel songs was a joy. We also had a church library which furnished me weeks of good reading. I sang in the choir at an early age and also became a Sunday school teacher. We were also urged as young girls to go to the sewing circle and learn to embroider articles to be sold at the mission sale."

*   *   *

Little did I realize during my growing up years how much music and singing were part of our worship and praise. It was customary each Sunday morning for the entire congregation, including all the children, to gather for an extended period of hymn singing before going to Sunday School. My husband and I continue to be amazed at the storehouse of hymns and songs we know by heart from those early years. Music and four-part harmony are an important part of our worship heritage.

Helen Peters Epp: We sang *"Hallelujah, Schöner Morgen"* every Sunday morning and knew it all by heart.

Ann Voth Ratliff, a professional musician who grew up in the Mennonite Brethren Church in Hillsboro, remembers, "There were six hundred people in our church and we had six active choirs. No one ever missed choir practice, no matter what. The singing of the Mennonites has always been great. It seems we don't hear that kind of singing anywhere else. Years ago when I'd bring friends home from college, they just couldn't believe their ears. The singing was very important in all our lives."

At the 1984 centennial celebration in the town of Hillsboro, the Mennonite churches of the area joined in a mass worship service in the large Tabor College gymnasium. The "house" was packed. Eloquent speakers recalled the difficulties of pioneer days and expressed gratitude to

God for His leading and strength through those first one hundred years. What I remember is the singing.

When the people rose to sing (many from memory) *Grosser Gott, Wir Loben Dich,* in four-part harmony, a most glorious overwhelming sound filled the hall. In that shining, blessed moment, singing that magnificent old hymn of praise to God, I felt the strength and depth of my roots—a family belonging to that simple white frame church. I felt ties to the Ukraine from which my grandparents came. I remembered and felt connected to the Anabaptists of the sixteenth century who gave up their lives rather than their faith. Their beliefs had inspired generations of my family. These bonds stretched still farther to include the men and women of the early Christian church. In the power of that singing I affirmed along with others praise for my roots and those who made this faith possible.

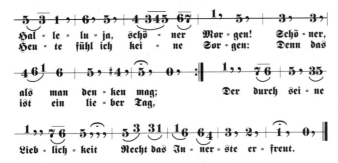

Translation
Hallelujah to this Fair Morn

Hallelujah to this fair morn,
Fairer than we all can dream.
This day I feel no heavy cares;
It really is a lovely day.
It brings to us its beauty
And gladdens our internal self.

—From a *Choralbuch* printed in Leipzig in 1865, used in Russian Mennonite village schools and brought to North America by a Mennonite immigrant.
—English translation by Herman Rempel.

The Festive Sabbath

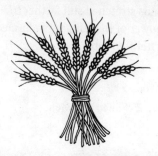

Mother always made Sunday special. Sunday morning she wore a clean white, ironed apron, put a fresh cloth on the table. When my older sister came home for Sunday, Mother made everything so festive.

—*Nellie Lehn*

Sunday—A Day of Celebration

Grandmother and Grandfather Jost rarely missed Sunday church. Even with a large family, they managed to be there regularly. The older children often walked the distance into town along the railroad while the younger children rode with the parents.

Sunday was a big day and everyone looked forward to it. The hard work of the week came to an end. The Sabbath provided welcome rest as well as spiritual refreshment and fellowship with friends. In the early years in North America there were few social functions. The main way to get together was to attend church. Sometimes the congregation shared a simple Mennonite-style meal after the service.

Every woman prepared extra food for the day so guests might join her family. Afternoon visits were made without formal invitation. Everyone expected company on Sunday afternoons and holidays. If you did not receive visitors, you got into the buggy and went to see someone. If visitors arrived when you were gone, they were not offended. They simply turned around and headed for another place. It was common to have three or four families visiting in the same house on Sunday, all staying for afternoon *Faspa*.

My father, Edward G. Jost, lived with this informal visiting philosophy all his life. The welcome mat was always out, and he anticipated the same in return. He expected Mother to be ready to entertain on the spur of the moment and she often complied.

My grandparents, the Martin Josts, were good friends with the George Peters family who lived down the road. Recalling early years of this friendship, Willard Peters, one of the sons, commented, "We went to see the Josts whenever the wind blew from the west. And the wind always blew from the west."

The following stories testify to the joy and festivity of the Sabbath as celebrated by the Mennonites of those years.

We Just Loved Sunday *by Bertha Fast Harder*

Our life in Mountain Lake, Minnesota, was very church-centered. Sunday morning church was the best time of the week. My best friends were there. We went to a country school the other direction from Mountain Lake, so none of my closest friends attended that school. I had friends at school but not the same kind. So on Sunday morning I could hardly wait. Whenever it snowed, we were sad. But then we would play church at home.

We always wore our best dresses on Sunday morning. My dad would back the car out of the garage and drive it up in front of the gate. When we girls were all dressed (we helped with the dishes first), we would go out and sit in the car and wait for Dad and Mother. We didn't mind waiting. It was Sunday. All day it was going to be Sunday. We usually sang during the four-mile drive to church.

It was so great to see our friends. Sometimes Mother would let us sit with them, if we promised to be good. I remember one beautiful Sunday morning I sat in the very front pew. There was a big door over to the east side and I could see out that door from the front pew. On

MENNONITE FOODS AND FOLKWAYS FROM SOUTH RUSSIA

that beautiful Sunday morning the minister announced that we were going to sing number 1 from *Gesangbuch Mit Noten*. That song was *"Hallelujah, Schöner Morgen"* [Hallelujah, Beautiful Morning]. I remember I sang with my heart and soul. To this day it is a beautiful memory.

Our Sunday dinner was almost always something my mother had prepared the day before. All she had to do was put it on the table. Or she would fry potatoes that had been cooked on Saturday. She would peel them in the morning before church and quickly fry them later. Often we had summer sausage, bologna or cold ham that she had fried the day before.

It was taken for granted in our community that we would visit during the afternoon. Either friends would visit at our house or we would go to other houses. We would usually go about 1:30 and later have afternoon *Faspa*.

There were numerous families with whom we shared repeated visits. It seems to me we exchanged visits at least once a summer. My mother or dad would say, "Hey, we haven't been over at Quirings," or "We haven't been over at Friesens or Penners for a long time." Of course, we children preferred to go places where they had children of our own age.

Sometimes my mother would invite someone already Saturday afternoon. Or maybe during church she would ask someone, "Do you want to come over in the afternoon?" Sometimes three or four families would come over at once. If they didn't have too many children, that was great. The adults would sit in the living room and visit and my mother would serve her *Faspa:* coffee, homemade *Zwieback,* jam, homemade pickles and always several kinds of cakes. Once in a while someone would bring baked goods along.

When the adults were through eating, we children would come in from playing outside. The men would go outside to the barn to see the new calves or something my dad was doing or, perhaps, admire our prize bull. The women, after their coffee, would go out and look at mother's flower beds and her vegetable garden. They'd walk around the yard and admire things. They would visit from twenty minutes to half an hour or longer. Then it would be time to go home, particularly if they were farmers.

We children would play and play. Sometimes we got carried away and trampled over some crops or garden things. My father did not like that. He also got upset with us when we played in the grain.

But playing in the haymow, that was permitted. We usually wore everyday clothes when people came, and that haymow — climbing up into it and jumping down into the hay — was as good as a trampoline.

Sunday afternoons with company, friends to play with and Mother's good *Faspa* helped to make it the best day of the week.

* * *

Marie Loewen Franz came with her parents from Russia in 1912. The family settled on the barren, western Kansas prairie near Meade, Kansas. Church was a very important part of their life. Marie Franz shares Sunday experiences from those early years in her book, *Word Pictures of Yesteryear*. Several of the following anecdotes are taken from that work.

Peter Wiebe's grocery store in the Chortitza Colony, Ukraine.

Russian Mennonite men's choir on an outing in 1913.

Stories of Sunday Church *by Marie Loewen Franz*

When our parents settled on the prairie near Ingalls, Kansas, church services were held either in people's homes or in the schoolhouse. People took their faith seriously. No one missed church on Sunday, even in the wintertime. I remember going to the service on the wagon, lined with new straw, all of us children sitting on the flat wagon floor with heavy quilts over our heads, covering us completely. It was very cold.[1]

*   *   *

Usually on the way to church with the family tightly packed into the car we had to sing, even when we weren't always in the mood. When Father said, "Sing," we sang. He'd start a tune and the rest of us were supposed to join him. It's amazing how this changed our attitudes. Maybe this is why he did it. By the time we reached church, we were usually in a good mood.[2]

*   *   *

In the early twenties in our Mennonite Brethren Church, people knelt facing the pews while praying. There was a short prayer session before the sermon. At times when the prayers weren't audible from those farther away, several prayed simultaneously. There was much praying in the churches in the past, probably largely due to the difficult times.

We looked forward to Sundays when we dressed up in our best clothes and attended church, usually twice, both morning and evening. No one ever missed except for illness, even during harvest time. Almost all places of business were closed on Sundays.[3]

*   *   *

Everyone loved the ever-popular *Jugendverein* (Junior League) held on Sunday evening. The programs were rendered entirely by our small local church talents and sooner or later involved everyone. We often played our guitars and sang.

Then there were the long-winded "Themes," usually by older men on any subject of their choice, which were sheer torture for the children because they were usually in the German language and not understood.

After the evening service it was fun time again, especially for the teenagers. There was considerable coupling up, but always in a group, on the church yard. Since this was in the country, with no place to go but home, we took full advantage of this time, while our parents visited with their friends and the small children lay stretched out on the pews fast asleep.

I've always felt that Sundays were special, the day our Lord set aside for a purpose.[4]

The Night We Forgot My Little Sister in Church *by Marie Loewen Franz*

In our early years the church building was only a quarter of a mile away from our house out in the country, so naturally we walked. One evening after the services, as usual, mothers had to awaken little children who had fallen asleep on the pews.

We never went home together. The older kids usually went on ahead. On one particular evening my little sister, Bertha, even though she had been awakened, just couldn't stay up. She immediately lay back down on the pew and in no time was fast asleep. Meanwhile, Mother, thinking she had gone on home with some of the rest of us, also went on home with Dad and the baby. Our parents didn't always take a head count.

Around midnight a bad thunderstorm suddenly came up. There was much blinding lightning and crashing thunder, followed by threatening rain. All this commotion awakened Bertha. At first she didn't know where she was, and everything was cold and dark. When she finally realized that she was in church all by herself, with no one around, she became terribly frightened. Luckily, the door was unlocked so she started for home. Only she walked very slowly because she had the idea that if she ran when she was frightened, she would fall down dead, a holdover from ghost stories she had heard. No sooner had she come home and into her bed when a heavy downpour of rain started which lasted for several hours. Bertha had made it back all by herself, safely.[5]

Sunday Entertaining *by Marie Harms Berg*

When guests came for Sunday *Faspa,* a tablecloth was spread over the oilcloth on the table. Only on very special occasions did we use the white damask tablecloth, which belonged in Mother's hope chest. Mother also had a large dinnerware set, white with small blue flowers. For *Faspa* the small plates of this set were used. On very special festive occasions the large dinner plates were set on the table.

When setting the table for a dinner, the knives, forks and teaspoons were all placed on the right side of the plate. If soup spoons were needed, they were put above the plates. We did not have silver cutlery or stainless steel, rather a steel that rusted easily, with wooden handles. When this cutlery was washed, we were not to put it into the water, for the wood would lose its shape or break off. It had to be dried carefully, otherwise it would rust. We knew the only way to clean it was with elbow grease and brick dust.

On Sunday dinners Mother usually prepared a kettle of *Mooss,* which she served with cold ham and fried potatoes. Sunday was a great day for the girls of the family because the dishes were washed only at breakfast. At noon and in the evening, they were stacked and waited until Monday morning.

Sunday Dinner *by Agnetha Duerksen*

Food for Sunday was prepared the day before. Simplicity was the key word. Going to church by horse and buggy made Sunday dinners late, especially for those who lived far from the church. I recall one particular Sunday when father invited Elder Heinrich Banman and his family to stop for dinner. Mother had planned a simple meal of *Brocke Mooss* (hot milk with *Zwieback*). She thought this too plain for guests like the Banmans, so she improvised by frying ham and eggs.

On Sundays we were not permitted to do any work other than that which was absolutely necessary. Those of us who grew up in this culture feel less tolerant of some of the practices today. If weather prohibited attendance at church, father would read a sermon from an *Andachtsbuch* (Book of Meditations). These sermons seemed long to us and we could hardly wait for the "Amen."[6]

Sister Wiebe's Sunday Dinner

The door to Sister Justina Wiebe's home was always open. Being the wife of Elder Jacob Wiebe, pastor of the Gnadenau congregation, Hillsboro, Kansas, she did much entertaining. Her Sunday table apparently was regularly filled with grateful guests. This was not uncommon among Mennonite people in the early pioneering years.

B.E. Ebel: Sister Wiebe, a small chubby woman, was very industrious, friendly and hospitable. Scarcely a day passed that she did not entertain guests, and often she offered needy persons food and shelter for days and even weeks at a time. On this particular Sunday she made everyone feel welcome.

When the meal was ready, some sixteen adults sat down to eat while the children were obliged to wait for the second service. At the invitation of her husband, Brother Jacob, all rose to their feet and folded their hands with bowed heads while the elder of the Gnadenau congregation rendered thanks to God for the food.

The dinner consisted of fried potatoes, fried slices of smoked ham, a big bowl of *Plümemooss, Zwieback* and coffee. The food was delicious, and the bowl as well as the *Zwieback* plate had to be filled repeatedly to satisfy the farmers' healthy appetites. There were no appetizers or cocktails, no salads, no relishes and no desserts; there was only one course. The above-mentioned dishes were eaten together and constituted a delicious meal.

Justina Friesen, daughter of the mayor of Halbstadt, Molotschna Colony, married Jacob A. Wiebe on April 11, 1857. Wiebe later was elected minister and was one of the founders of the Krimmer Mennonite Brethren Church, Annenfeld, Crimea. This entire congregation immigrated to Kansas in 1874. My own octogenarian uncle, John Toevs, of Hillsboro, remembers this kindly couple from his early boyhood days.

Other Sunday Activities

John F. Jost: In one of the early years of the Gnadenau settlement, a big blizzard blocked the roads around Hillsboro. On Saturday the immigrant men joined together and hand shoveled a mile of road, opening the way for village families to attend services on Sunday.

Frieda Pankratz Suderman: The only day of the week I found boring was Sunday because we were not supposed to do some things on Sunday. We were not even allowed to do the sewing for our dolls. In the forenoon we always went to church. When the weather was not pleasant, the afternoons dragged. We changed our best dresses into our next-best ones. As soon as my sisters and I had washed the dishes we were ready to go [visiting]. Mama took some of her fresh Saturday baking and we felt sure of a welcome.[7]

John H. Enns: For the young people of the Reesor, Ontario, settlement, Sunday was the day for common activity. It began with a walk to church. Afterward they did not go straight home. It became a custom to be invited by a friend one met at church and to follow him to his home for dinner, even if he happened to live two to three miles from the church. After dinner more friends arrived. On cold winter days the time was usually passed playing social games, making music, singing four-part songs or simply bantering with animated youthful talk. Sometimes they stayed for supper and the whole group attended a planned gathering, walking in the dark on the long, high-trodden snow paths amid snow-covered spruce trees that threw weird shadows in the light of the swaying lanterns. It would not be unusual for a young person to cover seven to ten miles on foot. During the summer visiting back and forth continued as in winter. There were sometimes excursions to one of the lakes. Some fished or went boat riding or played games and sang. Ordinarily they stayed in the settlement and went for walks after dinner.[8]

* * *

Sunday afternoon visiting brought large numbers of my cousins together at an uncle's farm or at Grandmother Jost's home. At one time there were fifteen cousins, all within compatible ages for playing together. The sedate ways of our elders, sitting in the house and visiting, held little appeal and seemed downright boring to us. If forced by winter weather to remain indoors, we children played parlor games such as cards or checkers or we just told stories. In summer we played hide and seek, tag or tried our hand at games of horseshoe or croquet. When the older boys had had enough of younger girls, they headed for the pond to fish, or they played basketball.

It seemed great sport to chase squirrels or walk on stilts behind the barn. A large pasture afforded us a chance for long walks, picking wild flowers or sampling juicy wild plums along the road. In late afternoon everyone was called back to the house to share in *Faspa,* a tradition which we all enjoyed. Today it seems amazing how we spent long afternoons away from the house (and our elders) playing in a carefree manner, unsupervised, yet safe in that tranquil, country environment.

Guests and Food

Fäl Jast moakt n'ladjet Nast.

Many guests make an empty nest.
Meaning: The girls in a family at-
tract many visitors. They soon marry.
An empty nest!

Oppe Somma Sindach
Wann't Plüme onn Kjielkje räanent,
Kom wie wada.

On a summer Sunday when it rains
plums and noodles, we'll come again.

Mitsch, pitsch, Päpa Mäl.
Dien Kjinja fräte fäl!

My, but your children devour
a lot of food!
— *Low German Maxims*

$\mathcal{D}$RIED FRUIT *MOOSS*
(*Plümemooss*)

1½ cups prunes
1½ cups raisins
6 cups water
¾ cup all-purpose flour
¾ cup sugar

½ tsp. powdered cinnamon or 2
sticks cinnamon
2 cups buttermilk
1 cup cream

In a large saucepan or kettle combine fruit and water and bring to a boil. Simmer until almost tender.

Make a paste with flour, sugar and cinnamon and a little water. Gradually add paste to the hot cooked fruit. Bring to a boil and cook about 5 minutes.

Set aside to cool. Before serving stir in buttermilk and cream.

— *Helen Peters Epp*

ℱRESH CHERRY PLUM *MOOSS*
(*Kjoasche-Plümemooss*)

Ethel Ewert Abrahams: This is a delicious combination of two very fine *Mooss* fruits.
Agnes Rempel Braun: We loved this in the Molotschna — big red plums and cherries combined in *Mooss!*

1 cup fresh red plums, pitted and sliced	1 – 2 Tbsp. flour
1 cup fresh sour cherries	½ cup sugar
5 – 6 cups water	½ cup cream

In a large saucepan combine cherries, plums and water and bring to a boil. Cook until skins pop.

Combine flour, sugar and cream, mixing to a smooth paste. Add slowly to the hot fruit, stirring constantly until mixture comes to a boil. Continue cooking briefly. Remove from heat. Serve hot or cold.

ℐTEWED CHICKEN WITH ANISE
(*Jeschmuadne Heena*)

Anise seeds add an interesting flavor to this one-pot dish of chicken, potatoes and apples. The secret of this tempting meal is long, slow cooking in a heavy pot on the back of the stove. Agnes Braun, Winnipeg, Manitoba, adds dried plums or apples to the pot.

¼ cup butter	¼ – ½ cup water
1 chicken, cut in pieces	Potatoes, peeled and quartered
Salt and pepper	3 – 4 tart cooking apples
1 tsp. anise seed	

Melt butter in heavy, iron kettle with lid or a Dutch oven. Add chicken pieces. Sprinkle with salt and pepper. Sprinkle lightly with anise seed. Cover and simmer slowly. From time to time, add a little water to keep chicken from burning.

Before chicken is tender, add peeled and quartered potatoes and unpeeled, quartered apples. When chicken is done, uncover and let brown, turning the pieces occasionally.

Remove chicken from pot. The juices and liquid from the kettle may be used as gravy for the potatoes. Add a little extra water and butter to the pan juices, if necessary, and bring to a boil. The chicken should have a nice glaze when ready to serve.

ℱRUITED YEAST BREAD DRESSING FOR CHICKEN
(Obstbobbat)

This is a delicious "new" kind of dressing for fowl. Dried apricots also make a tasty addition. Says Sara Zacharias Ens, "When mother didn't make fruit stuffing for chicken, she sometimes served stewed fruit with the chicken."

1 pkg. active dry yeast	½ tsp. salt
¼ cup sugar	1 egg
¼ cup lukewarm water	2½ cups unbleached or bread flour
1 cup lukewarm milk	1 cup raisins
2 Tbsp. margarine	

Sprinkle yeast and sugar over water and stir briskly. Set aside. Warm milk over medium heat, add margarine and salt and cool. In mixing bowl beat egg. Add milk and yeast mixtures. Gradually add 2 cups flour and add raisins. Gradually add remaining flour. (This should be the consistency of thick cake batter.) Beat well. Cover bowl with plastic wrap and set in warm place until doubled in bulk.

When duck or chicken is half roasted, spoon dressing into fowl and bake at 325°F. Any remaining dressing may be spooned into a greased baking pan and baked alongside the chicken.

Faspa

Faspa, a late afternoon lunch or coffee time, is a Russian Mennonite tradition, adopted in farming communities for very practical reasons. Interrupting busy farm operations in late afternoon to eat a large meal was considered poor use of time. However, everyone was hungry and found waiting until the men had finished their fieldwork and chores too long.

Therefore, around 3:30 or 4:00 o'clock in the afternoon women served *Faspa — Zwieback* or buns, cheese and sometimes cold meats. There might be *Schnetje,* crullers or waffles. During busy times *Faspa* was taken to the field where the men worked.

On Sunday it became a festive social gathering, a time when relatives and friends exchanged visits and took time to relax and eat. The menu became more elaborate, but always there was *Zwieback,* coffee and jelly.

The Low German word *Faspa* means afternoon tea or coffee. In the following selections memories of this pleasant hour are recalled by some for whom it was an important Sunday tradition.

Remembering Sunday *Faspa*

Marie Harms Berg: The Sunday *Faspa* custom has changed very little from the time when I was a young girl. Mother used to bake coffee cake, cookies and dark bread. People would buy a chunk of nice cheese. Real butter was served, homemade jellies and jams and also home-canned fruit. Today, here in Hillsboro, we still bake *Zwieback* on Saturday.

My son, when he came to live with me after being on his own for about twenty-eight years, said, "Mamma, it pays to live through the week just to eat your nice Sunday *Fespers*.

Mary Dirks Janzen: For *Faspa* in Russia the children had *Prips,* the adults had coffee. In summer we had *Rosinenstriezel* bread and fresh fruit.

Ann DeFehr Dueck: I never remember eating at a bare table in Russia. We had a beautiful cloth and lovely napkins.

Marie Loewen Franz: When visiting someone's home the children ate from plates the adults had used. Of course, the adults, knowing this, always left a clean plate by swabbing it clean with the last piece of bread. I remember looking at all the women, then picking out the prettiest one. It was her plate I chose. Five couples could have as many as thirty or forty children, maybe more. No way could the mothers spend all the time it would take to wash so many dishes. And who ever heard of paper plates? We didn't mind, we were used to this and it never hurt anyone.[9]

Saturday Summer *Faspa*
(Russia)
Sunday began on Saturday with all the baking preparations. Saturday afternoon *Faspa* was a foretaste of the Sabbath celebration.
Served outside under the spreading pear tree
Samovar Tea
Zwieback
Plum or Cherry Jam

* * *

Sunday *Faspa*
(Kansas, 1930s)
Zwieback
Butter & Jelly
Cinnamon rolls or coffee cake
Cheese
Sugar cubes
Coffee and Cream

Sugar Cubes Only on Sunday

Very little sugar was used in the preparation of food in Russia. It was put on the coffee table only on Sundays when there were guests. Even then, grownups were polite and seldom took any. Children, if they had their way, showed less moderation. But there was usually little choice. They had to do with one piece beside their cups and saucers.

Minnie Jost Krause: We always had sugar cubes on Sunday for *Faspa* and at weddings. Sugar cubes and *Zwieback* go together. They were like candy. We'd dip them into the coffee and suck on them. Mother always kept the sugar cubes hidden.

Helen Peters Epp: Faspa was always *Zwieback* and cheese and sugar cubes and coffee. At Grandma Hiebert's we had as many sugar cubes as we wanted. If we were sick when we stayed with her, she would put peppermint drops on them. Oh boy! That was special. Since that was good for bellyache, we often had aching bellies. Sugar cubes were not as refined as now; they were coarser. Sometimes it came in a hunk, almost like salt. You had to chip away at it. It was hard as rock and you couldn't use that kind for baking. Other times we bought sugar in a sack cloth.

Mary Dirks Janzen: On Sundays we had sugar in a container.

Peter Epp: On Saturday evening we had tea and fresh *Zwieback* and we could put as much sugar in our tea as we wished.[10]

Anna Epp Entz: I was not fond of sugar cubes, so all my cousins wanted to sit next to me at the *Faspa* table.

The *Faspa* Song

A Low German musical comedy group, *Heischraitje & Willa Honich* (Locusts and Wild Honey), based in Winnipeg, Manitoba, Canada, has in their repertoire an original song, *Faspa*, sung to the tune *Killigrews Soiree*. The words tell of a modern day *Faspa* that takes place after a football game. Since the menu is more like a banquet than afternoon coffee, everyone would surely be stuffed, rather than well fed. English and Low German mix in this humorous rendering of Sunday *Faspa*.[11]

1. *No Footbaulspeel onn Meddachschlop,*
Hop daut jeft noch Faspa.
Dennet Jelle onn Schinkjefleesch,
Sindach opp Faspa.
Dee goode Jips, ekj jrips no Prips,
Sindach opp Faspa.
Met aul dee Jast, doa woat jemast,
Sindach opp Faspa.
2. *Maunjchmol nu en Barbeque*
Sindach opp Faspa.
Foake uck daut Fleesch fonne Han,

En Han, ne Kün opp Faspa.
Mie es't ne Lost, dee scheene Kost
Sindach opp Faspa.
Onn dan nom äte, Päpanät,
Sindach opp Faspa.

Chorus: *Daut jeft Rintfleesch, Schinkjefleesch,*
Heenafleesch onn Tweeback reesch,
Kommst Borscht, Foarmaworscht,
Sindach opp Faspa.
Schnetje, Portselkje,
Varenikje onn Paskja.
Nü sie toofräd, fonn deiete.
Es kjeene Räd opp Faspa.

English Translation

1. After football games and afternoon naps,
   I hope we still have *Faspa*.
   Runny jam and thick sliced ham,
       Sunday at *Faspa*.
   The best oilcloth (table), I grab for coffee,
       Sunday at *Faspa*.
   With all the guests we have plenty of food,
       Sunday at *Faspa*.
2. Now and then there's a barbeque,
       Sunday at *Faspa*.
   Often, too, there is chicken, a rooster,
       or a turkey at *Faspa*.
   I'd like to have a good repast,
       Sunday at *Faspa*.
   And after all that some peppernuts,
       Sunday at *Faspa*.

Chorus: There'll be roast beef, roast pork,
   Chicken and toasted *Zwieback*.
   Cabbage *Borscht*, farmer's sausage,
       Sunday at *Faspa*.
   Finger biscuits, New Year's fritters,
   Varenikje and Easter bread.
   Now enough of dieting.
   There'll be no such talk at *Faspa*.

ZWIEBACK — A CONTEMPORARY VERSION

2 cups milk
⅔ cup vegetable oil
⅔ stick margarine
3 tsp. salt
4 Tbsp. sugar

1 cup warm water
2 Tbsp. yeast
2 tsp. sugar
8 – 10 cups flour

In a saucepan combine milk, vegetable oil, margarine, salt and 4 Tbsp. sugar. Heat to very warm; cool to lukewarm.

In mixing bowl combine warm water, yeast and 2 tsp. sugar. Allow to stand until bubbly. Add cooled milk mixture.

Stir in half the flour gradually and beat with electric mixer for five minutes. Add remaining flour gradually and knead with dough hook or by hand until dough is smooth and elastic.

Grease bowl and cover. Let rise in warm place until double in bulk.

Pinch off small ball of dough the size of a small egg. Place on greased pan. Place another ball, slightly smaller, on top and lightly press down. Let rise until double in size. Bake at 400°F. for 15 – 20 minutes.

SUMMER FRUIT *PLAUTS* FROM *ZWIEBACK* DOUGH
(*Obstplauts*)

The most tempting variation is a fruit *Plauts,* made with almost any summer fruit. Your family will love you and beg for more next week. *Plauts* has long been a favorite, as these women tell:

Mary Dirks Janzen: We always made *Plauts* all summer long with *Zwieback* dough.

Agatha Schroeder Fast: When you made *Zwieback,* you made fruit *Plauts* too. In summer we did this almost all the time.

Agnes Rempel Braun: Sprinkle sugar over the fruit before baking. Sprinkle some more over it as soon as it comes from the oven.

Press *Zwieback* dough about ½ inch thick into a greased 9″ × 12″ pan, pushing dough up and making an edge all around the pan (to catch the fruit juice).

Fruits such as apricots, apples, peaches, plums or cherries may be placed on top of the dough. If desired, peel the fruit, halve or quarter it and arrange so it completely covers the dough. Sprinkle with sugar and cinnamon or sprinkle generously with the crumb topping given below.

Crumb Topping for Fruit *Plauts*

¾ cup sugar
¾ cup flour

½ tsp. baking powder
2 tsp. butter

Cream all ingredients between fingers until crumbly.

Celebrations among Russian Mennonites

Niejoa (New Year)	January 1
Helje Dree Kjeenijch (Three Kings' Feast/ Epiphany)	January 6
Jreendonnadach (Green Thursday/Maundy Thursday)	March or April
Stelle Friedach (Good Friday)	March or April
Oostre (Easter)	March or April
Himmelfoat (Ascension Day)	40 days after Easter
Pinjste (Pentecost)	7th Sunday after Easter
Maidach (May Day)	May 1
Säwenschlopadach (Seven Sleepers' Day)	June 27
Dankfast (Harvest Festival)	October
Martien (St. Martin's Day)	November 11
Wienachtowent (Christmas Eve)	December 24
Wienachte	December 25
Niejoaowent (New Year's Eve)	December 31

Christmas in Russia

Ekj wensch, ekj wensch,
Ekj sie en kjleena Mensch.
Wan ekj eascht woa jrata senne,
Woa ekj bäta wensche kjenne.

I wish, I wish,
I'm only a little person.
But when I will be bigger,
I will make better wishes.
— *Old Low German Wishing Rhyme*

* * *

"Isn't it a wonderful time, these weeks in winter, when one is rained or snowed in and waits for Christmas?

"Hans agrees that now, a short month before Christmas, a beautiful mood prevails in the house. There is no excessive hurry, no pushing, no chasing while people work. It doesn't matter at all if Hans occasionally spends a half hour in the feed shed with Ivan, chasing sparrows who come there for shelter from the winter weather. There is time for Olga to tell him, while peeling potatoes, about her experiences when she walked in Christmas processions, carrying a star from house to house." [1]

* * *

For Russian Mennonite children the greatest excitement of the year came with the celebration of Christmas. There were three full days of festivity — programs at church and school, exchanging visits with relatives and eating to one's heart's content.

The celebration, by today's standards, seems simple. There were no decorated trees in the homes. Only the children received small gifts. Every family had its own private celebration with Scripture reading, singing and prayer.

For weeks the children prepared long poems to recite to their parents. These were called "Wishes" and were presented on Christmas morning. After church there was a traditional menu, served many other times during the year, but somehow on Christmas the plums in the *Plümemooss* were tastier and plumper, the ham slices thicker, the potatoes fried to a more golden crisp. Never before had the peppernuts tasted so good. Large bowls of oranges, apples and nuts added luxury to the occasion. In the evening the family sat around the table eating the rich, meaty Brazil nuts or picking fat brown pieces of pecan from their paper shells. The mingling fragrance of fresh oranges and spicy peppernuts was a once-a-year happening.

The day after Christmas there were more family gatherings at the grandparents. Children lined up to recite their long "Wishes" before the uncles and aunts and Grandpa and Grandma. In return, grandparents gave treats such as a sack of candy, a kopek or a dime. It was a holy time of quiet and simple celebration.

* * *

Among the Mennonites in Russia the Christmas, Easter and Pentecost holidays were each observed for three consecutive days. This tradition dates back to the time of the Reformation when Mennonites separated from the Catholic church. The Eastern Orthodox church had a custom of holding one day of devotion for each member of the Trinity — Father, Son and Holy Spirit — on these particular holidays. This was one Catholic tradition not discarded by the Anabaptists and has been maintained through the years by some Anabaptist groups.

Christmas in Gnadenfeld *by Mary Dirks Janzen*

Christmas in Gnadenfeld was exciting for a young girl. Each year we memorized a Christmas poem. The teacher ordered special booklet covers for the poems, which we copied in our very best penmanship, as neatly as possible. The covers of the booklets were so beautiful — decorated with branches and walnuts and sprinkled with glitter. Some had little winter birds sitting close together on a bough, or a Christmas tree decorated with shiny balls and lighted candles.

On Christmas morning, after breakfast, each of us would give our *Weihnachtswunsch* (Christmas wish) to our parents. We then recited the poem while mother and father followed the lines in the folder. When each child had given this wish, the Christmas gifts — the only gifts we got all year — were presented to us.

There was so much secrecy surrounding Christmas. Father would buy a beautiful spruce tree and hide it so that no one would get to see it until it stood decorated in the living room on Christmas Eve.

Children would, under no circumstances, help decorate the Christmas tree. The older members of our family, brothers Kornelius and Jacob, sister Agatha, maybe a sister-in-law and my father, did the decorating while we three younger children, Heinz, Miche and Katja, had our baths before going to church to take part in the grade school Christmas program. The two doors leading to the *Grootestow* (living room) were safely guarded from curious little eyes, which for us was extremely difficult to endure.

Secrecy hovered everywhere on Christmas Eve. It was an old Mennonite custom that Christmas gifts were put on a plate for each member of the family. Presents were kept a complete surprise until Christmas morning. Plates were always filled with goodies and when times were good in Gnadenfeld — from the year I was born, 1905, until 1914 when World War I broke out — little girls received beautiful dolls with china heads and later a wardrobe for the doll. Sometimes there was a new dress or an apron among the gifts. There might be hand-knit mittens, a shawl or gloves, aprons or petticoats and German storybooks. For the boys there might be a carved wooden horse or lamb, a penknife, a small wind-up metal train that ran along the floor or hand-sewn shirts made by our two older sisters. Candy was very rare; only the well-to-do had such a luxury.

After the tree was decorated and the gifts safely hidden from our little eyes, the whole family went to the church Christmas program. This was so different from any other worship service. To a seven-year-old the decorated Christmas tree in the church seemed to reach a height of thirty feet (which, of course, was not the case) but it must have been at least fifteen feet high, standing right in the center in front of the elevated pulpit.

We sat in pews facing the Christmas tree. Such wonderful things happened on this evening — reciting our short memorized pieces, singing with the entire grade school and watching the huge tree being lighted by a single white string. The string was lit by a match and allowed to burn until all the candles on the tree were ablaze.

Our old schoolmaster, Abraham Braun, was experienced in putting on children's programs in which everything went smoothly. After the last child had said his piece and the last note of *Stille Nacht* had faded away, he brought out our rewards — large baskets filled with small paper bags. Each bag was filled with nuts, an orange, some hard candy (no chocolate), an apple and a German storybook.

How our hearts pounded with excitement! This evening, indeed, was filled to capacity with wonders. The secrets of the Christmas tree and gifts at home, the white string which by sheer magic lit the Christmas tree lights in church, the privilege of reciting aloud in church (on other Sundays children were to be absolutely quiet) and the paper bag filled with good things to eat.

Furthermore, we always had new clothes for this special day. Before the Revolution, a local seamstress made our clothes from fine material, trimming our dresses with velvet edging and pretty buttons. Girls wore high-button shoes and boys high, lace-type boots.

All of us children knew well the Christmas story from Luke. Abraham Braun had drilled this Bible story into us, beginning with John the Baptist to the birth of our dear Lord Jesus. On Christmas the story of the Christ Child's birth was very special to us.

*   *   *

In Gnadenfeld there were three full days of Christmas celebrations. Visitors who came brought their children along so we could play. Each day there was church with a Christmas message and beautiful a cappella singing by the choir. After church there were dinners of *Plümemooss*, baked ham with dill and beet pickles, two kinds of bread and milk. Coffee was served for *Faspa* along with *Zwieback*, butter and jam or watermelon syrup. The coffee, for the grownups, and coffee substitute, *Prips*, for the children, were cooked in the tile oven, which also warmed the house. There were other baked delicacies for this occasion.

Our mother was a fine cook. She would have enough *Mooss*, ham, *Zwieback*, cookies, white and rye bread, butter and homemade spirited mustard to last for three days of festivities as the family and all the relatives came.

If relatives brought children, they would recite their *Weihnachtswünsch* and expect a gift. As a rule, the reward for reciting the Christmas poem was a bright blue, flowered handkerchief tied at its four corners and filled with nuts, hard candy, cookies and an apple. We children would go to the neighbors and relatives just to recite our Christmas poems and come back with gifts.

To accommodate three days of celebration, a house had to be big and have many rooms. The children usually played in one room, the young people visited in another and the older people were in a third. At day's end the distant guests would drive home with horse and carriage. Close neighbors bundled up and walked home, crunching through the crisp snow by the light of the moon.

Christmas in Osterwick *by Kaethe Kasdorf Warkentin*

At the time I lived in Russia, the churches still celebrated Christmas. It was much like here in North America, except everyone celebrated for three days.

On Christmas Eve there was always a big tree at church—decorated with lighted candles, apples and a few paper pictures. Our tree decorations, as well as our ideas and traditions, came from Germany. The Russians did not have trees.

After the church service on Christmas Eve, we went home and put our plates under the tree. While Dad prepared the plates, we listened from our beds to the nuts rattling, counting how many candies he dropped into each plate.

Mom and Dad bought all the treats long before Christmas and hid them in an old Russian chest. On Christmas morning we children got up very early, while it was still dark, ran and pounded on the doors of the *Grootestow*. We wanted to peek through the keyhole because we hadn't seen the tree and candles.

However, before we received our gifts, we had to say our Christmas poems for our parents. So we lined up properly to recite the *Wünsche* while Mother, Dad and Grandma sat listening. Then we were allowed to see the tree and get our plates. There were *prjaniki* from the Russian bakery. Those were the best filied cookies I've ever tasted, and my mouth still waters for them. There was an apple and, if we were very lucky, an orange. The oranges, we were told, came from far away, all the way from the Crimea or across the water.

Our gifts were mostly practical things—a new skirt, a blouse or an apron. When our parents were well-to-do, there were special gifts like our first little purses. These cost 80 *Kopeekje* each we found out later. We were terribly proud of that. All of this took place before breakfast. Later the adults went to church, and we children were allowed to stay home with a servant. After the service we had baked ham, cherry or *Plümemooss* and *Zwieback*.

On the second day of Christmas, the grandparents and others would come. We had all learned a Christmas wish. We always waited for someone to invite us to come, *"Nü kommt mol Wensche"* [Now come and recite your verses]. We waited anxiously for that invitation because it always meant a little gift from a neighbor, a friend or an aunt. If it was close by, we children were allowed to go alone. If it was far, Dad went with us. Most of the time we received a handkerchief that had been tied together and filled with candy and nuts. Long before Christmas each of us had been counting how many places we could go well-wishing. It was almost like Halloween.

Christmas in the Kuban *by Anna Reimer Dyck*

[Anna Reimer Dyck grew up on a large farm estate in the Kuban. However, the Christmas celebration at home and in the church resembled those in the villages.]

The rustle of paper, the chattering, all kinds of secrets—these were all part of getting ready for Christmas. We embroidered, made colorful paper designs, and crocheted. It was comfortable and cozy to sit at the round table over which a lamp hung, while in the oven some apples were being baked.

As Christmas came even closer, all of us children waited impatiently. When darkness began to fall, all of us would get ready for the Christmas program, which was presented alternately by the school one year and by the Sunday school the next. Carols were sung, and poems and plays were presented. Naturally, everything was presented in German. Although we also studied Russian at school, our mother tongue was our main language. At the close of the program, all students and other children were given a bag of treats.

Afterward, our family would go to Aunt Anna's home for the evening meal, since she was the oldest of Father's brothers and sisters. Here we would sing the beautiful old carols again. Later we children received small gifts from Aunt Anna and bags of sweets. When we arrived at home, we went to bed quickly for we knew there would be more gifts the next morning.

On Christmas morning mother found it easy to waken us. Quickly we dressed, washed and combed, then waited for the clock to chime. All the servants came to join the celebration including those who lived on our farmyard. Later, when refugees had come to stay on our farm, they also joined us. Everyone waited and when father rang the bell, all hurried into the room where the gifts and treats had been prepared.

There the lights brightened the Christmas tree, while the pungent aroma of the candles filled the room. Then father would read the well-known Christmas story. Each time it still seemed new. Following this, we sang carols, such as *"Welch ein Jubel, welche Freude"* [What Rejoicing, What Joy], and then we recited poems for our parents. Only then would mother remove the covering from the gifts, and when she did so, we could see at once what lay there, for in those days we did not wrap our gifts. Beside each dish lay a practical gift.

When the excitement had calmed down somewhat, and our gifts of sweets had been put away, we had breakfast. Following this there was church and dinner at home; then the visiting began. On the second day we would have church service again. In the afternoon we enjoyed visiting and feasting. Then, on the third holiday, after we had had church service, everyone came to our home.

There was also a fourth holiday, only for visiting. In fact, the celebrations continued until Epiphany.[2]

Christmas Caroling

Mia Reimer DeFehr: At the close of the Christmas Eve program the families would go home, but the young people, accompanied by their youth leader, went caroling into the wee hours of the morning. They stopped at as many as forty places to sing and every now and again to enjoy a cup of tea and cookies. But none were too tired to be on hand Christmas morning to sing in the choir for the very important Christmas service. For three consecutive mornings the church family celebrated Christmas.[3]

Christmas in Communist Times

Suse Rempel: During Communist times Christmas was no longer celebrated. People were forced to work on Sunday. Outwardly, they celebrated New Year, but deep, deep down they were celebrating the birth of Christ. There were usually humble gifts. Beautiful ammonia cookies were on a plate. This was a real treat for we rarely got anything like candy.[4]

𝒴EAST PEPPERNUTS

Helen Peters Epp: My mother made these yeast peppernuts. We called them *Eenbacksel* [single bun] or "Bachelor's Peppernuts." These are pinched off like *Zwieback* dough. Mother made only the yeast peppernuts, not the hard ones. She used lard in the recipe and the spices were cinnamon and maybe a little nutmeg or pepper.

This bun is typical of the very old standard recipes.

2 Tbsp. active dry yeast	1 cup sugar
½ cup lukewarm water	1 tsp. cinnamon
1 tsp. sugar	½ tsp. black pepper
1½ cups milk	¼ tsp. nutmeg (optional)
½ cup lard, shortening or margarine	5 – 5½ cups bread flour

Sprinkle yeast over lukewarm water and 1 tsp. sugar; stir briskly. In a saucepan combine milk and margarine over medium heat until very warm. Stir in 1 cup sugar. Cool to lukewarm. In mixing bowl combine yeast and milk mixtures. Stir together flour and spices. Gradually add half the flour and beat five minutes with electric mixer. Gradually add enough flour to make a soft dough.

Turn dough out onto floured board and knead until smooth and elastic, about 8 – 10 minutes. If using dough hook, knead according to mixer directions. Place dough in greased bowl, turning to grease top of dough. Cover with plastic wrap and set in warm place until doubled in size. Punch down.

Pinch off 2-inch pieces of dough and place touching in 9″ greased cake pan or baking sheet. Cover lightly and let rise until doubled in size. Bake at 350°F. about 25 – 30 minutes or until done. Cool on racks. Cover with clean Turkish towel to retain soft crust. Makes about 2½ dozen buns.

—Helen Hiebert Peters
—Helen Peters Epp

ЅYRUP PEPPERNUTS WITH YEAST
(Häwpäpanät)

One of Agnes Braun's secrets for good yeast dough is the generous addition of eggs. Mrs. Braun says the watermelon syrup they used in Russia gave these buns a special flavor which you do not get using molasses. "They are very slow. *Dee sulla en poa Stund gona lote."* (They should rise about two hours.)

1 cup milk	2 tsp. sugar
½ cup margarine	½ cup lukewarm water
¼ cup vegetable oil	4 eggs
¾ cup sugar	1 – 1½ tsp. cinnamon
½ cup watermelon syrup, dark	6½ – 7½ cups bread flour
Karo® or molasses	Egg glaze
2 Tbsp. active dry yeast	

In a saucepan combine milk, margarine and oil over medium heat until very warm. Stir in ¾ cup sugar and syrup. Cool to lukewarm. Sprinkle yeast and 2 tsp. sugar over lukewarm water and stir briskly. Allow to become bubbly. In mixing bowl beat eggs until light. Add yeast and milk mixtures. Stir cinnamon into flour. Gradually add half the flour and beat five minutes with electric mixer. Gradually add enough flour to make a soft dough.

Turn dough out onto floured board and knead until smooth and elastic, about 8–10 minutes. If using mixer with dough hook, the entire amount of flour may be added and then complete kneading according to mixer directions. Place in greased bowl, turning to grease top of dough. Cover with plastic wrap and set in warm place until doubled in bulk (about 2 hours or more). Punch down.

Pinch off pieces of dough the size of a lemon and set close together on greased 9″ cake tin or baking sheet. Cover lightly and let rise until doubled in size (allow plenty of time). Brush with 1 egg beaten with 1 tsp. water. Bake at 350°F. for 25–30 minutes or until golden and done. Cool on racks. Cover with a clean, Turkish kitchen towel to retain soft crust. Makes 32–34 buns.
— *Agnes Rempel Braun*

One Russian Mennonite Candy Recipe

Among the Schapansky family treasures is a black, ledger-style notebook their mother, Maria Martens Schapansky, brought from Russia to Manitoba. The recipe collection was started when she was married in the village of Steinfeld, South Russia, in 1923. It is filled with her favorite recipes written in old High German script as well as in Russian.

Candy (*Pomashka*) and confection recipes were rare in Mennonite kitchens. However, the family says Maria made this every Christmas. Only in later years did they have store-bought candy. Her children still make this candy, adding peanuts for variation. The recipe was translated from High German.

MARIA SCHAPANSKY'S CHRISTMAS *POMASHKA*

2 cups white sugar	2 tsp. vanilla
1 cup heavy cream	Crushed peanuts (a recent addition)

Mix cream and sugar in heavy saucepan. Over medium heat bring to a boil and cook until a drop hardens in cold water. This would be approximately 234°F. or "soft ball" stage on a candy thermometer. Add vanilla. Add peanuts if desired. Pour into buttered pan and cool. While still warm, cut into squares.

— Maria Martens Schapansky
— Valerie Schapansky Belknap

Christmas in America

Old Traditions in a New Land

Mennonite families who chose to leave Russia in the 1870s to forge a new life in America found the first Christmases difficult. There was poverty, grueling hard work and, sometimes, homesickness.

In spite of this, they found reassurance in their celebrations. In Mountain Lake and Steinbach and Hillsboro, they tried to preserve the old ways from Annenfeld and Alexanderwohl. This bound them together and reminded them of their homeland.

For three days they gathered in worship and celebration. Their children learned long, religious poems (often in German to preserve the language) to recite to the parents. There were programs in church and school. And there was food. The same familiar menu—ham, fried potatoes, *Plümemooss* and peppernuts—continued without change.

In the following accounts you will see the traditions that were kept in Mary Dirks Janzen's and Kaethe Kasdorf Warkentin's families in Russia also being observed by Mariam Penner Schmidt's grandparents and Bertha Fast Harder's family though they were separated by an ocean and thousands of miles.

Traditions provide a link to the past. They bring comfort, security and blessing in times of change and transition.

Christmas at Grandmother Penner's
by Mariam Penner Schmidt

Christmas! How simple the preparations we made seem to me now in all our feverish scramble to do everything we think necessary for the great day.

As I remember, there was much activity in the kitchen before Christmas, baking cookies and breads. Aunt Marie always baked several dark fruit cakes around Thanksgiving, wrapped them in a damp cloth and stuck them among clothes in a chest to age.

My Grandmother Penner, with whom I lived in Mountain Lake, Minnesota, was always knitting. Every grandchild received a pair of new mittens for Christmas. We did not send Christmas greetings to friends — too great an expense!

I always wrote a short note to the *Weihnachtsmann* [Christmas man], listing a few things I would like to have, not really expecting to receive them. I usually asked Aunt Anna, who was only eleven years older than I, to help make something for Grandma and the other two aunts. It might be a hanky with a bit of embroidery or a book mark; something that I could afford on my weekly allowance of a quarter. For many years I believed in Santa Claus. The Christmas after I was told by my little friends Santa was a myth, I was so disillusioned.

*   *   *

On Christmas Eve I never fully undressed, so I could hurry the next morning when Grandpa called, *"Mariam steh auf, es ist Weihnachts Morgen."* [Get up, Mariam, it's Christmas morning.] I did not need a second call.

That morning we always entered the parlor as a family. The tree was always lovely, a beautifully decorated, fragrant pine with real candles. I can still see some of the ornaments. It had been decorated the night before and no one was permitted in that festive room until Christmas morning.

Each of us always gave Grandpa a soup plate (the deeper the better) with our names on a piece of paper. In the morning the plate was filled with candies and nuts and a very precious orange. What child treasures an orange today? The gifts were not wrapped — no ribbons and paper to worry about. They were a child's delight — a doll, dishes and, one magic year, my much longed for writing desk.

*   *   *

After a Christmas morning breakfast, we went to church. I usually had a new dress to wear, thanks to my Aunt Helen, who was an excellent seamstress. I vividly remember one such dress — navy blue velvet with a lace collar and bright buttons down the left side of the dress. How proudly I walked into church that day.

After church all the children and grandchildren came to Grandpa's. How I loved that. Aunt Kate Klein had twelve children. Uncle Abe and Aunt Agnes Penner were there with their four. My dad was usually not there because he was a missionary and lived in India. He came home on furlough in 1909 and spent that Christmas with us. Three of my aunts were not married at that time.

The big table in the dining room was made larger and all the grownups sat there while "the little fry" sat at a long table in the kitchen. Usually at birthday celebrations and Sunday *Faspas* we children had to wait until the grownups had eaten. But not on Christmas day.

After dinner Grandpa and Grandma would excuse themselves and take a short nap. The grownups visited; the aunts did dishes. And if the weather was good, we children were encouraged to play outdoors.

When the nap was over, we were called back into the house. Grandpa read the Christmas story and we sang a number of German carols. Those children who learned short recitations, poems or songs would get up in front of the grandparents and recite them—often being prompted by the elders. Grandpa would reach into his pocket and give each one a nickel!

Grandpa then brought out bowls of candies and nuts. Grandma and the aunts fixed *Faspa* with Aunt Marie's aged fruit cake, Christmas breads and cookies. Everyone was too full to really enjoy the goodies.

In the evening there was a Christmas program at the church where many of us children gave our little *Gedichte* (poems) and sang Christmas carols. There was always a huge tree in church with real candles. I vividly remember two men standing on either side of the tree, holding long poles with rags on the ends. Every so often they dipped their rags into two buckets of water standing under the tree. They were very careful to watch each candle so there would be no fire. We children were fascinated by this.

My Childhood Christmases in Mountain Lake, Minnesota *by Bertha Fast Harder*

We knew that Christmas was coming when Mother got out the book of *Wünsche*. In it were a great variety of Christmas wishes, most of them religious. The poems were handwritten and the booklet had a cover with pale, pastel designs and was tied with yarn. Most of the poems had to do with thanking God for the gift of His Son and asking Him to bless our house. We memorized them and recited them to our parents and grandparents.

*   *   *

After supper on Christmas Eve things started to get exciting. We decorated the house with red tissue paper bells and greens. Our gifts were put on special plates which were filled with nuts and candy. My plate, which came from Russia, was a deep, white soup plate with a pink, fluted edge. We were always so excited and had been counting the nights until Christmas.

Mother put her best tablecloth and candles on the table. We set our plates at our regular places. Then it was time to go to bed, but we were far too excited to sleep. We would lie there listening to Father—clink, clink, clink—put the nuts and candies on our plates. The plates were always topped with marshmallow cookies on a vanilla wafer sprinkled with pink and white coconut.

*   *   *

On Christmas morning the door would be shut. We waited impatiently for Dad to finish the chores and wash up. Before we went in to see our presents, we recited the Christmas wishes we had memorized. We lined up — youngest first, my oldest sister and I in the back. Then Mother would go in and light the candles. When she opened the door, my eyes were riveted on that place around my plate. What did I get for Christmas?

One particular Christmas stands out in my memory. I was about eight years old when I got a little box purse of imitation alligator with a strap that snapped around. Inside the lid was a little mirror. I was the envy of all my friends at church.

*   *   *

In the afternoon of Christmas Day we would go to our grandparents. My mother came from a family of thirteen. Five of them were married and had children, so we had hordes of cousins. We also had five single aunts, some of them school teachers who came home for Christmas. We thought they had such beautiful clothes. And what a treat when they let us play in their bedrooms in the back of that big, old, long house. We admired their clothes and tried on their shoes and sat on their beds and played games.

When it was time for dinner, Grandma and Grandpa and all the parents filled the table. Children ate at the second shift and the aunts who had cooked the food waited till the third shift. When we girls were in high school, we helped serve the table and ate with the aunts.

Christmas dinner was always *Plümemooss,* beautiful, lean, home-cured boiled ham, creamy potato salad, *Zwieback,* rye bread, homemade mustard and horseradish. It was quite good.

*   *   *

We would have a Christmas worship service in the afternoon. At the one grandmother's house there was a long living room and the adults and Grandma and Grandpa would sit in a circle around the living room. There must have been eighteen people or more. When we were a little older, we stood around the edge, behind the grandparents. The younger children sat in the middle of the floor.

The smaller children recited verses for the grandparents, who sat in the center of the room. After each poem they smiled and nodded. We would get a squishy, soft warm kiss from Grandma and a mustachioed, wet kiss from Grandpa. Then he'd put a dime in our hands. We were not rich, so a dime was a great thing for all of us. We had Scripture and prayer and we sang and sang. One neighbor told us, "Oh, when you have a family reunion we always go for a walk about the time we know you will be singing — such wonderful music comes out of that house."

We had all exchanged names, so there was a gift exchange. It was our custom to write a poem with each gift. There were plenty of humorous and clever, but also corny poems. It was a marvelous time.

*   *   *

In the evening our church always had a Christmas program. We girls had new dresses which

Mother had made. The church was beautifully decorated and smelled very much of Christmas. In the corner stood a huge tree with real candles which were lit with those long tapers on a pole. The candle lighters had to be very careful in case a candle would flicker. Our grandfather was one of the "guardians" at the tree; each person had a long, hollow tube pole through which to blow out a candle if it looked risky.

Under the tree there were bushel baskets filled with *Tütjes* (paper sacks) — one for each child in the church and any visitors who came with children. Every child got one of those lovely sacks filled with peanuts, nuts, candies and goodies.

Of course, there were poems and songs by each of the Sunday school classes. The church was always packed. It was such a happy, warm, joyous occasion, even though it might be bitter cold outside. Inside everything was warmth, light and beauty. It was Christmas!

How Beautiful It Was *by Minnie Jost Krause*

Right after Thanksgiving Mother started her molasses peppernuts. Those were the ones "to fill us up." With ten boys around the house, they only lasted a couple of weeks. Later she made the "good peppernuts." Of course, they had to be hidden to keep them for Christmas.

We always had a small tree. When the family gathered in the front room on Christmas morning, Dad read the Christmas story and we children recited the poems we had learned in church. We had put our plates around the table on Christmas Eve. They were filled with candy, nuts and an orange, which was very special. Beside the plate might be a handkerchief or a cap or socks.

The big event at Christmas time was the Christmas Eve program at church. Mother always made new dresses for the girls and shirts for the boys.

I remember one year we had snow. Dad put straw and buffalo robes into the sleigh and we covered with wool comforters. It was so beautiful going down that country road. Dad was driving the horses and Mother was holding the baby in her arms. We children just lay there in the back of the sleigh, watching the stars in the quiet night with the sleigh bells jingling all the way.

Inside the church was a big tree with real candles. We were so proud of Dad since he was the tallest man and would walk around the tree with a wet mop, checking on the candles. He was so tall he could reach the top of the tree. The candles burned throughout the whole program.

When I was very young, we still had gas lamps in church. I remember how they turned them down real low for singing *Stille Nacht, Heilige Nacht.* That still thrills me when we sing it. It was something very special for us children. All the Sunday school classes had their different poems and songs and the choir sang. Then we would get our sacks with all the wonderful treats.

More about Christmas Trees, Programs and *Tütje*

Tina Harder Peters: Christmas was something that was done for the children. I remember someone picking me up one year to blow out one of the high candles on the church Christmas tree. I was so amazed at the beauty of the tree that when I got up to say my Christmas piece I thought only of the wonder of the tree, the darkness and the lights from the candles.

Suddenly I heard my mother prompting me from the audience. I was standing right beside the tree and forgot all about my piece. I can't remember if I was ever able to say it.

Helen Taeves Jost: We drove to Grandma's house in the village [Alexanderfeld, Kansas] in our old spring wagon. As I remember, we made a stage of boxes and performed our verses and songs for her. We had such a good time.

Sara Zacharias Ens: People who had no children of their own would ask us to come over and say our *Wünsche.* They always gave us a present.

Katherina Jantzen Prieb: Oranges were very rare — just to be looked at! We didn't have a tree in those difficult years, but we did put plates on the table Christmas Eve.

Alden Voth: I guarded my Christmas sack so carefully and ate so sparingly that I still had candy left at Easter.

Edward G. Jost: Everyone had a "private" hiding place for his Christmas sack.

Anna Epp Entz: In the early years there was no Christmas celebration in church, no festive decorations. There was only the sermon and the singing of hymns.

Nickel sisters: We didn't have a Christmas tree in the first years in Buhler, Kansas. It was considered heathen. Most people didn't have a tree.

Helen Peters Epp: I always kept my orange until it was about dried up. My brother, George, would get so hungry for it he couldn't stand it. I finally sold it to him. He actually gave me money for it.

H.B. Friesen Diary (1837-1926): We attended the Christmas program at the public Schlehuber schoolhouse [near Hillsboro]. There were poems and songs with organ music and horn and violin music which made a racket as if a dance were being held. In contrast to that, we always had a nice, quiet program at the Steinbach schoolhouse.[5]

Helen Harder Peterson: If we ever had an apple, we were greatly blessed. I don't know that we ever had an orange unless it came from school.

Lisle Stockings and Gilded Walnuts *by Hildred Schroeder Wiebe*

On Christmas morning our plates were always filled with peppernuts, candies and all kinds of nuts — Brazil, hazel, walnuts and almonds.

It was customary to put out plates for Santa to fill. As we grew older and read about how stockings were hung by the fireplace, we wanted to hang up stockings, too. However, we had no fireplace. We soon solved that. We borrowed Mother's and Grandmother's everyday lisle hose and pinned them with big safety pins on the backs of our wooden kitchen chairs.

Christmas morning we found them stuffed and bulging with apples and oranges and at least one special gift such as a ring or locket down in the toe. A delight we especially enjoyed was a gilded walnut shell glued together. Inside was a surprise. We would shake the shell and try to guess what treasure it held. It was always a contest to see who could wait the longest before opening it.

I also remember the first time we found Hershey kisses in our stockings. They were so good and sweet. As we grew older we helped with stringing popcorn and cranberry garlands. We made gilded walnut shell decorations for the tree. Each one hung by a ribbon and was filled with little treasures like coins or candies. Mother usually invited our friends to choose one of the ornaments to take home when they visited us. She thought it a good way to learn to share.

Taking Down the Tree at Church

Hildred Schroeder Wiebe: How we looked forward to the time when they would take down the big Christmas tree at First Mennonite Church in Hillsboro, Kansas. This was done the first Sunday after New Year, and everyone wanted to be there. There were apples and oranges and decorations made with marshmallows stamped in the shapes of houses, trees, drums, toys and horns. I'm sure they were hard, dry and dusty by that time, but no one cared. How we yearned for some of those candies. This was the after-Christmas highlight!

Minnie Jost Krause: One year we had such a snowstorm on Christmas Day that we couldn't go to the program at church. There was still snow on New Year's Day, but Dad hitched up the sled and took us to church. We got our candy. Going home, on North Main Street, there was a huge drift. The horses started to flounder in the deep snow and got scared. The sled flipped over and all of us were dumped into the snow. That didn't matter. All we cared about was saving our candy.

We Did Not Miss a Thing! *by Frieda Pankratz Suderman*

"You missed so much," I'm sometimes told, "because as a child you never believed a jolly Santa Claus could bring the things your heart desired. You did not send him lists of wants, then wonder deep in sweet suspense if you had been quite good enough to rate the things for which you asked. In missing this you were deprived and cheated of a small child's right to view the world in fantasy and shiver with suppressed delight."

But did I miss the best of Christmas when this one thing I always knew—the gifts that magically appeared were there because God's love was true? They were not brought by a jolly ho-hoing elf sliding down the chimney vent. The gifts were there because the Christ Child had been given by God to save all men, and those who received this gift of love gave gifts to others in gratitude. Was it I who was cheated when I knew that our parents had spent many hours in planning and making new playthings because they loved us like God loved His children?

No, I never missed a thing. The surprise and suspense were there. The surprise was in the beauty and loveliness of giving. The suspense came because of a sense of unworthiness. I am glad that I was taught that love inspires love and that to love means to want to give.[6]

RUSSIAN WAFER COOKIES
(Knick Knack)

Agnes Wieler Quiring: Knick Knack were very thin like wafers. We baked them in Zagradov [Crimea].

½ cup butter
2 cups sugar
3 eggs
½ tsp. vanilla

1 tsp. baking soda
3 cups (or more) sifted all-purpose flour
¼ cup sour cream

Cream butter and sugar until light and fluffy. Add eggs and continue beating until light. Add vanilla. Combine baking soda with sifted flour. Set aside. Now alternately add the sour cream and sifted flour.

Allow dough to stand and chill in refrigerator. Roll out very thin on floured board. Place on greased baking sheet. Bake at 375°F. for 7–8 minutes. Cool on racks. Store in airtight container. Flavor improves with age.

— **Mennonite Treasury of Recipes**
— *Annie Fast Peters*

RUSSIAN JAM-FILLED COOKIES
(Bachelor Buttons)

½ cup shortening or margarine
¾ cup brown sugar
1 egg
½ tsp. vanilla

½ tsp. each baking soda and cream of tartar
1½ cups sifted all-purpose flour
thick jam or apricot filling

Cream shortening or margarine and brown sugar. Add egg and vanilla and beat well. Stir together baking soda, cream of tartar and sifted flour. Gradually add to sugar mixture. Mix well.

On floured board roll out small amounts of dough to ⅛-inch thickness. Cut into 2-inch circles. Place a spoonful of jam (preferably one made without pectin, such as apricot jelly) in center of one circle. Place second circle on top and seal edges. Place on greased cookie sheet and bake at 400°F. for 8–9 minutes. Cool.

— *Mrs. J.C. Sawatsky*, **Altona Women's Institute Cookbook, 1954 edition**

ᴀPRICOT FILLING

If you don't have a thick enough jam for making Jam Jams, you might try this filling which works very well. It is not runny and has a delicious flavor.

1 cup chopped dried apricots	2 Tbsp. sugar
1½ cups water	2 Tbsp. lemon juice

Combine ingredients in saucepan and cook until tender, 20 – 25 minutes. Mash or blend. Let cool and use for filling any jam-filled cookie.

�YELLOW AMMONIA COOKIES
(*Gruznikje*)

Margaret Klassen Sawatsky: Every year we had Russian friends who came to wish us well at Christmas. They came from nearby villages and threw grain in our front door. Occasionally, we were also visited by strangers. If you weren't out of bed, they came in anyhow. They always sang a blessing, wishing us riches for the coming year. Mother always had plenty of *Gruznikje* on hand to give to the Russians.

1½ cups sugar	1 Tbsp. baking ammonia
½ cup butter	dissolved in 1 Tbsp. hot water
2 large or 3 small eggs	1 cup cream, sweet or sour
5 drops oil of peppermint	4½ – 5 cups unsifted all-purpose flour

Cream sugar and butter. Add eggs and beat well. Add peppermint oil. Dissolve ammonia. Add cream and ammonia. Add enough flour to make a soft dough. (If the dough sticks to your fingers when touched, it is too soft.)

Roll out on lightly floured board to about ⅛-inch thickness (not less or it will be too spongy). You may sprinkle with colored sugar before baking. Place on greased baking sheet. Bake at 375°F. for 9 minutes. Cookies should be white. Makes 5½ – 6 dozen.

—*Ida Epp Hildebrand*
—*Helen Peters Epp*

AMMONIA COOKIES
(Pfefferminzküake/Gruznikje)

Helen Peters Epp, a lifelong collector of cookie recipes and her own cookie book editor, says this is her favorite recipe. The dough is easy to handle and the cookies puff up nicely. The recipe uses less sugar than some. Sweetness may be added with a light icing.

¾ cup sugar
½ cup butter
3 small eggs
½ tsp. peppermint extract or 5 drops oil of peppermint

1 cup rich milk
2 Tbsp. baking ammonia
4½ cups (about) unsifted all-purpose flour

Cream butter and sugar. Add eggs and beat well. Add extract or oil of peppermint. Dissolve ammonia in a little of the milk. Add dry ingredients and milk alternately.

Roll ¼-inch thick on lightly floured board. Cut into 2½-inch circles. Place on greased baking sheet and bake at 350°F. for 10–12 minutes.

—*Anna Androes Epp*
—*Helen Peters Epp*

CANADIAN PEPPERMINT COOKIES
(Dreppeküake)

Russian in origin, this cookie is still very popular among the Mennonites in Canada. This recipe, which uses more peppermint oil than many others, has a clear, robust peppermint flavor.

1½ cups white sugar
½ cup butter
2 eggs
2 Tbsp. baking ammonia

½ cup milk
1 cup sour cream
15 drops oil of peppermint
5–5½ cups sifted all-purpose flour

Cream butter and sugar. Add eggs and beat well. Set aside. Dissolve ammonia in the milk or in a small amount of hot water. Add sour cream and peppermint. Add milk mixture, alternating with flour, to batter to make a soft dough.

Roll out small portions of dough ¼-inch thick on floured board. Cut with 2½-inch cutter. Bake on greased sheet at 350°F. for 10 minutes. Makes 6 dozen.

MOTHER'S HONEY COOKIES

Helen Peters Epp: Helen Jost's honey cookie recipe is the best one I've ever had. I think she got the recipe from the Schaeffler family who had the department store in Hillsboro, Kansas. They came from Germany.

Helen Taeves Jost: The longer the honey cookie dough stands, the better. [From my mother's recipe notebook, 1913.]

2⅔ cups honey	4 eggs
Grated rind of 2 lemons or 2 oranges	8–9 cups sifted all-purpose flour
4 Tbsp. baking soda	Pinch of salt
Vinegar	

Melt honey over low burner; add grated rind. Remove from burner. Dissolve baking soda in a little vinegar and add to the honey mixture. Let this stand an hour or two, stirring frequently. Beat eggs well and stir into honey. Gradually add flour and salt. Knead the dough.

Let the batter stand for three days in a warm place. Roll out small portions of dough and cut into Christmas shapes, circles or diamonds. Place on greased baking sheet. Bake at 425°F. for 5 minutes or until gently browned. Allow to cool briefly on pan and remove to wire rack. Cover with honey cookie glaze while cookies are still hot. This recipe may be cut in half. Store honey cookies in tightly covered container. They improve with age and remain fresh a long time.

—*Helen Taeves Jost*

LEBKUCHEN

1 cup honey	½ tsp. each cloves, cardamom, salt
¾ cup dark brown sugar	and baking soda
1 egg, beaten	⅛ tsp. nutmeg
1 Tbsp. lemon juice	⅓ cup finely chopped candied orange
1 tsp. grated lemon peel	peel and citron combined
2½ cups unsifted all-purpose flour	½ cup ground almonds
1 tsp. cinnamon	

Heat honey in small pan over medium heat only until it begins to bubble. Do not boil. Remove and cool. Stir in brown sugar, egg, lemon juice and lemon peel until blended. Set aside and cool to lukewarm.

In a large bowl stir together flour, spices, salt and baking soda. Add honey mixture, candied peel, citron and almonds, stirring until well blended. Cover and refrigerate for several days. Bring to room temperature.

On a heavily floured board roll out a small amount of dough to ⅜-inch thickness. Cut dough into rounds with a 2½-inch cutter. Grease baking tin and line with parchment or sprinkle with flour. With fingers round up cookies toward center. You may decorate with blanched almond halves in the shape of flowers. Bake at 375°F. 10 – 12 minutes or until set. Remove and brush with glaze while still hot. Store in airtight container. Age at least 3 weeks or longer before serving.

Glaze: 1 cup powdered sugar, 5 Tbsp. water or lemon juice.

SOCKANÄT OR *ZUCKERNÜSSE*

Margaret Klassen Sawatsky: This old recipe comes from my father's diary (1912 – 1913), written in German while we still lived in Russia. Soda was measured by price — three kopeks worth.

1 quart *Milch*
1 *Pfund Schmalz*
3 – 4 *Pfund Zucker*
Soda für 3 *Kopeken*

25 *Tropfen Zitronenöhl*
15 *Tropfen Pfefferminz Öhl*
Mehl

— *Margaret Klassen Sawatsky*

SOCKANÄT OR *ZUCKERNÜSSE* WITH AMMONIA
(Sugar Nuts)

Margaret Klassen Sawatsky: In Russia *Päpanät* were also called *Päpaküakje* [little pepper cookies]. Our ammonia peppernuts were larger than the size of a walnut.

Two young boys strike a formal pose for the photographer.

A group of Mennonite school children pose with their teachers beside the village school in 1907.

This is the typical large, soft, sweet peppernut made in Russia.

1¾ cups sugar
¾ cup lard*
3 – 4 drops peppermint oil
1 cup milk

1 tsp. baker's ammonia
½ tsp. baking soda
3 – 4 cups sifted all-purpose flour

*For health reasons you may want to substitute margarine, butter or shortening.

Cream shortening and sugar until light and fluffy. Add flavoring. Stir together dry ingredients. Add alternately with milk, beating well after each addition. (If using ammonia, mix with a small portion of the liquid.) The dough should be quite soft.

Form into 1-inch rolls. With sharp knife cut off ½-inch pieces and place close together on greased baking sheet. Bake at 350°F. until golden brown. Watch closely. You may lay the peppernuts in a Turkish towel while cooling to help retain softness. Store in airtight container.

ЅYRUP PEPPERNUTS

This is a light, slightly hard peppernut with a subtle flavoring of spices and a perky seasoning of pepper. The dough is smooth and easy to work with.

1 cup sugar
½ cup margarine
1 cup dark corn syrup
½ cup each sour cream and whipping cream
¾ tsp. each baking soda and baking powder

¾ tsp. cinnamon
½ tsp. each ground star anise, allspice and nutmeg
¼ tsp. cloves
¼ tsp. (rounded) black pepper
7 – 7¼ cups sifted all-purpose flour

Cream sugar and margarine until light and fluffy. Add syrup, sour and sweet cream. Mix well. In a bowl stir together baking soda, baking powder, spices and flour. Gradually add to margarine and sugar mixture and knead well. This is a fairly stiff mixture. Finish with a dough hook or by hand. Refrigerate overnight.

Roll small amounts of dough into ½-inch ropes. Slice dime-sized pieces with sharp knife. Place on greased baking sheet. Bake at 350°F. 7 – 10 minutes or until golden brown. Cool. Store in airtight container.

—*Ruth Brandt*
—*From* **Pluma Moos to Pie**

SIAROPPSPÄPANÄT

Many of the older recipes use syrup as a partial sweetener. This old Penner family recipe provides ample peppernuts for big family gatherings. It is medium sweet and lightly spiced. I have included both the original recipe and a modified version, which is easier to handle.

Original Version	Modified Version
4⅔ cups dark corn syrup	1 cup + 3 Tbsp. dark corn syrup
2 Tbsp. baking soda dissolved in	1¼ tsp. baking soda dissolved in
½ cup water	2 Tbsp. water
2⅓ cups sugar	½ cup + 1½ Tbsp. sugar
2 cups margarine	½ cup margarine
6 eggs	1 egg + 1 egg yolk, or 2 eggs
1 Tbsp. each cinnamon and cloves	¾ tsp. each cinnamon and cloves
20 cups sifted all-purpose flour	5 cups (about) sifted all-purpose flour

Bring syrup to a boil. Carefully add baking soda; remove quickly from burner and stir in. Soda may cause syrup to boil over. Cream margarine and sugar. Add eggs. Add syrup and combined dry ingredients. Knead dough well. Chill dough overnight.

Roll into ½-inch ropes and cut into small pieces. Place on greased baking sheet. Bake at 350°F. for 9–10 minutes or until golden brown. Store in airtight container.

— *Mariam Penner Schmidt*

EASY PEPPERNUTS

Florence Balzer Penner: This was both my mother's and grandmother's recipe. Peppernuts were always part of our Christmas baking. I can't remember a time when we did not have them. Mother made at least a half bushel, storing them in tins in the pantry and in a dark hallway upstairs.

There were other recipes, but this is definitely our family's favorite. I still make at least three batches. Even so, we run out. Peppernuts work well with small children. They don't leave crumbs like cookies.

My dad, Rev. J.P. Balzer, began his ministerial training after my parents had three children. This meant moving the family to Hesston College and then on to Chicago where he attended Moody Bible Institute. The Great Depression in 1929 necessitated our early return to the Inman community.

1½ cups sugar
1 cup butter, lard or margarine
4 eggs
2 tsp. baking soda mixed with ½ cup buttermilk or sour cream

3¾ – 4¼ cups sifted all-purpose flour
2 tsp. each cinnamon, nutmeg, cloves, ginger

Cream shortening and sugar until light and fluffy. Beat in eggs one at a time. Mix baking soda into liquid and set aside. Sift flour into separate bowl and stir in spices. Gradually add flour and baking soda mixture in alternate quantities, kneading batter thoroughly. If adding fruit or nuts, work in evenly. Cover and chill several hours in refrigerator.

Roll small amounts of dough into finger-sized ropes. Slice into ½-inch pieces and place on greased baking sheet. Bake at 350°F. for about 8 – 10 minutes or until golden brown. Remove, cool and store in airtight container.

Variation: Add 1 cup finely chopped walnuts, coconut, diced citron or raisins.

— *Marie Neufeldt Balzer*
— *Florence Balzer Penner*

ANISE PEPPERNUTS

Anise peppernuts are one of the enduring recipes baked for more than a quarter of a century by the peppernut bakers at First Mennonite Church, Hillsboro, Kansas. Sylvia Unruh Abrahams recalls the early years when their fund raising project first got underway. "Many of us helped roll and cut peppernuts, but it was Fern Goering [Mrs. Roland], our pastor's wife, who always rolled hers in her hands, about ¼-inch in diameter. Every peppernut was perfect and looked exactly the same. Hers were much smaller and daintier than the ones the rest of us made!"

¾ cup lard
1 cup sugar
¼ cup brown sugar
1 cup brown corn syrup
1 tsp. baking soda dissolved in
1 Tbsp. hot water

1 egg
1 tsp. each ground cloves, Cinnamon and anise seed
4½ cups unsifted all-purpose flour

Combine lard and sugars in mixing bowl. Beat until light and fluffy. Add syrup and baking soda. Beat in egg. In a bowl stir flour and spices together. Add gradually to creamed mixture. Cover dough tightly and chill overnight.

Roll into ropes and cut into dime-sized pieces. Bake at 350°F. 7–8 minutes.

—First Mennonite Church, Hillsboro, Kansas

CRUNCHY BROWN SUGAR PEPPERNUTS

This peppernut recipe has become a real favorite in our household. It is crisp, crunchy, rich in brown sugar and chock full of nuts. It appears in a cookie book compiled by Helen Peters Epp, who got it from Selma Voran Graber. It is also a favorite with Evelyn Wiebe, whose husband is on the teaching staff of Fresno Pacific College. She adapted it from Linda Epp's recipe in the *Dorcas Fellowship Cookbook*, Western Oaks Mennonite Brethren Church, Bethany, Oklahoma. Evidently, good recipes sometimes travel many miles.

4 cups light brown sugar	½ tsp. nutmeg
1 cup butter or margarine	¼ tsp. cloves
4 eggs, beaten	7 cups (about) sifted all-purpose flour
1 Tbsp. baking soda dissolved in	3 cups finely chopped English walnuts
1 Tbsp. hot water	
1 tsp. each cinnamon and ground	
star anise	

Cream shortening and sugar until fluffy. Add eggs and mix well. Add baking soda. In separate bowl stir together flour and spices. Gradually add half the flour and mix well. Add remaining flour and mix. Stir in chopped nuts and knead thoroughly. Chill overnight.

Roll dough into thin ropes and slice into nut-sized pieces. Place on greased baking sheet. Bake at 375°F. for 7–10 minutes. Cool. Store in airtight container. (This is a slightly crumbly dough. Keep working the broken places back together. Try to keep sliced pieces small enough or they will become like small cookies.)

—Helen Peters Epp
—Selma Voran Graber
—Evelyn Fischer Wiebe
—Linda Epp

RAISIN NUT PEPPERNUTS

Good recipes always find their way into many collections. This popular recipe circulated among many kitchens in Hillsboro, Kansas. It has been used for more than a quarter of a century as one of the favorite peppernuts to be baked in huge quantities at First Mennonite Church for the annual fund raising event.

1 cup chopped raisins
3 cups sifted all-purpose flour
2 cups sugar
½ cup lard (or margarine)
2 eggs

1 tsp. baking soda dissolved in
1 Tbsp. water
1 tsp. vanilla
1 tsp. each cinnamon and nutmeg
½ cup finely chopped walnuts

Mix the raisins with part of the flour and chop in blender or food grinder. Set aside. Cream sugar and shortening until fluffy. (Substituting margarine for lard will give you a different texture.) Beat in eggs. Add baking soda dissolved in water. Add vanilla. In separate bowl stir together remaining flour and spices. Add to batter. Knead in raisins and nuts. Knead well. Chill dough overnight.

Roll out in long finger-sized ropes. Slice pieces the size of a hazelnut and place on greased baking sheet. Bake at 350°F. for 8–10 minutes. Cool. Store in airtight container.

—*First Mennonite Church, Hillsboro, Kansas*

DUTCH PEPERNOTEN II

½ cup brown sugar
1 egg yolk
2 Tbsp. water
2¼ cups sifted all-purpose flour

¼ tsp. baking powder
⅛ tsp. salt
¼ tsp. each cinnamon, nutmeg,
cloves, powdered anise

Combine all ingredients and knead together into a soft ball. Form into about 90 marble-sized balls and place on greased baking sheets. Bake at 350°F. for about 20 minutes or until golden brown. This recipe was not tested.

—*Heleen Halverhout*
—*Eunice Jonkman*

ĐUTCH *KRUIDNOOTJES*
(Little Clove Nuts)

Ida Feyen-Rÿkens, a teacher in Hoofddorp, The Netherlands, has this to say about peppernut baking in her country. "We usually buy our *Pepernoten* (pay-per-noten) for *Sinterklaas* Day from the baker. However, I also make them with my students, using a box mix. We like to make them to keep the tradition. They smell so nice while baking. *Pepernoten* are baked and eaten the week before December 5.

"In Holland there are two kinds of peppernuts, the old kind which are frosted and are somewhat sticky. These *Kruidnootjes* are crisp like the ones *Zwarte Piet* throws into the houses, classrooms and chimneys in the days before *Sinterklass* Day."

This peppernut is crisp, spicy and simple to make.

1½ cups sifted all-purpose flour	7 Tbsp. butter or margarine (chilled)
½ tsp. baking powder	½ cup brown sugar (packed)
Pinch salt	¼ cup white sugar
½ tsp. each cloves, cardamom and nutmeg	3–4 Tbsp. beaten egg or milk
½ tsp. curry powder	2 tsp. grated orange rind
1 tsp. cinnamon	

Sift flour and stir together with baking powder, salt and spices. Cream butter and sugar. Add egg or milk and orange rind. Add sifted dry ingredients and knead together well. Roll into finger-sized ropes and place on baking pan in freezer for 15 minutes. [The original recipe suggests rolling ropes in sugar; this is optional.] Snip or slice into small hazelnut-sized pieces and place on greased baking pan. Bake at 350° F. for 10–12 minutes or until golden brown. The cookies should not be soft, but crisp. Cool on towel. Store in airtight container. If using milk, it is not necessary to grease cookie sheet.

The original recipe calls for 2 tsp. prepared *Speculaas* spice, plus pinches of additional spices. The spices have been adjusted.

—*Ida Feyen-Rÿkens*

CULTURAL CONNECTION—DANISH *PEBERNØDDER*

"These peppernuts are light, dry and crunchy, the way a peppernut should be," says tester Phyllis Miller Reimer.

1¼ cups sugar
¾ cup butter
2 eggs
4 tsp. fresh, grated lemon peel
1 tsp. baker's ammonia mixed with 1 tsp. hot water

1¼ tsp. cinnamon
1 tsp. each white pepper and ginger
4 cups sifted all-purpose flour
¾ cup finely chopped, unblanched almonds

Cream butter and sugar until light and fluffy. Add eggs and beat well. Add lemon rind and baker's ammonia dissolved in hot water. In a separate bowl combine the flour and spices. Add and mix well. Add the almonds. Chill dough overnight.

Roll into pencil-thin ropes. Cut into bite-sized pieces and place on greased baking sheet. Bake at 375°F. for about 7 minutes. Cool. Store in airtight container.

RUSSIAN PEPPERNUTS

Minnie Jost Krause has baked lots of bread, *Zwieback* and rolls since she was a little girl helping with the baking in her very large family. At one time she baked for a local grocery store in Hillsboro. Her baked goods were always popular. She was one of the best among several good bakers in the Jost family.

2 Tbsp. active dry yeast
2 Tbsp. sugar
½ cup lukewarm water
⅔ cup shortening or margarine
¾ cup sugar
½ cup molasses
2 eggs

2 cups lukewarm milk
1 tsp. salt
3 tsp. cinnamon
1 tsp. cardamom, ground
¾ tsp. black pepper
7–8 cups all-purpose unbleached or bread flour

Sprinkle yeast and 2 Tbsp. sugar in warm water; stir to dissolve. Cream shortening, ¾ cup sugar and molasses. Beat in eggs. Add warm milk, yeast and spices mixed with half the flour.

Beat 5 minutes with electric mixer. Gradually add remaining flour.

Turn onto floured board and knead until smooth and elastic (5 – 10 min). If using dough hook, finish kneading according to machine directions. Place dough in greased bowl, turning to grease top of dough. Cover with kitchen towel and let rise in warm place until doubled in bulk. Punch down and let rise again until doubled in bulk. Punch down.

Pinch off 2-inch pieces of dough, making balls between palms of hands. Place close together on greased baking sheet or in 9″ cake tins. Cover and let rise until almost doubled in size. Bake at 350°F. for 25 – 30 minutes or until golden brown. Cool on racks. Cover with kitchen towel to preserve softness.

— *Minnie Jost Krause*

New Year's Day

New Year's Day is another day rich in tradition and custom. For Mennonite families *Silvesterabend* or *Niejoaowent* began in church with prayers and songs, thanking God for his faithfulness, remembering those loved ones who had departed in death and asking His blessing for the coming year. There were bells in the Russian Mennonite villages at midnight but little of the frivolity and few manifestations of the superstitious customs practiced by their neighbors.

New Year's Day was for visiting friends and family. In the Vistula Delta children who had learned long poems to speak at Christmas had yet another to recite to parents and grandparents. Here are two such rhymes: one in Werder *Plattdeutsch* and the other in High German.

Daut oole Joa es wa' febie,
Daut nie kjemmt enoan.
O daut ekj soo jlekjlijch sie
Daut ekj noch wensche kaun.

The old year is gone again,
The new one comes around.
Oh how lucky I am
That I can still wish!

A New Year's Wish

Hochgeehrter Herr, wohlgeachtete Frau,
Ich wünsch Ihn'n soviel Glück und Segen,
So wie Tropfen in dem Regen,
So wie Flocken in dem Schnee,
So wie Fischlein in Haff und See.
Ich wünsche auch von Herzensgrund,
Ach lieber Gott, lass die Herrschaft gesund.[7]

Highly honored master, well esteemed mistress,

I wish you as much luck and blessing
As there are drops in the rain,
As flakes in the snow,
As fish in the sea.
I wish you also from the bottom of my heart,
O dear God, give the master and mistress good health.
— *Vistula Delta Saying*

Portselkje and Poems

In every Mennonite home New Year's festivities centered around the kitchen. Here the mother baked mountains of sugared raisin fritters for the noon meal. This tradition may have come with the Dutch Mennonites from Holland in the sixteenth century for the Dutch still make fritters for the New Year. In fact, throughout northern Europe frying cakes on this day symbolized fatness and prosperity.

In the Grosses Werder (Vistula Delta) it was also customary to make fritters on New Year's Day. In Werder *Platt* they were called *Portseln* which means tumbling over. When fried in hot fat, they do "tumble over." Children stood beside their mothers at the stove, chanting a little rhyme which earned them a handful of *Portselkje* as the Mennonites called them.

Ekj Kjeem soo häa jerant,	I came here a-running,
Dee Bekjse seen jetrant;	My pants are ripped,
Dee Fuppe senn jebläwe,	My pockets stayed behind.
Nü mott jie mie waut jäwe.	Now you must give me something.
Doa kjikjt ekj äwr'm langen Desch,	I'm looking over the long table.
Waut wea doa fe Jabackniss?	What have you been baking?
Scheene Niejoaschküake.	Wonderful New Year's fritters!
Jäw jie mie eent, dan sto ekj,	Give me one, and I will stand,
Jäw jie mie twee, dan go ekj,	Give me two, and I will go,
Jäw jie mie dree toojlikj,	Give me three at the same time,
Dan wensch ekj jü ḍaut gaunsse Himmelrikj.	Then I wish you the kingdom of heaven.

*   *   *

Wishing

Ekj wensch, ekj wensch.	I wish, I wish,
Ekj sie en kjleena Mensch;	I'm only a little man;
Ekj hab nich fäl jeleat.	I haven't learned much,
Ne Portsel sie ekj doch noch weat.	But still I'm worth a *Portselkje!*

PORTSELKJE

We make this recipe every year at our Lincoln Glen church bazaar here in San Jose, California. I make them every New Year's Day — without fail.

¼ cup lukewarm water	2 cups milk
2 Tbsp. active dry yeast	4 cups sifted all-purpose flour
½ cup sugar	2 cups plumped raisins
6 eggs, well beaten	Cooking oil
3 tsp. salt	1 Tbsp. vinegar
1 tsp. cinnamon	Sugar

Combine yeast, water and sugar. Stir briskly and allow to bubble. Add salt and beaten eggs to the yeast mixture. Beat well. Add cinnamon.

Then add milk and gradually add the flour. Mix well. Add raisins. Do not knead. Cover and let rise until doubled in bulk.

Add 1 Tbsp. vinegar to the COLD oil. Heat to 350°F. Take dough from the side of the bowl, rather than from the middle. Try not to disturb the risen dough. An ice cream scoop (about the size of two walnuts, not too big) is ideal for scooping out the dough. They should not be too big, so they will finish through. Turn when golden brown.

Drain on paper towels. While still warm, roll in granulated or powdered sugar. Serve warm. Fritters may be frozen and reheated. Sugar before using.

—Adaline Becker Karber

SCHMECK HAUS PORTSELKJE II

Here is another version of *Portselkje* used in the *Schmeck Haus* at Bethel's Fall Fest. Different bakers use different recipes. This version uses baking powder and is also found in *The Thresher Table,* the Bethel College centennial cookbook.

2 Tbsp. active dry yeast	4 eggs
½ cup lukewarm water	6 – 8 cups sifted all-purpose flour
2 cups milk	½ tsp. baking powder
½ cup sugar	1 lb. plumped raisins
2 tsp. salt	

Dissolve yeast in lukewarm water. Scald milk; add sugar and salt. Cool. Beat eggs slightly and add to milk mixture. Add yeast mixture. Gradually add flour and baking powder. Add raisins coated with part of the flour.

Cover bowl and let rise until doubled in bulk. Drop by spoonsful into deep hot fat, 375°F. Fry until golden brown. Turn once.

Drain on absorbent paper. Shake in plastic bag with sugar. Serve warm. Yield: 50–60 *Portselkje.*

Note: Dough should be a "hard stir" consistency.

— *Rubena Schmidt Friesen*

Celebrating the New Year in Russia

In the new colonies of Chortitza and the Molotschna, Mennonite women and children continued their old West Prussian traditions of baking *Portselkje* and chanting coaxing rhymes to receive the fritters.

In addition Mennonites in the Ukraine began to participate in some of the local customs. They welcomed little "Russian beggars" who came to the door scattering grain on clean, polished floors and wishing the master and his household a prosperous New Year. In return the beggars pocketed cookies and *Portselkje.*

Mummers also brought pageantry and excitement. They followed an ancient custom of frightening away evil spirits in their costumes and masks. They sang and danced and hoped for kopeks. Most of the time they were given cookies or fritters in the Mennonite homes.

New Year's Eve in Church *by Anna Rempel Dyck*

There were many wonderful celebrations and holidays where song enriched our festivities. Not to be forgotten was New Year's Eve, a night when celebration reached its peak in Gnadenfeld.

Mother baked her wonderful New Year's cookies called *Portselkje.* The goose hung in the attic, ready to be fried. The small singing Russian boys marched from door to door, from village to village, wishing everybody a Happy New Year. They usually departed with heavily loaded bags on their backs.

We wore our Sunday shoes which had been carefully polished by our brother. The ordinary wooden slippers which usually decorated our feet were set aside. We were ready. When Daddy put on his big fur coat and took his walking cane in his right hand, the time had come!

It was icy cold outdoors. We tripped blissfully along with Father and Mother over the crackling snow, steering toward the church. The road to the church led through a beautiful elm avenue in the center of the village. As we passed the village school and crossed the middle of the street, the large, illuminated church with its high bay windows greeted us. Songs and sounds were heard from a distance.

The New Year's Eve service started at 9 p.m. and let out at 12:30 a.m. The entire last half of the service was singing. Preachers and precentors started the songs, then single groups joined in and finally the entire church was singing. This was customary for the New Year's Eve service. Yes, Gnadenfeld was blessed with good singers and song leaders.[8]

New Year's Eve in the Kuban

Mia Reimer DeFehr: On New Year's Eve [*Silvesterabend*] the church in the Kuban once again welcomed worshipers. The evening was spent in reflection and sharing with each other the experiences of God's goodness throughout the past year.

Fittingly, on the first morning of the year, the Christian church looked with hope, trust and gladness into the year before them, beseeching God's guidance for each step of the new, unknown path ahead.[9]

Prayer at Home on New Year's Morning

Each family had its own tradition for worship, but special days called for special prayers. In his book, *Lost in the Steppe,* Arnold Dyck describes young Hans Toews listening to his father's New Year's prayer.

"On Christmas and New Year's morning before sitting down to the breakfast table, all kneel before their chairs, and Father says a prayer aloud. At other times each prays silently before his own bed. Hans is wondering at his father's proficiency and at his warmth. Only he finds his High German pronunciation strange, because he has never before heard him speak High German." [10]

The Russian Wheat and Barley Blessing

The Russian wheat and barley blessing practiced in the Ukraine developed from ancient festivals related to the winter solstice and represented a time of agricultural celebration called *Korochun.* Peasant farmers wished to ensure a good crop for the new year and bring blessing to the entire household. At harvest time the last sheaf of wheat was saved and brought into the house for New Year's Day.

Children of the family threshed this grain and scattered it over the farmstead and in their neighbors' houses. Those who lived in the Mennonite villages remember the ceremony. "The property owner considered it a great honor to be wished well," says Cornelius Jantz.

Johan W. Dueck: Around New Year's time, whole groups of Russian children went from village to neighbouring village in order to "scatter." This represented a blessing of prosperity for the forthcoming year. These groups usually entered the bedrooms of the houses early in the morning and scattered several handsful of grain around the room, which they took from a bag of mixed grain that they carried. They particularly enjoyed spreading grain on the beds, especially if someone was still lying in them. As they were doing this they raised their voices in a harmonious chorus, singing a *Gospidi* [O Lord, have mercy], which was not unpleasant to hear. In such a manner the group wandered from house to house, always anticipating a small gift. At some places their entry was prohibited but in most cases the farmers allowed themselves to be given a New Year's Wish and Blessing.[11]

Kaethe Kasdorf Warkentin: On New Year's morning the Russians from nearby villages came to wish us well. They carried a bag of rye or oats from which they threw handsful of grain across the kitchen floor and chanted this wish:

> I am sowing, sowing, reaping.
> May the New Year give you a plentiful yield.
> With the New Year I congratulate you.
> May the Lord bless you richly.

Anna Reimer Dyck: On the morning of New Year's Day the Russian servants would sometimes push their way into our parents' bedroom. Their pockets were full of grain which they would then throw on our parents as they recited the verse:

> We scatter the seed both far and near
> And bring good wishes for the New Year.

This was a custom that was supposed to ensure a good crop. In return Father would give them some money, for it was our custom to give money to the servants and their children on New Year's morning.[12]

New Year's Day—The *Brommtoppers*

An old tradition with its roots in the Vistula Delta came with the Mennonites to their villages in Russia. On New Year's Day young boys dressed in outlandish costumes painted their faces black and went from house to house singing and performing to the accompaniment of a homemade drum. (In the Vistula Delta it was common to play a "devil's fiddle" as well.) They entertained with little skits and serenaded each household member with an earthy Low German version of the *Brommtopp* song. Herman Rempel says the *Brommtoppspieler* (players, mummers) were primarily Mennonite boys possibly joined at times by Russian servants who were treated as part of the family. They were given *Portselkje*. This custom evidently died out in the Mennonite communities soon after World War I.

Following is the Vistula Delta version of a *Brommtopp* song written in Werder *Platt* and recorded by Siegfried Rosenberg in his book, ***Geschichte des Kreises Grosses Werder***. The Mennonite *Plautdietsch* version with words and music for the *Brommtopp* song may be found in Victor Carl Friesen's *The Windmill Turning*.

Brommtopps Leet

Wie kome hia häa one irjent Spott,
En scheena good'nowent jeft ons Gott;
En scheena good'nowent, ne freelijche Tiet,
Dee ons dee Brommtopp haft jeliet.
Wie wensche däm Harn en gooden Desch,
Opp aule fea Akje en jebrodna Fesch;
Enne Medd 'ne Kruck met goldna Wien,
Doa kjemt dee Har met Lost doabie.
Wie wensche de Frü 'ne goldne Kroon,
Onn ferr't Joa en junga Sän.
Wie wensche däm Sän en jesoldeldet Peat,
En poa Pistoole onn en blanket Schweat.
Wie wensche daut Määkje selwane Fadadoos,
Onn näakjst Joa en junga Matroos.
Wie wensche däm Kjnajcht ne Schrop onn ne
  Schea,
Daut hee kaun putse däm Har siene Pead.
Wie wensche dee Kjäakjsche en rooda Rock
Onn dan omm'n Joa eent mett'm Bassemstock.
Wie wensche däm Koohoad ne Scheffel enne
  Henj,
Daut hee kaun foare dän Growe felengd.[13]

The Brommtopp Song

We come here to you without making fun,
A nice good evening give us God.
A nice good evening and a happy time
Which the *Brommtopp* can provide.
We wish the master a well-laden table,
On all four corners a good fried fish.
In the middle a jug with golden wine,
With that the master may jolly be.
We wish the mistress a golden crown,
And in the coming year a fine young son.
We wish the son a saddled horse,
A pair of pistols and a shining sword.
We wish the daughter a silver pencil case,
In the coming year, a fine young general.
We wish the hired man a currycomb and shears
So he may groom the master's horse.
We wish the kitchen maid a red skirt,
And during the year (a licking with) the
  broomstick.
We wish the cowherd a shovel in hand,
So he can work the length of the ditch.

New Year's Day and the Mummers

Agnes Quiring of Winnipeg recalls that in Zagradovka Russian boys came to her parents' house on New Year's Day dressed in costumes and masks. She also remembers a "stuffed goat." The boys danced and sang in Russian. They were probably mummers. Other Mennonite women were not familiar with this tradition.

According to Marie Halun Bloch, who grew up in the western Ukraine, mummery was practiced by the Ukrainians. After dinner on the First Day of Christmas, young people who were not going caroling gathered to make the rounds from house to house. These mummers, dressed in strange costumes with masks, posed as many different characters—beggars, gypsies, doctors.

Like the Russian grain blessing, mummery had its origin in the ancient festivals of the winter solstice. During this season the days were short and the nights long and dark. Most European peasants, whose homes were lighted only by candle, believed that the demons of winter lurked in the shadows of the house, the barn and the field. Mummers went around driving out the demons of winter. Later, in less superstitious times, the custom continued, but the sole purpose was entertainment. Marie Halun Bloch says this custom died out after World War I.

Ukrainian Star Boys Visit Mennonite Villagers

In the Mennonite villages Epiphany or Three Kings' Day, January 6, was celebrated with a service in the church. In the Kuban a week of prayer services preceded the celebration. January 6 was also a day for Mennonite children to plunder the Christmas tree. Also on this day families sometimes received a visit from the Russian "Star Boys." Russian children from neighboring villages celebrated the coming of the wise men to visit the Christ Child by going about with songs and New Year's wishes.

"On this day there was great fanfare along with beautiful decorations," says Kaethe Kasdorf Warkentin. "Star boys, depicting the wise men, came to our village each year wearing long white robes and carrying a large paper star on a long pole. The star represented the Star of Bethlehem.

Marie Halun Bloch described this event in detail. "One of the group carried a miniature manger. Others dressed as the angel, the three kings and the shepherds. At times a comic character accompanied them. A lighted candle shone through a large star made of thin, colored tissue paper stretched over a frame. More elaborate stars were made so that you could twirl the star. It was an honor, of course, to be chosen to carry the star which was carried about from house to house by the carolers."

One child was also designated "sack carrier" in which the boys gathered gifts offered by the families they stopped to visit.

Star Boys and *Prachaküake*

Kaethe Kasdorf Warkentin: Each year it was my task to stand at the door with the whole dishpan of *Prachaküake* [beggar's cookies], passing them out, three, four, five at a time to the carolers or star boys. Sometimes it was frightfully cold and stormy and I nearly froze standing in the wind and cold at the door. Sometimes Grandma would relieve me while I went in and warmed my hands at the stove.

We made a lot of *Pfefferkuchen* [spicy bar cookies] since there were many carolers who came to the door. They all expected a reward. We called the cookies *Prachaküake*. Mother made them with a lot of rye flour after the Revolution. Other flour was much too dear. Actually I liked these cookies even better because the rye flour gave them a little zest.

The New Year in the New World

In the new Mennonite settlements in North America, church services continued to close out the old and welcome the new year, just as had been done in Russia. In many places as the English language became more common New Year's morning services were still always held in German.

Anna Epp Entz: New Year's Eve in our Mennonite church in Newton, Kansas, was spent reminiscing. It was the *Jahresschluss* [year's end]. We sought God's leading and God's

111

guidance for the coming year. We didn't watch the old year out. We came back again the next morning to greet the New Year with song, praise and a sermon.

The day had its somber overtones, as Mariam Penner Schmidt recalls. "In the home of my grandparents, the Abraham Penners in Mountain Lake, Minnesota, it was a serious day because what was God going to send us in the coming year? Joy? Sorrow? Death of a loved one? I have kept that impression of New Year's Day. Our noon meal was always the same as Christmas: *Schinkjefleesch,* fried potatoes, *Plümemooss* and *Portselkje.* The afternoon was spent visiting — either we had guests or we went somewhere."

Bertha Fast Harder: I don't remember New Year's Eve until I was in high school. By that time we always had a New Year's Eve program in our church in Mountain Lake, Minnesota. It would go until midnight. Then we would line up around the church with candles. For me it was a beautiful time. I remember one time I stood next to the pastor, Rev. P.R. Schroeder. I didn't know him very well but really revered him. It happened that we held hands and prayed for the one next to us. My heart welled up within me to think that that minister was praying for me personally.

The baking of *Portselkje* continued in every home in North America on New Year's Day, just as it had in West Prussia and Russia. "It took a lot of *Krutzkje* [dry corn cobs] to keep the fire hot enough to make the fritters tumble over," says Bertha Harder. "Mother's *Portselkje* were usually ready by noon and that's all we ate."

Kaethe Kasdorf Warkentin also emphasizes, "*Portselkje* were special and you had to have more than one. We always recited a New Year's request, which was a way of politely asking for *Portselkje.*"

Portselkje baking continues in some Mennonite homes. They are quite popular at folk festivals and fairs where they are often baked and sold by the thousands.

* * *

Russian Mennonites never adopted most of the Ukrainian New Year's Day traditions that had helped to make the day entertaining. North America had no Russian servants to bring a wheat and barley blessing. Mothers who had swept up the scattered grain from the kitchen floor may have counted this a blessing. The star boys, too, were part of the Eastern Orthodox tradition and were never adopted by the Mennonites.

The *Brommtoppspäla* were one remnant of the old traditions which came to the New World, but only into southern Manitoba. This masquerade gave the young Mennonite teenage boys an opportunity for pranks and merriment which livened a rather somber, perhaps, otherwise uneventful village New Year's Eve.

The *Brommtopp* tradition never came into the midwestern United States. It has completely disappeared in Canada. The only memories are a few pictures of a Springfield, Manitoba, group and the *Brommtopp* song (Mennonite version) which appears in *The Windmill Turning* by Victor Carl Friesen.

Holy Week Celebrations among the Russian Mennonites

Father always greeted us in
Russian on Easter morning:

Christos Voskres!
Christ is risen!

And we replied,
Voistynu Voskres!
He is risen indeed!
— Nellie Lehn

Easter Sunday, 1788

It was Easter Sunday, March 22, 1788, when the first group of fifty Dutch Mennonite emigrants left the Vistula Delta. They departed by wagons from the village of Bohnsack near Danzig. A crowd gathered to bid them a sad farewell on their long journey into a strange "promised land," Russia.

After five weeks of trudging along muddy roads and camping outdoors, they stopped and rested for a while. Four weeks later they resumed their journey, finally reaching the town of Dubrovna where they were to spend the winter. Another group of immigrants joined them there. Five months later, they began their journey along the Dnieper River. Finally, they were assigned a location which was to be the beginning of the Chortitza Colony and the first village of Rosental.

Other Easter Weeks in Russia

Easter is the greatest celebration of the Christian church. In Russia the day was celebrated by Orthodox Christians with great pageantry and ceremony. Mennonites, who lived in the small villages surrounded by Eastern Orthodox, Catholics and Lutherans, observed the ceremony but celebrated with an Anabaptist simplicity, seeking to focus on the spiritual aspect of the death and resurrection of Christ. Their Holy Week observances began on Thursday.

Maundy Thursday/Holy Thursday *(Jreendonnadach)*

Maundy Thursday or Holy Thursday, as it is sometimes called, commemorates the Last Supper of Jesus with His disciples. The word *maundy* is from the Latin *mandatum* (commandment), referring to Christ's words to His disciples, "A new commandment I give unto you, that ye love one another."

Mennonites called this day *Gründonnerstag* or *Jreendonnadach* from their days in the

113

Vistula Delta. It was common on "Green Thursday" for German and Austrian Christians to prepare green vegetables such as dandelions. In some areas penitents, wearing sprigs of green herbs to express joy, were readmitted to the Church.

In West Prussia Green Thursday was also celebrated with a special traditional baking— *Gründonnerstag Kringel* or *Jreendonnadachkjrinjel*. This was a large pretzel-shaped yeast bread made with white flour, milk, eggs and lemon rind flavoring. When Mennonites were first introduced to it, it was baked by professionals, which is why it is not a standard part of old Mennonite cookbooks. Those who could afford it purchased it from the "bread women" who brought baskets filled with *Kringel* to the Prussian villages. It was customarily served with coffee in the afternoon.

Mary Dirks Janzen remembers that foot washing was observed on this day in their church in Gnadenfeld (Molotschna). "Our parents went to this service, as did our older brothers and sisters."

Good Friday *(Stelle Friedach)*

On this day the churches in Mennonite villages observed Jesus' crucifixion. It was a day of mourning and sadness. In some places the women wore black. Anna Bergen Franz remembers, "Good Friday was a very quiet day. We children were somewhat restricted and couldn't play with others because of making noise and activity." Families attended special church services.

Kaethe Kasdorf Warkentin: Before Easter there was a time of Lent. The Russians started fasting six weeks before Easter. We Mennonites did not do that. However, during the Easter week we were not allowed a lot of "big deals." There was never a wedding in the Lenten season. The funerals, of course, you couldn't help. But weddings and other noisy celebrations were not permitted.

During the Easter Week school was out, but we were not allowed to play ball or any other games which created noise. All was to be quiet.

I always dreaded Good Friday (*Stelle Friedach* [Quiet Friday] as it was known in Low German) because it was such a dark day and we had to sit still and be quiet. We went to church in the morning and had a very simple dinner after which we mourned. We had to sit still wherever we were. There was no visiting done on that day. All the baptized members wore black and the fathers had their long-tailed coats on when they went to church. I just dreaded that day. I was so glad when Easter morning arrived, and I could laugh and run around again.

Holy Saturday

Holy Saturday was a day of preparation for Easter. In some families children and mothers colored Easter eggs. It was also the time for baking *Paska*. The mood of the day was less somber.

On Easter Eve the Mennonites' Ukrainian neighbors decorated baskets with spring flowers and myrtle leaves, filled them with *Paska*, sausage and colored eggs and took them to the Orthodox church for the priest to bless. Mennonites never adopted this custom. "I remember the women walking in a line, one behind the other, wearing white *babushkas* and holding their *Paska* high, on their way to church. They looked almost like a row of white geese," recalls Margaret Peters Toews.

"On Saturday we did just the necessary things," remembers Kaethe Kasdorf Warkentin. "The workers were all at home. Father had let them go on Thursday noon. There were just one or two to help in the household and feed the cattle. Only the necessary baking was done — the *Paska,* the *Zwieback* and the lamb had to be prepared before Sunday. On Saturday things started to liven up a little more."

Easter Sunday *(Oostre)*

In West Prussia Mennonites celebrated Easter at home with a simple table covered with a white cloth and decorated with a bouquet of pussy willows. Raisin *Striezel,* a "milk bread" filled with raisins, was the typical baked food prepared for the day. Not until they lived in Russia did the Mennonite Easter celebration become really festive.

Mennonite homes and churches adopted the wonderful Russian greeting, "*Christos Voskres!*" (Christ is risen!), and the resounding response, "*Voistynu Voskres!*" (He is risen indeed!). Mennonites baked and enjoyed the tall, stately Russian *Paska* and admired the artistry of the Ukrainian Easter eggs. Mennonite children learned about the "willow switch tradition" from Russian workers. Most Mennonite homes welcomed the Ukrainian visitors who came with the traditional grain blessing.

Many older Canadian Mennonites remember the bells in distant and nearby Russian Orthodox churches. "The bells could be solemn and mournful or bright and joyous. It seemed to me the happiest tune these bells rang was on Easter day. The sunshine and warmth, the green grass, the flowers and blossoming fruit trees, the happy children and the bells ringing caused an exhilaration possible only in the hearts of the young," says N. J. Kroeker.

Easter was celebrated for two days in most churches. "Our choir director, Johann Jacob Derksen, and his singers had prepared all the songs so close to the hearts of the worshipers — songs of the sacrificial death of God's beloved Son, Jesus, His triumphant rising from the dead and the life everlasting for all who believe in Him," recalls Mia Reimer DeFehr of her youth in the Kuban. "It was a day of triumphant joy."

Anna von Kampen Funk remembers Russian carolers walking through the villages on Easter day and evening singing beautiful hymns. Some Mennonite Brethren groups adopted this custom, often singing until after midnight on Easter Eve. Helene Rempel says, "We would sing '*Er Lebt!* '[He Lives!] and people would come from their homes and thank us profusely."

Preparing for Easter in Gnadenfeld *by Mary Dirks Janzen*

Since there were quite a few Russian Orthodox people who lived in Gnadenfeld, the priest would come to our village on the Saturday before Easter for a service in which he blessed the *Paska* and the colored Easter eggs.

We three children watched this unusual service one time and were filled with mixed feelings because of how different it was. The priest sprinkled holy water on the *Paska* and on the colored eggs. He spoke in Latin which we could not understand. Even if he had spoken Russian, we wouldn't have understood because he talked too fast.

On holidays after their chores were done, the Russian boys and girls congregated on a short, side street in the village where there were benches. They would visit, sing, play the accordion or mouth harp and dance. You could hear them from most any place in the village. These people were a part of Gnadenfeld.

Before Easter morning our whole farmyard was raked and swept so everything would be clean and festive. Mother carefully laid the colored Easter eggs among the green grass of some oat seedlings which she always planted two weeks before Easter. Of course, she also never forgot the *Paska*. Father always brought the swing down from the barn so we could properly sing the following little song:

Schockel, Schockel, scheia,	Swing, swing, *scheia* —
Oostre ät wie Eia.	Easter, we eat eggs.
Pinjste ät wie wittet Broot,	Pentecost we eat white bread;
Stoaw wie nijch dan woa wie groot.	If we don't die, we will grow tall.

Easter was celebrated for three days. The first day there was a service in the church. That day was also designated for visiting grandparents. Grandmother always had something special for the children.

Easter Dinner in Osterwick *by Kaethe Kasdorf Warkentin*

We did not have an Easter Sunrise service. But we usually had an early eight o'clock church. Before leaving we put the lamb into the outside oven. Sometimes when we had a number of visitors, we roasted a sheep. The wood had been prepared the week before and everything was ready to go. Occasionally we had *Soljanka* soup which we cooked in the *Miagrope*. We had white bread, *Bulkje,* which had been baked ahead of time, too. Our *Paska* was always served at an afternoon *Faspa* and also with *Zwieback* later in the evening.

When the workers came back from their homes after Easter, they always brought beautifully decorated eggs as gifts. We could hardly wait for the workers to come back from the holidays because they had their square head-scarves tied with a whole bunch of eggs in them. We had our own eggs to eat, of course, but these *pysanky* were so beautifully painted. I always waited anxiously for that.

Easter Dinner in the Kuban

Anna Reimer Dyck: Our mother baked *Paska* in the Russian style in round tall pans or pails which gave them their distinctive mushroom shape complete with icing and decoration. She also made *Käse Paska* (cheese *Paska*) with cottage cheese, sugar, cream and vanilla. This was beaten until smooth and served with a spoon as an accompaniment to *Paska*.

The Easter meal consisted of marinated fish, a variety of meats such as baked ham, sausage and chicken, all of which were served cold. The tables were beautifully decorated with flowers and eggs.

At each mealtime in the three-day festivities, relatives gathered at different homes for a meal. On the last day the youth, breathing a sigh of relief after the many church services, went on an outing, usually to the woods.

* * *

In the previous account Anna Reimer Dyck recalled Easter celebrations from her youth in the Kuban. Some years later, before immigrating to Canada to join her fiancé, Willy Dyck, she lived for a year in Moscow with the Peter Froese family while she tutored their children in German.

A house in that city served as headquarters for the *Mennobschestvo* (the Menno Society), leaders of the Mennonite Agricultural Association, the American Mennonite Relief Commission and Mennonite emigration authorities. Among the families living there were the Froeses and the Jacob Lehns. Mrs. Lehn, a former actress, was Russian and entertained in the warm, gracious manner of the Russian people. In the following account Anna Dyck describes a true Russian Easter and dinner at the Lehns.

Easter in Moscow—1925–26 *by Anna Reimer Dyck*

The celebration of Easter marked the end of a period of fasting. For six weeks the believers were not supposed to eat meat or meat products, but rather fish and vegetables. Then, on Easter day, the tables would be loaded with food of all kinds. It was a festive time, when people visited each other and found it very easy to eat and drink too much. We too were invited to join the Jacob Lehn family in its celebration of Easter. When we arrived at their home, we found that Mrs. Lehn's table was indeed a work of art. Among other things, there was a whole small roasted pig with an apple in its mouth; platters of ham with wreaths as decorations; colored Easter eggs; the special Russian Easter bread, *Paska,* with its colorful frosting, cheese *Paska,* in the form of pyramids; crab; and, of course, various beverages. Naturally, the samovar was there, so that the tea was always ready. As invited guests, we stayed for the day, and watched the Easter visitors, in typical Russian style, come and go.[14]

Remembering the Ancient Willow Branch Ritual

It was the Ukrainian young folks living and working in Mennonite homes, who brought their ancient traditions and rituals into the family circle. Anna von Kampen Funk remembers Easter in her home. "The Russian servants had decorated the house with green branches and grass was strewn in the kitchen. Then they used a willow switch to awaken us. As they brushed us with the willow they said, 'Not I hit you, but the willow.'"

Marie Halun Bloch, who lived in the Ukraine, explains the ritual. "The willow is a symbol of Easter because it is among the first plants to sprout in the spring. The pussies of the willow used

117

to be eaten as a source of energy and good health. Touching a person with the willow branch has the same effect."

Another Tradition — Sowing

"At Easter Russians used to come to our door. Older adults and children came and threw seed wheat into the door and said, 'Christ is risen!'" says Helen Penner Lingenfelder of her childhood in Russia. "Mother offered them hospitality and invited them in. She gave cups of flour and potatoes to the poorer people."

The tradition of scattering wheat at Easter was very similar to the New Year's Day wheat blessing. Also tied to ancient agricultural celebrations, it pointed forward to harvest. For Ukrainians Easter was a forty-day cycle when age-old associations with man and nature came to a religious climax in the resurrection of Christ.

Coloring Eggs in Mennonite Russia

Long before the first Easter, people greeted the springtime by transforming common yard eggs into objects of honor and beauty. Peasant folks believed the egg to be symbolic of new life and fertility. After a cold dark winter spring was the time to rejoice. To celebrate the return of the sun to warm the earth and the appearance of new life, ancient peoples dyed and adorned eggs with designs expressing new life. These eggs were exchanged as gifts of friendship.

With the coming of Christ and the spread of Christianity, some of the old pagan designs took on new Christian meanings representing the Trinity, Christ or everlasting life. They were mixed with deer and roosters and horses along with the fish, a common sign among early Christians. Pagan and Christian symbols remain mixed together to this day.

In no place in the world has the art of decorating Easter eggs reached greater perfection than in the Ukraine. During Russian Mennonite times it was customary for Ukrainians to greet each other after the Easter mass, to embrace and to exchange these exquisite, colorful eggs. Great love and pride went into their decoration and distribution. Kaethe Kasdorf Warkentin remembers beautiful eggs being brought to her family as gifts at the end of the Easter holiday.

In Mennonite homes coloring eggs was part of the Easter celebration with children. "We colored a hundred eggs at Easter," says Helen Pankratz Siemens.

"For each child there was a nest containing as many eggs as the child was years old," says Anna Reimer Dyck. "Each servant also received a dozen hard-cooked, colored eggs." Mothers planted bowls of oat and barley seed which grew tall enough to hide the eggs. However, the Mennonite decorations never reached the artistry and beauty of those done by their Russian neighbors.

Anna Bergen Franz offers a possible explanation. "We didn't adopt the Russian custom of adding decorations to our colored eggs. We took things from the Russians that were practical. Probably the philosophy was that if you were going to do something artistic, it should have value. Time was valuable. You didn't just sit and spend all that time on something that had no use. It probably would have been acceptable to put such artistry into a pillow case, but not on eggs. We lived with a work philosophy. You shouldn't be sitting and reading or doing art when you could be sweeping under the bed."

There were some exceptions. "In our home there was a great emphasis on decorations at Easter," remembers Anna Reimer Dyck. "White-clothed tables were decked with bouquets of pussy willows from which hung painted, half eggshells filled with sweet-scented violets. The Easter table was always decorated with many, colored eggs. Some had country scenes painted on them; others were decorated with silver and gold trimmings."

Coloring Eggs When Times Were Hard

Times changed rapidly in Mennonite homes after the Revolution. Easter was celebrated with great simplicity because even necessities were often scarce.

Anna Bergen Franz: Colored eggs were a luxury. We usually sold our eggs. However, on Easter we could eat as many as we wanted to. Sometimes we sort of hung onto them. Mother planted oat seeds and we hid eggs in there.

Helene Rempel: Eggs were a delicacy and were not normally served in our menu. They had to be traded or sold for needed things. At Easter, though, we colored eggs and the children could eat as many as they wanted. We would write "Easter" in wax on the eggs. Then we colored them with onion peelings and walnut shells.

Russian Mennonite women became very creative and found substitutes for the commercial egg coloring which they could no longer buy. These delicate colorings were often quite different from the bolder colors of former years. A description of these natural colorings comes from a former resident of Osterwick.

Kaethe Kasdorf Warkentin: In the good days we bought coloring for eggs. But in the days after World War I we used red beet soup for a nice red. We saved walnut shells to use for brown. We also dried onion skins for a golden brown. We saved all our dry onion peelings in a jar and just before Easter we boiled them down to a cup of juice. The eggs colored with that were a soft, beautiful, golden brown. They were so pretty.

We also had wild lilac with purple berries. The juice was pressed out of these berries in fall and kept in a bottle with a little alcohol. For yellow we used saffron. Green was made from tender, young leaves, early herbs or green wheat. We also used carrot soup for an orange color.

Anna Peters' mother also used carrot juice from grated carrots to color eggs. "We also used onion skins and colored pencils to color from thirty to fifty eggs."

Agnes Rempel Braun remembers her mother boiling red paper in water to get out the color. All of the families continued to hide their eggs in bowls of barley and oat grass.

Easter and Hard Times

Easter memories from Mennonite village life during the "golden era" were peaceful and good. Then came World War I, the Revolution and famine. This succession of tragedies—political oppression, religious persecution, destruction of property, famine, disease, slave labor, deportation, family separation and massacre—completely changed the Easter memories.

During the time of severe famine, a young woman, Anna Baerg, removed the wrappers from cans of condensed milk sent to Russia by American Mennonites and on the back side of these labels recorded the happenings of those terrible days. A few days before her Palm Sunday entry, she wrote of receiving rations from the American soup kitchen three times a week. She also wrote of sending people, all like skeletons, away from her door and described the horror which that brought. Following is her entry of March 23, 1922, Alexanderkrone, Molotschna Colony, South Russia.

It is Palm Sunday, in the morning the choir sang in church, but I could not be there, nor at choir practice today or the day before. The body just doesn't have the necessary strength and I always feel tired. We always want things different from the way they are, but somehow I had to think that really we are not worthy of this suffering. Is it not true that through suffering even the best people have been refined and purified? There is a greater blessing in suffering than we realize, but the problem is we understand suffering so little. We think of it as martyrdom, but in reality it is one of the most valuable lessons in the school of our God. Those who sit there with deaf ears, hear nothing, of course.

The relief kitchen now has supplies for only two weeks because the Americans have withdrawn their help here in order to help in other places. The only hope now is Mr. Willing (of the Dutch Mennonites) and when he also declines, then humanly speaking there is no hope for us—we will all die of starvation.

Easter—After World War II

After the Revolution and famine there was a massive exodus of Mennonites from Russia. In 1941 the Soviet government organized an evacuation of the so-called German Volga Republic. Most men had been sent away earlier; now women and children were deported to the east. In 1943 another evacuation occurred—an endless trek toward the Polish border and finally refuge in western Germany. After the war many Mennonites lived in refugee camps. Others found places to live on farms with German families. Herta Funk remembers an Easter in such a place.

Herta Funk: During the years of 1945–1948 we got one or two eggs a year. We were refugees, traveling around in Germany after the war. For a while we lived and worked on a large farm. My father and we children worked. There was a school, which we attended, right on the farm. One year we had an egg hunt at the *Herrnhaus,* the manager's two-story house. Our school teacher provided the eggs for the hunt.

EASTER PASKA

Jennie Duerksen was a food manager in the Reedley, California Community College cafeteria for many years. She loves to do yeast baking. Now retired, she occasionally fills in as substitute baker at the college. She has tested most of the sweet bread recipes in this section. This is her family *Paska* recipe which originally came from Anna Rogalsky of Reedley. "*Paska* is best eaten the day it is baked or one or two days later," says Mrs. Duerksen.

3 Tbsp. active dry yeast	¾ cup lukewarm milk
2¼ cups lukewarm potato water	⅓ cup shortening or butter
2 tsp. salt	1 cup sugar
2¼ cups bread flour	7½ – 8 cups bread flour
5 eggs, separated	

Sprinkle yeast over potato water. Add salt and mix in 2¼ cups bread flour. Stir well. Set aside and let rise until doubled in bulk. Beat egg whites until stiff; set aside. Beat egg yolks and set aside. Over medium heat warm milk and butter or shortening until very warm. Cool to luke-warm. When sponge has risen, add beaten egg yolks, sugar, milk and 3⅓ cups of the flour. Beat 5 minutes with electric mixer. *Gently* fold in egg whites. Then gradually add another 4¼ cups bread flour, reserving 1 cup for kneading on the board. If using dough hook, finish according to mixer directions. If kneading by hand, turn dough out onto floured board, incorporating last 1 cup of flour as you finish kneading.

The dough should be as soft as possible, but not sticky. Knead until smooth and elastic. Return dough to greased bowl. Cover and let rise in warm place until doubled in bulk. Punch down. Grease three 3-lb. coffee or shortening tins. Divide dough into three equal parts, shape into balls and place in tin cans. Cover with kitchen towel and set in warm place. Allow to rise until doubled in size. Bake at 350°F. for about 40 minutes. Cool on racks and decorate with powdered sugar icing. Sprinkle with decorative candies.

—Jennie Jost Duerksen

HOT MUSTARD
(Samp)

Frieda Lehn Neufeld: If you like strong mustard, here is my mother's version. One friend, when eating it, remarked, "It sure opens up the sinuses!"

2 Tbsp. dry mustard   Sugar
1½ tsp. (approximately) water   Vinegar
¼ cup boiling water

In a small bowl combine mustard and water; stir to make a paste. With spoon mound the mustard into a small heap. Carefully add boiling water to the bowl until the water covers the top of the mustard. Let this stand for several hours or overnight to "leach out" the flavor. Carefully pour off water. Add sugar about equal to the remaining mustard. Add vinegar to taste and mix until you have a spreading consistency. Spoon into covered jar.

—Ann Bartel Lehn

ℛOAST LEG OF LAMB FOR EASTER

Kaethe Kasdorf Warkentin: In Russia we raised our own sheep, so we usually had roast lamb for Easter dinner. The salted meat from winter was gone and the young chicks were not yet ready for butchering. Mother used the shank or whole leg of lamb. She sprinkled it with salt and pepper and pressed whole cloves into the meat and added a little water.

It was roasted in the big oven indoors. When the coals had burned down somewhat, Mother banked the embers up around the pan. The lamb was always ready when we returned from our Easter Sunday worship service. Mother served the meat plain with homemade mustard or horseradish, boiled salted potatoes and *Plümemooss.* For dessert she served *Paska* and coffee.

Preheat oven to 450°F. Sprinkle or rub whole leg of lamb with salt and pepper. Insert whole cloves. Place meat, fat side up, on a rack in an uncovered and greased pan. Reduce heat to 325°F. and roast about 30 minutes to the pound. Make a pan gravy with the drippings and serve with horseradish or mustard.

— Kaethe Kasdorf Warkentin

TRADITIONAL *PASKA*

Simplified Version (Rapidmix Method)

1½ cups half-and-half	1 tsp. vanilla extract or vanilla bean
½ cup unsalted butter	2 tsp. salt
5 eggs, separated	2 Tbsp. SAF or commercial instant
¾ cup sugar	yeast
Grated rind of 1 lemon	5½ – 6 cups bread flour

Over medium burner heat half-and-half and butter until butter melts. Set aside to cool to lukewarm. Beat egg whites until stiff. Set aside. In electric mixing bowl combine egg yolks and sugar. Beat until light and lemon colored. Add lemon, vanilla and salt. Add cream and butter mixture to eggs. Beat in half the flour, mixing until smooth. Add the yeast, which is made to add with the dry ingredients, and mix well. Fold in the egg whites.

Gradually add remaining flour, only enough so the dough is not too sticky. Use electric mixer as long as possible. If using dough hook, knead 8 – 10 minutes. If kneading by hand, turn out onto lightly floured board and knead until smooth and elastic. This should be like sweet roll dough — not heavy like bread dough. Cover and allow to rise until doubled in bulk. Punch down.

Prepare coffee cans (two 2-lb. and two 1-lb. cans, or three 2-lb. cans) as indicated in the Traditional Easter *Paska* recipe. Set in warm place to rise until doubled in size. Bake at 325° for about 40 – 45 minutes. Smaller cans bake shorter time. Cool. Frost with powdered sugar and lemon frosting. Decorate with nonpareil candies or icing flowers. Serve with cheese *Paska*.

Note: This recipe was tested in a Bosch® kitchen machine using SAF instant yeast (available at bakers' warehouses or through Bosch® dealers) and using the Bosch® 1-rise method. Total preparation and baking time was 2½ hours. Other quick yeasts are available in local supermarkets but may not be as fast.

ℱRIEDA NEUFELD'S CHEESE *PASKA*

¾ lb. hoop (dry curd) cheese or
baker's uncreamed cottage cheese
9 hard-cooked egg yolks
¾ lb. sweet butter or margarine,
softened

Sugar and vanilla to taste
Whipping cream (as needed)

Press hoop cheese and egg yolks through a sieve. If you use baker's cottage cheese, simply mix egg yolks and cottage cheese. (Pressing through sieve is unnecessary.) Blend well with softened butter. Stir in sugar and vanilla. If mixture does not have spreading consistency, add whipping cream. Store in covered containers in refrigerator. Freezes well.

Pentecost Sunday in Russia

Christians celebrate Pentecost (seventh Sunday after Easter) to commemorate the coming of the Holy Spirit to the apostles (Acts 2:1–4). The name comes from the Greek word for fifty; Pentecost occurred on the fiftieth day after the first day of Passover. The day was later called Whitsunday or White Sunday because newly baptized Christians wore white baptismal gowns on that day, marking the end of the Easter season.

It was traditional for Mennonite churches in Russia to hold baptismal services on Pentecost. Anna von Kampen Funk says, "The candidates had to know the whole catechism. For this day we baked *Zwieback* and *Streuselkuchen.*"

Because the Anabaptist church insisted upon believers' baptism, the candidates were usually older teenagers. Margaret Klassen Sawatsky remembers, "Young people, eighteen years old or so, would take part in the catechism class led by our minister [in Gnadenfeld], and would be baptized on Pentecost Sunday. They would be taken in as church members and were eligible for communion. What impressed us, as young girls, were the beautiful white dresses the girl baptismal candidates wore and the fine suits of the young men."

According to Agnes Rempel Braun, people in the Molotschna painted their fences red and white and whitewashed the trunks of their trees for Pentecost.

After the long Russian winter, Pentecost came at a most beautiful time of the year. "As children," says Kaethe Kasdorf Warkentin, "Pentecost had a special meaning to us. Nature stood in all its beauty—trees in blossom and flowers in bloom."

In the Kuban it was the same. "Pentecost was a time of great rejoicing. By now spring had come, the fields were green and flowers covered the hillsides," recalls Anna Reimer Dyck.

At Pentecost the Russians Decorated the Barn

Mary Dirks Janzen: Pentecost had three full holidays the same as Christmas and Easter. Our hired boys and girls did only the necessary chores, such as feeding and watering the cattle. The girls had to milk and separate the milk. There was lots of leisure time when they could visit with the other hired boys and girls.

At *Pfingsten* the Russians decorated our barn in Gnadenfeld. We had a windbreak around the village. We had planted five rows of trees. At *Pfingsten* the hired help decorated the barn with branches from these trees. It smelled like the forest. They even decorated the poles in the barn. It must have been connected with their Orthodox religion or else tradition.

Margaret Klassen Sawatsky: At Pentecost we always decorated our front and back rooms. We liked to decorate our school, too. The Russian girls loved to help, but we did it ourselves. But that was before the Revolution when we were little. The Russian girls that worked for us liked to cut the grass and put it in the hall.

Anna Reimer Dyck: On Pentecost we decorated our home with mayflowers and put green branches on walls and doors. On all the tables, the piano and the window sills, we placed fragrant flowers. For the first two days we had church services in the forenoon, but on the third day the choir and young people went for an excursion into the green, fragrant woods. Here, under the towering trees, we had our picnic.[15]

Pentecost—The Green Holiday

Marie Halun Bloch: In the Ukraine Pentecost is called "Green Holidays," which suggests it probably had pre-Christian origins. For the occasion the house is decorated inside with boughs of greenery. It was once and still is a celebration of vegetation, which revives with every spring. It is also a holiday of the dead, who now have eternal life.

Rev. Basil Rhodes: The grass and decorations of greenery used by the Russians at Pentecost are symbolic of the Holy Spirit giving life to the whole creation. [Rev. Rhodes is a priest at St. Nicholas Orthodox Church, Saratoga, California.]

A Russian priest, San Francisco: The palm is a symbol of victory. There are no palm trees in Russia, so green branches from trees are used. They symbolize the coming of the Holy Spirit to the apostles. They also symbolize the beginning of the Church in Russia.

Holy Week Celebrations among Russian Mennonites in North America

"Mennonite religious holidays were observed much more in days gone by than they are now," comments Herman Rempel. "Fifty years ago Christmas had three holidays. Epiphany or Holy Three Kings Day was celebrated and no work, aside from the regular chores, was performed. Easter and Pentecost were also observed for three days in the same way that Christmas was celebrated."

Good Friday

Good Friday in many of our North American Russian Mennonite communities was a day when many churches served communion during the service. It was a quiet day at home when no work was to be done. Businesses in the small towns all closed for the day. Social functions were discouraged and family meals were simple and plain.

Mariam Penner Schmidt remembers that on Good Friday Bethel Mennonite Church in Mountain Lake, Minnesota, observed "the washing of feet. How that intrigued me, and I begged Grandmother Penner to let me stay, just once to see how it was done. Children and people who were not baptized were asked to leave after the sermon. Grandmother allowed me to stay once and I saw how the women would wash each other's feet — and the men, the men's feet. Grandpa, I remember, always washed his feet real well before he went to church on that day."

At First Mennonite Church in Hillsboro where I grew up there were special Holy Week services every night. Sometimes these were evangelistic in nature. Frequently, the speaker was the popular Dr. J. E. Hartzler, a professor at Witmarsum Seminary and later at Hartford Theological Seminary. He spoke with eloquence and drew a full house most every evening. In addition it was his custom to show slides with narration of his travels in the Holy Land. In those days before television, when motion pictures in our town were rare, he captivated the entire congregation. His pictures and narration remain a vivid memory. Holy Week services were common in many of the surrounding churches.

Getting Ready for Easter

If there was good weather before Easter, it was customary to do a spring cleaning before the holiday. In any case the house was thoroughly cleaned on Saturday while Mother attended to the baking. She started a sponge the night before and continued adding and kneading until the high, mushroom-shaped *Paskas* came from the oven in mid-afternoon. They were lined up on the kitchen table, reminiscent of a bakery, waiting to be frosted. In the evening she loaded them in Dad's old black Chevy and made her rounds — delivering *Paska* to the minister, the sick, special friends and relatives. We were allowed a tiny sample on Saturday. The rest waited for Easter breakfast and Sunday *Faspa*.

In America it became traditional to have something new to wear on Easter Sunday. Martha Letkeman Funk remembers Hillsboro Mennonite women having new hats for Easter. Their dresses were quite plain, with long skirts, but their hats were fancy with big flowers, lace and trailing ribbons. Schaeffler's Millinery, where they sold hand-decorated hats, did a brisk business just before the holiday.

Many little girls regularly got new white shoes for Easter Sunday morning. This was tradition in my own growing up days. Even when it rained or snowed, and sometimes it did, spring and summer clothes were ushered in on Easter Sunday. To wear a new dress with ruffles and frills and white shoes was very special.

Easter Sunday in Church

Wilma Toews has a fond memory of her Grandfather Flaming coming to their home early on Easter morning. "He always asked us children with such excitement, 'Have you seen the Easter Lamb in the rising sun?'"[16]

In Hillsboro, Kansas, there were special sunrise services out at the reservoir. Zion Lutheran was the only church in town with bells, and they seemed to ring with a special urgency and proclamation on Easter morning. There was a festive mood as people left for church, and everyone seemed to sing with more enthusiasm while declaring "He arose!" The choir, too, had practiced for weeks to sing the "Hallelujah Chorus." Whatever garden flowers might be in bloom stood in vases in front of the pulpit. Easter Sunday was indeed a wonderful day.

Mariam Penner Schmidt: At home Easter was a wonderful day much like Christmas. Our menu was nearly the same — baked ham, fried potatoes, *Plümemooss* and hard-boiled eggs. The family and other company was served a late *Faspa* of *Zwieback,* bread, cheese, cake and coffee.

Anna Epp Entz: On Easter families gathered at the grandparents. The men ate first, then the women and the children last. The tables weren't big enough to hold everyone. Grandma used to put a little sugar cube beside each person's place. Children had coffee and milk. We dipped the sugar cube into the coffee. Sugar was scarce. This was quite a ritual. All the cousins wanted to sit next to me because I wasn't fond of sugar cubes and they could have mine. In the afternoon the children played and the adults visited.

We had a second holiday. Sometimes we visited the other side of the family. It was a time of cousins getting together. We are missing something by not getting together like we used to.

Easter Dinner at my Grandmother Jost's

Holidays in my father's family were major celebrations. There were no special invitations. It was taken for granted that everyone would "go home to the folks" on those days. We children especially looked forward to those times because there were so many cousins. Eighteen under the age of twelve to be exact. Seven of Grandmother's children were married, making sixteen adults at the table. There were several unmarried sons still living at home making a total of about forty people.

How did Grandmother manage such an invasion, provide enough food and keep her sanity? She never missed church to prepare a meal even though the troops landed promptly after the service and expected to eat shortly thereafter. Late afternoon dinners were not in vogue with Mennonite menfolk and children. That was when you served *Faspa.*

Her secret was a simple meal much of which was prepared the day before. No three course affairs. She served the old standby meal that Mennonite women had been cooking since their Vistula Delta days — baked ham, fried potatoes and large bowlsful of *Mooss* that kept disappearing. There were usually dill pickles along with rye bread and butter. We ate in three shifts, washed the dishes, set the table for *Faspa* and still had time for an Easter egg hunt.

In fact, that was the most exciting part of the day. With so many older boy cousins, the hunt was a wild, rowdy affair. Following the noon meal the children were imprisoned in the living room with doors locked and shades drawn tight. Peeking was absolutely not permitted.

Meanwhile, out in the pasture, delight ran high as the uncles plotted the wickedest places for hiding eggs. They could make us hunt eggs all afternoon. When the starting whistle blew, children exploded through the door like circus clowns shot from a cannon. It was a mad race to see who could find the most eggs.

One year the prize egg and a dime floated on a board far out in Grandfather's pond. Whoever fetched it would get the grand prize — ten cents. The Siemens boys, both in new tweed suits with knickerbocker pants, launched out into the muddy water. They sloshed out of the water, dripping wet and victorious. Aunt Bertha was furious. No doubt they had another prize waiting on their return home. The day ended with everyone eating *Paska* and hard-cooked eggs at the *Faspa* table.

More about Easter Eggs and Egg Hunts

Helen Penner Lingenfelder: In the early days when I was small we always had Sunday school with another family. Dad taught the lesson. On Easter they made a nest for every child in the nearby field of oats which by this time was six or eight inches high. In the nest they hid the eggs while we were inside the house with the shades pulled.

Helen Peters Epp: When I was little, we dyed eggs with boughten dye. We had an egg hunt at Grandmother Hiebert's in the village. Aunt Justina hid the eggs among the irises in the vineyard. There were no prizes. Children didn't work for prizes in those days.

Anna Epp Entz: My husband, Pastor J. E. Entz, and I had a traditional egg hunt for all the children of our First Mennonite Church in Newton, Kansas. We cooked about 200 eggs in dishpans. About 50 – 75 Sunday school children and their friends came on Saturday before Easter to our country manse. They brought sack lunches. After they hunted the eggs, we had ponies for the children to ride. What a highlight. This ride was more important than any car ride anyone ever took.

Manitoba Easter Memories

Julius G. Toews: One morning early in spring, I awoke early as usual but to my surprise, Father and Mother were up and around already and I overheard them being engaged in an animated conversation. Mother asked Father whether he had been checking the hens' nests for eggs that previous evening. He said he had, but there had not been any. Mother seemed to be worried. "I can't understand why our hens are so slow in starting to lay. In two weeks' time it will be Easter and still no eggs."

This conversation between my parents had me worried. No eggs for Easter? What a calamity! It was the custom that on Easter Sunday there was no limit to the number of eggs we were allowed to eat. In fact, there usually was a keen competition between the boys as to

Children pose around the Great Oak in the village of Chortitza. The first Mennonites who came from Prussia in 1789 built their houses near this tree.

Young Mennonite women at an outdoor tea party in 1893. The grass in the foreground was grown for its decorative quality.

who would be the champion egg-eater of the family. The previous Easter, I remembered, I had eaten four, but our neighbor's boy, my age and my size, had managed five, and his adult brother had gorged himself with ten eggs.

Mother, later in the day, assured us that if our hens would not produce she would buy eggs from our neighbors. We would get our eggs on Easter Sunday. This was an appreciated consolation to me.[17]

Sara Zacharias Ens: In Canada we used to color eggs with water colors and crepe paper. The big boys found such awful places to hide them. I remember a picture of an egg sitting on the barn roof.

Ascension Day *(Himmelfoat)*

In earlier times Ascension Day was chosen as a time to examine the young baptismal candidates. Boys and girls were required to memorize the catechism and be able to answer questions during a meeting open to the public.

Other Holidays Observed by Russian Mennonites

In our small Mennonite town in Kansas there was rarely a parade. Fourth of July fireworks and large community picnics were held in other parks and towns but not in ours. Independence Day came in the midst of wheat harvest and no farmer stopped such a crucial operation except for Sunday church. If we celebrated at all, it was with a small box of sparklers and a family ice cream feed in the evening. A few non-Mennonites hung flags on their front porches. Most Mennonite people avoided the celebrations because of the military overtones. The same was true of Dominion Day in Canada. However, some Russian Mennonite churches had all-day celebrations or all-church picnics on Fourth of July.

On Memorial Day it was the same. Parades took place in other towns with school bands and veterans marching in uniform. From a decorated podium a town father would honor the war dead. In Newton the drum and bugle corps played rousing marches and melancholy taps. But not in Hillsboro. Memorial Day in our family meant "Decoration Day," as it was called. We spent some time weeding and decorating family graves in a far-away country cemetery. Armistice Day and Remembrance Day (Canada) also were too military in nature to be observed by Mennonites.

There were few celebrations for children in our growing up years. Even birthdays and anniversaries remained simple. Perhaps it was our family's strong work ethic that frowned on frivolity and excessive festivity. It seemed that others, who were not Mennonite, had more fun on holidays and were allowed to celebrate with an abandon and freedom we did not know. "By the sweat of your brow you shall earn bread" left little room for play. Even on a holiday, there was work to be done before we could celebrate.

In the following section are firsthand stories of how various holidays were observed in the Russian Mennonite home, both in the Ukraine and in North America.

The May Festival *(Maidach)* in Russia

Henry B. Tiessen: At the May Festival all the people of the village would participate. In Ladekopp there was a special place where woods, meadows and river met and there the festivities took place. At the bank of the river were several natural springs and fresh cool water came out in abundance. It was an ideal place for picnics. Soon the *Droschkjes,* the *Drogge* [vehicle on springs with flat floor instead of curved body] and the box wagons arrived. Some of the young people arrived on their bicycles. Milk and perishable foods were placed in big containers filled with cool spring water.

There were games of ball or other games in the meadow. The young people congregated under the big trees, playing their musical instruments and singing folk songs. Occasionally a couple of lovers would break away and go for a stroll along the river bank. The older folks would sit in the shade, listen to the music, watch the children play and reminisce about the good olden days.

The highlight was a picnic lunch served on blankets under the big trees. There was milk, coffee, *Kvass, Zwieback, Zuckerkuchen, Torten,* cookies, *Kringel,* marzipan and even fresh cherries. There was much fun, laughter and a good time for everyone.[18]

Royal Visits to Russian Mennonites

"Mennonites generally held the imperial family in awe," says historian James Urry. "Rulers were often seen as legitimate leaders ordained by God who were to be obeyed as long as their dictates did not contradict Mennonite principles. The Emperor Alexander's religiosity was well known to the colonists. During his visit to the Molotschna in 1818, and shortly before his death in 1825, the emperor was welcomed with enthusiasm."

For many decades the Molotschna Colony served as an agricultural showcase in southern Russia. The royal family took keen interest in its development and a number of times visited the Molotschna.

In April, 1818, a rider arrived in the village of Lindenau informing Mrs. D. Hiebert that Czar Alexander I would be arriving on May 21 and would join the family for breakfast. The mayor was told to have 400 horses ready for the procession. An order came from Halbstadt that all houses, yards and gardens were to be beautified and the streets swept and decorated with white sand.

On the special day a great crowd gathered, Mennonites and neighboring Lutherans lining the street. A procession of nineteen carriages arrived. In the sixth, drawn by six horses, rode the emperor.

Welcoming him with a bouquet of flowers, Mrs. Hiebert invited the emperor to sit at the head of the table, a place of honor, which he refused. Instead he insisted the hostess be seated there. She claimed she felt too humble, but he answered, "No, dear child, just be seated next to me for we are all humans, created equal by God." The royal entourage enjoyed the meal and upon leaving the czar presented Mrs. Hiebert with a diamond ring.

Through the years there were other royal visits to other villages in the Molotschna. The visitors found it convenient to stop there on their way to the Crimean summer resorts.[19]

The Birthday Child in Russia

Anna Reimer Dyck: In my home in the Kuban children's birthdays were always celebrated at breakfast. The celebration included my parents, the children and occasionally a relative who lived nearby. The birthday child was seated on a chair decorated with flowers and vines and he or she would receive a special gold cup from which to drink.

As on every day, vases of flowers were to be found on the table and on the piano. The birthday cake would be a round sponge cake with decorations. The rest of the meal would be regular breakfast fare: fresh buns and bread, butter, jam, cheese and always fresh fruit. It was not customary to eat meat or eggs for breakfast.

After school the birthday child was allowed to invite ten to fourteen friends and they would come with us and play and eat outside, picnic style.

Grownups came to celebrate with us in the evening, if the birthday fell during the week. If on a weekend, more guests would be invited and the celebration would often include several mealtimes. A childless aunt and uncle of my mother-in-law would invite all their siblings to their birthdays and a feast of fantastic baking would be served: fruit *Plats* made with yeast dough, cakes, cookies and numerous other pastries.

My mother's birthday was a special occasion since the date, May 6, was shared with my eldest sister, Hulda, as well as the Russian czar. As a result it was also a national holiday and the family took the opportunity to go to the woods for a major outing. We always had "lamb on a spear" roasted over an open fire. We would take a lot of food, fresh fruit and baking and, of course, the samovar.[20]

ſYRUP CAKE
(*Siaroppsplauts*)

Herta Funk: Siaroppsplauts was a kind of dark, flat cake, fairly moist, with a flavor a little like gingerbread. It was baked in a large black pan.

This recipe fits Herta Funk's description very well. The brown sugar adds richness. It is relatively spicy.

½ cup shortening	½ tsp. cloves
¾ cup brown sugar	2 cups sifted all-purpose flour
1 cup dark corn syrup or molasses	1 cup milk
2 eggs, separated	
1 tsp. each baking soda, cinnamon, ground star anise	

Cream shortening and sugar and add corn syrup or molasses. Beat in egg yolks and mix well. Add sifted dry ingredients alternately with milk. Fold in beaten egg whites. Bake in two loaf pans lined with waxed paper at 350°F. for about 40 minutes. Serve plain or with a whipped cream topping.

ſOFT MOLASSES DROP CAKES

My mother's only recipe book was of her own making, a notebook filled with pages now crumbling and brown. She hand copied the following recipe when she was sixteen. It is a cake-like cookie, soft, light and mild with a touch of spice. It is a recipe with enduring qualities.

1 cup sugar
¾ cup shortening or margarine
1 egg
½ cup molasses
3 cups sifted all-purpose flour
2 tsp. baking soda dissolved in 1 tsp. vinegar

1 tsp. each ginger, cinnamon, salt
¼ tsp. black pepper (optional)
¾ cup milk
½ cup chopped walnuts (optional)

Combine sugar and shortening and beat until light and fluffy. Beat in egg and blend well. Add molasses. In separate bowl stir together flour, baking soda, salt and spices. Add alternately with milk. Add walnuts, if desired.

Drop dough by heaping teaspoonful onto greased cookie sheet about 2 inches apart. Bake at 375°F. about 8 – 10 minutes or until done.

— *Helen Taeves Jost (1913)*

SOUR CREAM DROP CAKES
(Schmauntküake)

A light, flavorful cookie. A little frosting or colored sugar adds a festive touch. Good for lunch boxes and picnics.

2 cups sugar
½ cup shortening or margarine
2 eggs
1 tsp. vanilla
½ tsp. salt

1 tsp. each baking soda and baking powder
3½ cups sifted all-purpose flour
1 cup thick sour cream

Cream sugar and margarine until light and fluffy. Beat in eggs and vanilla. Stir together the dry ingredients and add alternately with the sour cream.

Drop by spoonful onto lightly greased cookie sheet. Place about 2 inches apart. Bake at 375°F. 10–12 minutes or until done. Cool. You may frost, if desired. If using colored sugar, sprinkle over tops of dough mounds before baking.

ANISE SYRUP COOKIES
(Siaroppsküake)

Anna Derksen Rosenfeld says this is an old recipe from Russia. It appears in the *Mennonite Treasury of Recipes* from Mrs. A.D. Penner. The ingredients listed here are one-third of the original.

⅓ cup butter
½ cup sugar
1 egg
⅓ cup honey
⅔ cup dark corn or watermelon syrup

⅓ tsp. ground star anise
1 tsp. baking soda
4 cups sifted all-purpose flour (about)
½ cup cream
Glaze

In mixing bowl combine butter and sugar and beat until light and fluffy. Add egg and beat. Add honey and syrup. Gradually stir in dry ingredients, alternating with cream. Knead into ball and chill in refrigerator.

Roll into small balls in the palm of your hand. Place on greased baking sheet about 1 inch apart. Bake at 375°F. for 8–9 minutes, depending on size. (Nine minutes ensures a more rounded shape when cool.) Glaze over cooling rack.

Glaze: Mix together 2 cups powdered sugar and ½ cup hot milk. Stir until smooth. Keep warm in double boiler.

Säwenschlopadach (Siebenschläfertag) (Seven Sleeper's Day, June 27)

Säwenschlopa is a forgotten holiday among the Mennonites. Several elderly Canadians vaguely recalled such a day when given an explanation. The following information comes from Sigrun Golbeck Kebernick from Germany. Her mother remembers the day from the family's years in the Vistula Delta.

Legend has it that seven brothers were persecuted and locked in a cave near Corinth in 25 A.D. In 446 the cave was opened and the young men were found alive. On the 27th of June these seven brothers were celebrated.

Sigrun Kebernick also remembers that as a child she hoped for sunshine on this day. Tradition dictated that if the day were sunny, the next six weeks would be sunny. If it rained, wet weather was imminent.

St. Johannes Day in the Vistula Delta

The celebration of Midsummer's Eve on June 24 was an important event throughout Europe. It was the "night of destiny" when the future could be forecast. When the Vistula Delta area became Christianized, June 24 became known as St. Johannes Day. Many of the original customs remained along with old weather maxims for that time of year. The forecasts sound like those made on Groundhog Day in the United States.

Summer weather begins on St. Johannes Day.

As the weather on Johannes Day, so it will remain for forty days.

When St. Johannes is "baptized" in water, the summer becomes even wetter.

Thunder and lightning on St. Johannes forecasts many summer thunderstorms.

Rain on Johannes Day—expect a wet harvest.

Before Johannes Day you dare not praise the grain.

—Old Weather Maxims from the Vistula Delta

Harvest Festival *(Dankfast)*, Russia

Mia Reimer DeFehr: The Harvest Festival or Thanksgiving was celebrated in the church. This had been decorated by the young people with garlands and bouquets of flowers. Fruits and vegetables beautified the front of the altar, symbolizing gratitude for God's wonderful bounty. Long tables had been set under the many shade trees on the yard of the church. The large number of worshipers enjoyed the feast of love prepared by the women of the church. Each had brought her offering of fried chicken, ham or Mennonite sausage. There were always stewed dried fruits — apples, cherries, pears and peaches — set in bowls all along the tables. Potato salad was prepared in advance by the women, with *Tante* Liese heading them, at the caretaker's cottage on the yard.[21]

St. Martin's Day *(Martien)*

Jeft't ferr Martien en schwoare Frost
dan kjrie wie en linda Winta.
If there is heavy frost on St. Martin's Day
We'll have a mild winter.
— *Low German Saying*

St. Martin's Day is a feast day celebrated by the Roman Catholic Church on November 11, honoring St. Martin, bishop of Tours, France in the fourth century. The day falls at the end of the harvest season and is celebrated in Europe with feasts. In Great Britain, Martinmas marks the ending of one of the legal quarters into which the year is divided.

Herman Rempel: St. Martin's Day is a throwback to a Catholic religious holiday, but it took on quite a different meaning with the Mennonites. I believe it began in Prussia when large Mennonite families had a surplus of workers in the family. At an early age they were hired out to other well-to-do Mennonites or other neighbors.

The young Mennonites had little to say about where they would work. This was arranged by parents and the wages were usually low. The parents were poor and wages might consist of meat, feed grain, flour or perhaps a little cash.

The period of work always terminated on St. Martin's *(Martien)* Day when accounts were settled. The parents took the proceeds and the young worker had little to say about how the wages were spent or used.

United States Independence Day, July 4

The shiny Santa Fe train, belching steam and smoke from the engine, chugged to a screeching stop in front of the small depot at Peabody, Kansas, on July 4, 1874.

Eagerly the passengers peered from the windows at their new surroundings. Women in long, dark dresses, wearing *babushkas,* guided young children down the coach steps. Men, lifting wicker trunks and baskets, walked about on the platform looking for friends. These Mennonites, all new immigrants, had just arrived from Russia. Among them was the John C. Penner family from Pragenau, Molotschna Colony, on their way to a new home in Hillsboro.

But to the surprise and horror of the Penners, all seemed to be chaos — far from the peaceful reception they had expected. There was shooting followed by loud explosions all around. Even young school children stood about throwing firecrackers at their feet.

"What is this? What have we come to?" lamented a disappointed Penner. "We left Russia to escape the war!"

Friends, who had arrived earlier, were there to meet them and hastened to calm their fears. "This is part of the Fourth of July celebration," they explained. "This is how they celebrate America's independence."

Many of the immigrants, like the Penners, shared little enthusiasm for this day. Independence Day came and went in the midst of summer's harvest. For most Mennonites it was just another busy day of farm work.

As time went on, however, parents gave in to their children's wishes and allowed little celebrations at the end of the day. Here are memories of July 4 from the early part of the twentieth century.

Helen Peters Epp: We called the day "Four July." Sometimes the men would go to town but not the women. We would go with Mother to Grandma Hiebert's in the Alexanderfeld village near Hillsboro. She had a big apricot tree in the front yard. All the women would stay there and pick apricots to take home. The men may have celebrated with a few firecrackers, but we children didn't get any. It wasn't like it is now with all the fireworks. Sometimes we'd have a freezer of homemade ice cream.

Marie Harms Berg: When I was a child, they had a Balloon Ascension in Hillsboro one Fourth of July. The balloonist came down in a haystack and broke his leg. I had never seen anything but birds fly before. It was all very exciting for us children.

Martha Letkeman Funk: Hillsboro had a little celebration downtown. There was a platform where the band played a concert in the evening. I remember having a balloon on a stick and carrying it around until somebody put a firecracker to it. My balloon was gone, just like that!

Once there was an auto race on the Fourth. There were only two cars in our town. My friend Olga's father, Dr. Jacob J. Entz, had one purchased around 1909 and G. L. Klassen, who sold and serviced Model T Fords, had the other. Those two were to race from Main Street to the end of Grand Street. Olga begged to go with her father but he said, "Oh, no! I'll be going much too fast." They went about ten miles an hour! That was a big thing that day. Everyone came to watch.

Minnie Jost Krause: We lived on the farm and didn't get into town. It was harvest time and we girls still had to put up the shocks. "Now if you get all those shocks done by three or four o'clock this afternoon," Dad said, "I'll go to town and get some fireworks and we'll make a freezer of ice cream." He kept his word. What fun we girls had, sitting in the back of our wagon and riding home from that "forty," two miles south of our place shooting those tiny firecrackers all the way. Mother filled the freezer. Dad and the boys turned it. We girls headed for the pond for a swim. It was a good day.

Wilma Toews: Sometimes we had a few pennies for firecrackers and a box of sparklers. This was potato digging time and we had to stay home to work. In the evening there was time for sparklers and homemade ice cream.

Anna Epp Entz: The Fourth of July was an all-day affair in our church in Medford, Oklahoma. We had devotions in the morning, then dinner. There was a program by the Sunday school with singing, dialogues and poems. There was always an abundance of food. Children on the street had firecrackers.

Bertha Fast Harder: Somewhere along the way my father got the idea that we should be awakened on the Fourth of July with a bang. Father owned a double barreled shotgun that he may have used to kill the crows eating our grain. Anyway, on the Fourth of July we were awakened in our upstairs bedroom with Father standing below shooting straight up into the air — BANG! BANG! It was a very loud, reverberating sound. Fourth of July is here! We just loved that. And we always hoped and prayed for nice weather because we worked hard on the farm and Fourth of July would be one day we would take off *all* day. If the weather was nice, we would go to our lake for an all-day picnic and swimming. Oh, how we loved that. Then in the evening it was our custom to get into the car and drive to the town of Mountain Lake. We'd go to a local drug store and each have a banana split arranged in those long, narrow glass dishes with big scoops of ice cream and cherries and nuts on it. That was our big treat.

Russian Mennonite Wedding Customs

The husband is the brain,
The wife—the soul.
— *Old Russian Proverb*

Wan dü friee jeist,
dan besee die eascht de Mutta.
When you go courting to get married,
first observe the mother.
— *Old Low German Saying*

Love, Courtship and Marriage in the Russian Mennonite Village

Wedding customs among the Mennonites of Russia and those who came to North America were influenced by their lives in the Vistula Delta and sixteenth century Holland. Remnants of various traditions and folkways — many having their roots in the festive occasions of the Grosses Werder — could still be found in Canada up until World War II.

In the Vistula Delta when a young man wished to make a marriage proposal, he sought the help of the *Umbitter* (petitioner) who in turn visited the young girl's parents. She was given the information and allowed a period of time to respond. Sometimes a second elder accompanied the *Umbitter*.

Every congregation had a man filling the office of *Umbitter*. This man, an elder or deacon, had special responsibilities related to betrothals. It was his duty to announce the engagement to the congregation when it had been finalized and to go from house to house with a written wedding invitation.[1]

This tradition had been transplanted from Holland where preachers or elders also carried the marriage proposal to the girl and her family. Those who did not accept the arrangement and made their own proposals were subject to church discipline.[2] According to West Prussian church records this particular custom had fallen into decline by 1765.[3] By that time young men had become so bold as to go behind the elder and propose directly to the girls of their choice, sometimes even without the parents' knowledge. While it was continued in some Russian Mennonite circles, most traces of the practice disappeared in the 19th century.

Siegfried Rosenberg indicates that sometimes Delta farmers had their own ideas about marriage and weddings. They seemed more concerned about money than anything else. The children "especially in the Mennonite circles, whenever possible, married within the family relationship, with little consideration given to the feelings or wishes of the young people involved. Sometimes the arrangement was made between fathers without sending an elder or a relative ahead to make the proposal (as with the *Umbitter*). On occasion there were even written agreements made regarding the dowry."[4]

In West Prussia the engagement agreement was almost as binding as the marriage vows. In the Heubuden congregation (part of the Old Flemish branch of the church), during the time of strictest discipline, a broken engagement was dealt with so severely "that not only was marriage forbidden to both, but the one breaking the engagement was excommunicated and not received again until the other died." Until 1775 marriage outside this congregation was forbidden.[5]

Before the formal engagement ceremonies, a private meeting between the couple took place. They frequently exchanged rings. It was both a festive and solemn moment, an occasion of few words often accompanied by tears and kisses.

The actual formal engagement celebration, to which the families and church friends were invited, took place in the bride's home. A short religious service opened the celebration — Scripture reading, hymn singing and prayers for the welfare of the young pair. A *Faspa* hour or light meal followed, served to all the guests. Sometimes this occasion was nearly as big as the wedding.

Visiting Friends in the Vistula Delta

Engagement periods were short, usually lasting only two or three weeks. The bridal couple was showered with invitations from relatives and friends. This tradition continued in Russia and North America. It would have been a disgrace not to invite the honored couple for at least one meal.

At Delta gatherings the engaged couple sat in a place of honor, their chairs decorated with garlands, the table festive with greenery. According to Siegfried Rosenberg, "The bridal couple would sit for hours under the scrutiny of the ladies, during which conversation was often formal and stilted." Anna Rempel Dyck described these bridal visits during her engagement in the Molotschna village of Gnadenfeld in 1873. "Day in and day out, three long weeks were occupied with visits — sometimes two or three a day. Close relatives were always part of the company. To sit at well-spread tables and enjoy love and friendship was wonderful, but due to so much repetition, it became boring. How happy we were to snatch a little quiet hour for our privacy." [6]

The Wedding Invitation

Before the days of formal, engraved invitations, one single invitation was passed or carried from family to family throughout the village. In West Prussia it would have been the duty of the *Umbitter* to take this from house to house.

Among the Mennonites' Delta neighbors, the folk customs were even more interesting. A representative of the family decked out in colorful ribbons or bands rode by horse from house to house, carrying with him the bridal invitation. In some places a woman, called a *Kesterbeddersche,* went from house to house carrying a bouquet of flowers, a cane tied with a green bow, a red handkerchief (a greeting from the groom), a white handkerchief (a greeting from the bride) and the formal invitation. She recited a humorous poem bidding people to the bride's home on the wedding day, then to the church and again to the home for the reception.[7]

A Wedding Invitation in Russia

When the *Umbitter* no longer carried the wedding invitation, one was often artfully written by the village school teacher and passed from house to house. The biography of David Stoesz includes a copy of such an invitation on the occasion of his marriage to Maria Wieb, November, 1862.

Worthy Friends,
We have decided to tell you, through spiritual blessing, of our confirmation of our engagement for marriage bonds, if God wills, and have established this coming Tuesday, the 27th, as the

day of the wedding festivities. Therefore, on this stated day at 2 o'clock, all named friends and their worthwhile families are kindly, heartily invited to come here to the household of our dearest parents Heinrich Wieb of Heuboden, and be present at the marriage vows, and with us to ask the dearest Lord for a happy marriage. After the ceremony, a light, well-intentioned meal awaits you. If it is your good wish, please join us and be served.

Your friends,
Groom David Stoesz
Bride Maria Wieb
Hueboden the 25 of November, 1862

We pray you will send this further.[8]

Getting to Know Each Other

How did the young people of the isolated, segregated Russian Mennonite villages meet and fall in love? They lived in sheltered, strict home atmospheres and came under close scrutiny of neighbors and the watchful church community. Such a setting allowed little frivolity. Dating patterns which later developed in North America would have been far too liberal or "dangerous" in Russia. Still, young people met, fell in love and married.

In the village the common elementary school was probably the first opportunity for socializing between Mennonite boys and girls. Church was another place where they gathered in small groups before and after the service. It was also common for young people to meet in homes of their young adult friends on Sunday afternoons. Young fellows and girls dropped by to visit either the son or daughter of the home. Parents discreetly planned to be away to visit other friends or relatives. Boys would gather in one room and girls in another for part of the afternoon. Later everyone came together in the "great room" to talk, sing and play games. According to Gerhard Lohrenz, young couples who "had an understanding" but were not officially engaged sat together. The young people were always well behaved.

Some families chose to send their brighter children away to high school in another village.[9] This would be their first real social contact with young people from other villages. Another opportunity was the inter-church song festival. Joining the choir to sing at the songfest brought talented young people together. Visiting relatives in another village to celebrate birthdays (especially important in the Vistula Delta) and holidays provided other natural opportunities for intermingling and getting acquainted.

Most common were romances and marriages between young people in the same colony. Henry B. Tiessen estimates that forty percent of the young women married a partner from another village but from the same colony. Twenty-five percent married outside the colony. The girl next door or the boy from church were the best bet for romance.

Mary Dirks Janzen confirms this. "It was customary for a young girl to marry a Mennonite boy from her own or a neighboring village. Occasionally some Mennonites married Lutheran girls. Elopements were rare. However, I remember very well the day the Foth girl eloped with the telegraph man from our village. It was the same time the *Titanic* sank. The two events were of equal importance in our village."

In spite of restricted village life, romance blossomed. When a young man singled out the girl of his choice, he often courted with flair and style. When they decided to marry, the young man customarily sought the parents' permission. A date for the engagement ceremony was announced and a wedding date set. Weddings, which took place regularly in the spring and fall, were festive occasions, filled with merrymaking and entertainment, especially before and after the ceremony. They were also perfect settings for other young people to meet and often paved the way for another new romance.

Although patterns changed with the opportunities created by education during the years in Russia, the family and the father's wishes often proved more than a young girl could resist. Anna Rempel Dyck recalls how her mother, a young girl of seventeen, gave up romance with a younger man to marry a forty-four-year-old widower with children to keep peace in the family. "This marriage caused much grief for the (our) young mother, especially since she had been engaged to a brave man of her own age. Her grandparents thus committed a great injustice by appealing to her childlike obedience in order to persuade her to marry this widower because of his good financial condition." [10]

The Dashing Suitor in Russia

Often the events surrounding a young man's serious intentions of courting a girl were kept secret. In his book, *Lost in the Steppe,* Arnold Dyck describes the bewilderment of young Hanschen when his older brother, Peter, began acting in what seemed to him very peculiar ways. Hanschen observed that on certain days of the week Peter started making trips outside the village by himself. On those days the horses were curried especially carefully, "the brass studs of the harnesses polished to a shine and the carriage washed." When Hanschen inquired of his parents what his brother was up to, their answers made little sense to a young boy. Finally, the word was out that Peter was getting married.

The courtship ritual usually followed very definite folk patterns. After a young man had seen or met a girl he liked, he began making plans to court her. He would polish and shine his father's *Fadawoage* (buggy), the horses' harnesses and even the horses themselves, until everything was *blitsblank* (polished to perfection). Then he would dress himself in his Sunday best, shine his shoes and slick down his hair. He now took on the role of a *Fria* (suitor). A friend or older brother would be invited to go with him to be the driver of the buggy while he, the *Fria,* sat alone in the back.

Katherine Woelk van den Haak: To go courting it was necessary to show off a bit. In this everyone wanted to outdo the other. The *Kutscha* (chauffeur or driver) would pull hard on the reins, click his tongue and swing his whip. Off they would go at a speed they were sure none could duplicate.

Sometimes they went through several villages. The *Kutscha* made certain they arrived at the girl's home at the fullest speed possible.

The young girl invited the boy into the parlor or *Grootestow* and talked with him. They confessed their love for each other — on this very first occasion (!) and agreed to meet again. Shortly he would tell the girl's parents about his intentions. [11]

This courting ritual had its origin in the folk traditions of the Vistula Delta where a young man made a grand performance at the engagement celebration, driving a fine steed for which he had gotten a new saddle and harness. He then drove his dashing charger at unprecedented speed before the young bride, whom he wished to impress.

The "horse and buggy *Fria*" often came in for considerable good-natured teasing from his local buddies. In the village of Osterwick when a young *Fria* drove to the home of his betrothed some of his young friends, armed with shotguns, hid in the bushes and fired shots into the air as he drove by.[12] This naturally gave the horses a good scare and the suitor had all he could do to manage the horses and keep his buggy from tipping over, subtracting considerably from his attempt to make a dazzling impression on the entire community.

In some cases this pageantry of racing took place on the day of the wedding — passing the bride's home with great show, similar to the way Russian landlords raced through the villages in their *troikas*. Arnold Dyck says, "Under no circumstances may the bridegroom reach the place of the wedding on foot, even though it were the neighbor's place."

Kaethe Kasdorf Warkentin: When my dad got married, he raced through the town with his two black horses all by himself. From the bride's place they walked to the place of the wedding. Other young people joined them until it was a long procession by the time they got to the church.

The Bashful Suitor

First visits by a shy, young suitor could often be awkward and sometimes painful. One of these courtship meetings is described in an autobiographical account by Cornelius Goosen. He tells of his first meeting with Margaret Wedel, Nicolaipol in 1893.

The girl Cornelius admired, eighteen-year-old Margaret, had grown up in a step family where many of her duties almost made her a servant. One of her tasks was to tend the orchard. Cornelius often saw her there and regularly greeted her with a friendly, reserved, "Good day," as he passed by. One afternoon he mustered all his courage and asked permission of the stepparents to speak to her. Reluctantly granting the visit, they inquired if he had marriage in mind and also warned him not to stay long.

"Obtaining her consent, I asked her to come into the summer room. My heart beat violently. I walked up to her, gave her my hand, and asked if she was willing to go through life with me."

Margaret gave her consent, they kissed briefly and knelt down and prayed together. The second kiss, he allows, was "sweeter than the first. It was the beginning of our getting together."

Arranging meetings with Margaret continued to be difficult, but at times he would see her on the way home from meetings at church. A year later, when he still had to ask permission of her stepparents to meet her, they agreed on a wedding date.[13]

Haunskje onn Jreetje

The following Low German poem is about two children. Johnny is busy patching his shoes while Gretchen, the neighbor girl, watches him. She tells him that if he wants to court someone he should consider her. She has nice toys which she would give to him. He says toys are not enough because there are many other little girls. Sometime later they are both walking on a footbridge. Johnny falls into the water while Gretchen runs away. Johnny calls to Gretchen for help and assures her she will become his dearest bride.

Haunskje onn Jreetje

Haunskje saut em Schornsteen,
Flekjt sich siene Schoo,
Kjemmt doa Nobasch Jreetje aun,
Sach am flietijch too.
"Haunskje, we(11)st dü friee,
Dan frie dü doch no mie!
Ekj hab scheenet Spältijch,
Daut jäw ekj dan uck die!"
"Spältijch es too weinijch
Onn Kruschkjes senn soo fäl."
"Onn Haunskje, we(11)st dü friee,
Dan frie dü doch no mie."
Haunskje onn Jreetje jinje toop opp'm Stajch,
Haunskje foll 'nenn onn Jreetje rand wajch.
Haunskje roop: "Jreetje, komm halp mie 'rüt,
Sau(1)st uck woare miene leewe Brüt"

The *Polterabend (Pultaovend)*

Celebrating the evening before the wedding is an old European custom practiced by Mennonites both in West Prussia and later in Russia. In High German it is called *Polterabend* and in Low German *Pultaovend*. In the Grosses Werder among non-Mennonites, the parents of the bride saved up old dishes, bowls, cups or anything breakable to smash on this occasion. The guests then shattered the porcelain and pottery. The louder the noise, the better. The larger the rubbish heap, the happier would be the future of the bride and groom.

Mennonites generally held a more reserved evening of entertainment and gift giving. Anna Rempel Dyck remarks, "Many young friends came to celebrate on the eve of the wedding, but no rattling and rumbling took place."

Kaethe Kasdorf Warkentin remembers, "After the evening meal on Saturday, which included wedding guests, they had the gift giving. This was the *Pultaovend*. All the gifts were brought. It was held in the big barn that had been cleaned out and decorated for the wedding."

On this evening friends and relatives of the bridal pair often presented humorous poems, songs, special music and skits. The evening ended with games, especially popular with the young. During the Revolution this custom gradually disappeared.

The Wedding Ceremony

In Russia the village churches had no kitchens or fellowship halls for serving and dining. Therefore, most people were married at home, sometimes in the *Grootestow* (large room). More often than not, houses could not accommodate the whole village so the barn, usually the machine shed, would be emptied, cleaned of cobwebs and often lined with tarpaulin. Every inch of the yard had to be swept and groomed, gardens weeded and trails through the gardens raked and sprinkled lightly with fine white sand. Benches were placed throughout the garden and yard to provide a place for guests to relax and visit.

One or two o'clock was the customary hour for the wedding ceremony. Backless benches had been placed, "church fashion," with the women and children relegated to the back. The couple entered alone, sat on two decorated chairs in the front, with their close friends seated immediately behind them. There were no attendants or flower girls. Following are details of village weddings as women remember them from village life in Russia.

Anna Rempel Dyck: (1873) Our wedding was celebrated in our spacious barn. It had been swept very clean and decorated with flowers, beautiful green branches and garlands. At one end of the "giant drawing room" the wedding ceremony took place while at the other long rows of covered and decorated tables were set for the wedding dinner.

Kaethe Kasdorf Warkentin: The barn was decorated with evergreen branches and *wille Wiendrüwe* [wild grape vines] with wheat heads woven into them. If you knew there would be a wedding, you raised a lot of flowers. Garlands were made from the ropes used to haul big loads of wheat shocks. Girls did the decorating. Young people gathered benches from the village for the ceremony. The bride and groom came in, always alone, and sat on two chairs decorated with greenery.

Agatha Schroeder Fast: We were married in the barn where they set up tables and brought in the food. There were branches and greenery all over. They wove garlands from branches. My sister didn't want to get married in the barn. She said, "Every time I drive by it I will think, 'That's the barn where I was married.'"

The Wedding Clothes

Kaethe Kasdorf Warkentin: In my mother's time [late 1800s] the bride wore the black dress in which she had been baptized. But she had a white veil. The richer people already wore white for the wedding. This was about fifty years before the Revolution.

As time went on the dark dresses became less popular. "Late in the nineteenth century," says Katherine Woelk van den Haak, "the bride usually wore a long or a waltz length gown." The color might be black or white, as the bride preferred.

Before World War II brides wore long white dresses and veils attached to a myrtle wreath in Herta Funk's village. However, even the myrtle wreath was frowned upon and girls needed to ask the church elders for permission.

At one wedding Mary Francis recalls her *Onkel* Woldja "bearing himself with just the right amount of grace and dignity in his grey serge jacket and much admired *Büdelbekjse* [balloon trousers, similar to jodphurs] which were in style then." Most often the bridegroom wore a white shirt, black cravat and a long coat like those worn only by the minister or the baptismal candidates.

The Whole Village Came to Celebrate

Late fall was the time for weddings, when barns and attics and cellars were filled, and families could afford those leisurely, drawn-out days of celebration dictated by tradition. Whole villages were invited. Anna Rempel Dyck wrote that two hundred fifty families "with their children and grandchildren were invited to participate in the reception. Some had to drive many miles on their hackney-carriage, others came in covered wagons and, of course, had to stay overnight with us and with the neighbors."

The Wedding *Faspa*

In good times and bad it was customary to serve *Faspa* after the ceremony. No family had enough cream and butter to make enough *Zwieback* for 300 to 500 people for several days. Although no formal appeal for help was made, invited guests automatically shared from their larders. This was as traditional and natural as attending the wedding.

Mountains of *Zwieback* were baked for the guests and stored in the "small room" on a bed of very clean, fresh straw. Here they cooled until time to serve. Other times the buns were put into borrowed laundry baskets and lined up in rows for the wedding feast. Even though food was ample, the bride's mother tended to fret that there might not be enough *Zwieback*. It would have been thought stingy to run out of *Zwieback* or any other food, for that matter. The *Faspa* menu included *Zwieback,* sometimes jam and butter, sugar cubes and coffee.

The Wedding Reception *(Nokjast)*

Kaethe Kasdorf Warkentin: Weddings sometimes lasted for a week, so there were a lot of people to feed. If the whole village came, there was much cooking for each meal. Sometimes women were hired, *Kjast Tauntes,* to prepare the food.

Saturday night was the wedding supper. They often served *Rintsupp, Salankje* or *Borscht* with *Bulkje* and butter. There was *Mooss* for dessert. To play a joke the guests sometimes tried to make the host run out of food. They did this to my grandfather. "We'll get that Klassen," they said. "We want to show him that he will run out of food."

It would have been a disgrace to run out of food and tell the guests, "You will have to go home, we no longer have anything to eat."

Mary Dirks Janzen: In Gnadenfeld the wedding supper consisted of only four items: *Pflaumenmooss* [fruit soup made from a variety of dried fruit], cold sliced ham or lamb, homemade mustard and two kinds of homemade bread. The meal was eaten in the shed where our horse-drawn vehicles were kept. Teenage girls were asked to set the tables. We could hardly wait until we were asked to do this job.

Not all wedding meals were the simple style of the village with *Mooss, Zwieback* and coffee. Anna Reimer Dyck grew up on a large estate in the Kuban where weddings had become more elaborate and the wedding reception more sophisticated. She describes a typical wedding meal in the Kuban before the Revolution.

Anna Reimer Dyck: The wedding meal would usually be a cold meal, but there would be an abundance of food — ham, chicken, sausage, potato salad, steamed fruits, pickles, breads and buns. The desserts would be primarily pastries: cakes, syrup *Plats,* cookies and fresh seasonal fruit. Coffee and tea were served as well as milk and grape juice for the children.

Children were always included among the wedding guests, but they ate separately from the adults. In fact, tables were designated for age groups according to the color of flowers on the tables. For example, red flowers indicated the young people's table, white indicated the grownups and children would have something else. The tables were elaborately decorated with bouquets as well as garlands of flowers.[14]

*   *   *

Mary Francis: Preparations were going on in the summer kitchen. The scent of baked ham and *Plümemooss* hung heavy over the house. Thickly sliced ham that had been baked to perfection and was dripping with sweet, syrupy sauce, baked potatoes in melted butter and garnished with green chopped parsley, all the corn on the cob one could eat, *Zwieback* and seven kinds of sweet and sour pickles were on the menu. After the main course there were *Apfelplats* and *Plummenplats* [apple and plum coffee cakes] and all kinds of *Klein Gebäck* [small baked delicacies]. The *Tanten* [women] who served the table in the drawing room shook their heads in disbelief and amazement at the heaps of food we (the children) could put away.[15]

A Typical Mennonite Wedding Supper

1902–1912
Gnadenfeld, Molotschna Colony
Cold Sliced Ham
Homemade Mustard
Rye Bread
Bulkje
Plümemooss

After the Wedding — Games and Singing

Helene Rempel: After the wedding the young people sat and sang. The older folks talked and listened. There were musical instruments such as a violin, mandolin, guitar and *balalika.*

Mary Dirks Janzen: We young folks did a lot of singing after the wedding. We knew all kinds of folk songs and used guitars.

After the ceremony we played games such as "Hash Hash" and "Last Couple Out." There was one game, "*Schlüsselbund*" [Key in the Ring], which we all just loved. In this game a girl had to pick up the keys on a ring and go around the circle looking for a boy of her choice. She offered her arm to him and he accompanied her while she started a different song and jingled her key ring. Then all the girls had to find a boy to walk with. The girl who was "it" noisily dropped her keys and everyone scurried for a seat. The one left without a chair took the keys and started the game all over again as new partners were chosen.

The Ceremony of the Black Bow

During the evening of games and singing planned by friends, a special little folk ceremony was traditionally observed. This, too, was brought from the Vistula Delta, where at midnight after games and folk dancing, the friends and bridesmaids of the new bride exchanged her myrtle crown and veil for a bonnet.[16]

In Russia the bride and groom sat down on the benches, joined by their friends, and sang a song. While singing the first two verses, the bride removed her crown and veil and the bridegroom his boutonniere. They were placed on a plate.

During the singing of the third verse, the bride was guided to the middle of a circle, blindfolded and twirled around several times. She then gave her veil and crown to another young girl who was thereby designated the "next bride." The same was done with the groom's flowers. The new couple became the next "bridal pair" for the rest of the evening.

To replace her veil and crown the young bride was given a black bow, a sign of responsibility, which was pinned to the back of her head. Here is an English translation of the song.

> The bridal wreath you need no more
> For duties weight you by the score.
> To build a home where Christ shall live,
> May God enrich with joy and peace.
>
> The boutonniere is yours no more
> Your loving wife you shall adore.
> For duty calls you to arise
> Your happiness before you lies.
>
> Our prayers are that God will bless
> And crown your efforts with success.
> Serve Him, and gaily hand in hand
> Walk with Him to the Heav'nly land.
>
> Bow down thy head thou lovely bride,
> Thy crown of beauty laid aside.
> Now may this bow adorn your hair.
> God keep you happy in His care.

The Dowry

Anna Rempel Dyck: (1873) My husband received a $2,000 dowry, one beautiful horse, a clothes closet, six basket chairs, a bed with blanket and covers, much underwear, many good clothes, a fur coat and an overcoat.

I received a chest of drawers, much larger than the local ones here, filled with good linen and all kinds of clothing and bedding. I also received one excellent cow and many wedding presents along with large quantities of flour, ham, lard and butter. All this was loaded on a huge, white wagon, drawn by two strong horses.[17]

Hard Times and Weddings

After World War I the Mennonites remaining in Russia suffered a succession of tragedies — political oppression, religious persecution, destruction of property, famine, family separation and much more. Despite the tragic times, young people continued to be married. Some asked, "Why do you marry now?" Cornelius Wall married Agnes Dueck on Christmas Eve, 1917, at the height of the turmoil.

Cornelius Wall: The fall of the Czar triggered a three-year reign of terror and suffering in the Mennonite colonies. Bandits marched back and forth across the country, confiscating livestock and food supplies, plundering and killing. Repeatedly they came into the homes of our parents, opened doors and drawers and took what appealed to them. We had no choice but to endure them as we prepared for our wedding. Some people asked, "Why do you marry now? It's such a dangerous time." We had decided it was best to join hands and walk the rest of our lives as one. We never regretted that decision. On our wedding day, the Reds patrolled the streets. The guests filled only a small room, for the number had been restricted. We enjoyed our wedding day, even though some shooting took place to intimidate the people. Several bandits even came to our wedding to eat food served to the guests. Needless to say, we had to simplify the menu for our wedding guests.[18]

Agatha Schroeder Fast: During good times the whole village was invited to a wedding. During hard times we had only *Zwieback* and *Prips*. We could have only a few people. In the *Dorf* (village) they came only for *Faspa* on the wedding day. In the last years there was no sugar. It was impossible to have a wedding without *Zwieback* and sugar cubes.

Helene Rempel: During the poor and bad times we had to borrow everything, even the dress and the veil.

Anna Martens: We were married during hard times in Zagradovka. Things were so poor that my husband bought my ring by trading it for corn. Mother sold flour to make my bridal dress.

Herta Funk: After we fled from Russia to Germany, we lived on a large German *Hof* [farm]. If there was a wedding, it was held in a large barn. The meal was simple — only *Borscht* and *Jrettemalkj* [barley porridge].

A Beautiful Surprise

The year was 1947. Young Maria Penner, a Mennonite refugee student nurse, and Gerhard Weise, a young German, planned to be married at a Sunday (Mennonite refugee) church service in Munich, Germany. A wedding reception was out of the question. The war was over, but poverty was everywhere. Food was scarce and closely rationed. By going without many meals, the couple saved enough ration coupons to make a simple wedding meal for six. On the day of the wedding, however, their plans suddenly changed. The bride and groom were invited to a surprise reception. With much ingenuity and scraping together, the camp women managed to prepare a meal of real *Borscht* and almost-forgotten white bread. Even the tables were decorated with flowers. It was a king's celebration. The most lavish, expensive reception could not have been given with more love, prepared with so little and remembered with such deep affection.

Later the Weises immigrated to Canada where they raised a family and now have grandchildren. Maria last saw her father when she was six. Her mother, who had fled with her children to Germany, was sent back to a Russian prison camp. After years of painful searching, Maria was able to return to her childhood home in Russia. She found her mother, health broken from long years of hard labor. Mrs. Penner died a few years later. Maria and Gerhard Weise continue to live in Winnipeg, Manitoba.[19]

𝒦ORINTESTRETSEL FOR A WEDDING

Agnes Rempel Braun: At my wedding in Tiegenhagen we served this rich *Korintestretsel* along with *Zwieback* and coffee for *Faspa*. In the Molotschna there were two kinds of raisins — the large kind with seeds which the children liked to eat. The other smaller in size, were called *Korinte* (currants) and were used in baking.

2 cups milk	2 Tbsp. active dry yeast
½ cup shortening	2 tsp. sugar
½ cup butter	½ cup lukewarm water
2 Tbsp. sugar	6½ – 7 cups bread flour
2 tsp. salt	3 cups plumped raisins or currants

Heat milk, shortening and butter together over medium burner until butter melts. Stir in sugar and salt. Cool to lukewarm. Sprinkle yeast and sugar over lukewarm water and stir briskly to dissolve. In mixing bowl combine milk and yeast mixtures. Add about 4 cups of the flour and beat with electric mixer for 5 minutes. Gradually add 2½ – 3 cups flour and turn out onto lightly floured board and knead until smooth and elastic, about 8 – 10 minutes or finish with a dough hook.

Place dough in greased bowl, turning to grease top of dough. Cover with plastic wrap and set in warm place until doubled in bulk (about 1 hour). Punch down and work in the raisins or currants, distributing them evenly. Divide dough into 3 equal pieces, shape into loaves and place on greased cookie sheet or greased 9″ cake tins. Cover with clean kitchen towel and set in warm place until doubled in bulk. Brush with egg glaze of 1 egg beaten with 1 tsp. water. Bake at 350°F. for about 40–45 minutes or until bread is done. Cool on racks. Cover with a towel to retain softness.

—Agnes Rempel Braun

ZWIEBACK

Elizabeth Neufeld Buller: My mother, Helena Neufeld, who lived in Russia the first forty years of her life, always maintains that the *Zwieback* she bakes here in North America never did live up to those baked in the outdoor brick oven in Russia.

Mother used to sell her baked goods to Dester's Grocery in Buhler, Kansas. Every Saturday she baked ten to twelve dozen *Zwieback*. She also cooked in a nursing home and after retiring continued to make *Portselkje* every Friday morning for a fast-food place. Now she teaches her grandchildren her baking secrets. Although she no longer fills orders, she still bakes and no one leaves her apartment empty-handed.

1 cup very hot potato water	¼ cup *each* butter, good margarine,
2 Tbsp. sugar	and lard*
2 pkgs. active dry yeast	4 tsp. salt
2 cups milk	10–12 cups bread flour or enough
2 cups half-and-half	to make a medium-firm dough

* Helena Neufeld uses only fresh home-rendered lard.

Add sugar to potato water; let cool; add yeast. Meanwhile scald milk and half-and-half. Stir in margarine, butter and lard (if available). Cool to lukewarm. Combine yeast and milk mixture in a very large mixing bowl.

Add salt and 5 cups flour. Beat until reasonably smooth. Add remaining flour, 1 cup at a time, until dough is smooth and moderately firm. Knead until smooth and elastic.

Cover with a clean dish towel or plastic wrap. Set in a warm place and let rise until double in bulk. Punch down. Let rise again until double. Punch down. Working with a handful of dough at a time, pinch off pieces of dough the size of a Ping-Pong ball. Place balls on a greased baking sheet about 3 inches apart. Pinch off an equal number of slightly smaller pieces of dough and place them on an ungreased cookie sheet about 1 inch apart. Continue to pinch off pieces of dough until all the dough is used. You should have equal numbers of large and small pieces of dough. If not, bake the single ones along with the *Zwieback*.

Cover pans with clean dish towels and let rise for about 20 minutes. The ones you pinched first will probably be ready soon after you have finished pinching the last of the dough.

Just before placing pans in a preheated oven, 375°F., fill a small custard cup or other similar container with tap water. As you pick up a smaller ball of dough and before you place it on a larger ball, dip the underside of the smaller ball in the water. As you place the smaller on the larger one, press down firmly so it will adhere and not fall off as it bakes. (I usually take a quick peek in the oven after about 5 minutes of baking, and if any of the tops appear to be sliding off, I gently slide them back on to keep them upright.) Bake 15 – 20 minutes or until lightly browned.

Since oven temperatures vary, you may have to adjust the temperature of your oven. The *Zwieback* should be done and lightly browned in no more than 20 minutes. Remove from pans and slide onto cooling rack.

Zwieback are best when fresh. Any remaining *Zwieback* left over on Monday can be torn or cut in half, squeezed firmly, and placed on an ungreased pan and toasted in a 200 – 250°F. oven until evenly browned and dried. They can then be enjoyed through the week for snacks. They may be dunked in milk or coffee, sprinkled with sugar or eaten plain.

This is a large recipe and may be cut in half. If you have enough space and pans, *Zwieback* freeze very well and you won't have to bake them again for weeks.

— *Helena Neufeld*
— *Elizabeth Neufeld Buller*

Love, Courtship and Marriage in the Russian Mennonite Community in North America

Courtships, engagements and weddings among the Mennonite immigrants in the United States and Canada continued in much the same tradition as in Russia. One thing was certain, however: the rigors of pioneer life on the plains of Kansas and Canada demanded support and teamwork. Marriages most often resulted from love but also at times convenience. It was very difficult for a single man to pioneer alone.

The young met at churches, schools and social gatherings, but courting was done at home. The Model T Ford brought some changes into courtship patterns. Now with wheels and a motor, a young man could reach many more villages and meet more young women.

Entering a neighboring village still posed problems, as it had for the buggy driver whose horses were frightened by shotgun blasts from nearby bushes in Osterwick. One Canadian *Fria* took precaution against the pranksters by removing the steering wheel from his Model T and taking it with him into his girlfriend's house. After bidding his sweetheart goodnight, he picked up the steering wheel, walked back to the car, reattached it and puttered back home.[20]

Long, drawn-out courtships continued to be discouraged by the church. When a young couple decided they "wanted each other," they were, in Low German, *oppjebode* (announced). Their plans for marriage, which had been kept secret to that moment, were announced on a Sunday morning to the entire congregation. The engagement was celebrated at the home of the bride's parents where relatives, friends and many young people flocked that same afternoon.

Food had been prepared for days. The occasion was a time of feasting and celebration, a break in the hard work routine of the villagers' lives. The engagement celebration remained an important tradition in Kansas into the early 1900s. Marie Harms Berg describes her Uncle Frank's engagement celebration when she was a little girl.

Marie Harms Berg: My uncle Frank Wiebe and my aunt Agnes Ebel Wiebe celebrated their engagement in the home of my grandparents.[21] The whole front room was full of people. For me, as a young girl, this was all so exciting. Aunt Agnes wore a navy blue cape that was lined with red satin. She looked so pretty. I thought to myself, "If I ever grow up, I surely want a cape just like that."

Grandpa, being a minister, gave a speech. The couple had to kneel during the prayer. There was a lot of singing and praying. It was like Christmas and almost like a wedding.

Grandmother laid a long table with her very best service and fixed everything so nice. There were abundant supplies of *Zwieback,* coffee and cookies. The bridal couple sat at the head table smiling all the while. We children had to wait and eat later. This was two weeks before the wedding. After this *Verlobung* [engagement] ceremony, Uncle Frank and Aunt Agnes had to make the rounds of many homes for parties and dinner invitations.

* * *

After the engagement ceremony, tradition dictated a visit to grandparents and relatives, just as had been done in Russia. With a well-groomed horse and a shipshape top buggy, the couple set out on their visiting expedition. When they were spotted turning into a driveway, the first to see them proclaimed, *"Dee Brutlied sent hia!"* (The bridal couple is here!) All work stopped and there would be a frantic scramble to set the house in order. The man of the house took care of the horse and the young couple was invited in. If their schedule permitted, they would stay for *Faspa.* This tradition of visiting relatives before the wedding survived for a time but eventually disappeared.

Wedding Invitations

In American Mennonite communities, as in Russia, it was customary to invite the entire congregation to the wedding and reception. The invitation was usually extended by the minister from the pulpit on a Sunday morning. Special emphasis might be placed on invitations to the deacons and elders of the church.

Marie Harms Berg: When my parents, Henry S. and Anna Wiebe Harms, were married in the late 1800s, Mother's parents immediately planned a large wedding. Grandfather, being the elder of the church, invited everyone to attend. Also all the relatives and neighbors were invited.

During the 1920s printed, embossed invitations came into use. Among our own Toevs family treasures are three of those early invitations, all with the same pattern, probably ordered from the same printer. By 1925 formal, printed invitations were sent to individuals, although the custom of passing around a "family invitation" still lingered in a few families into the 1950s.

Food Preparation

"Everything was either baked at home or by the neighbors who offered help," says Marie Berg. "The day before the wedding large batches of *Zwieback* dough were stirred together and kneaded by the women. Chunks of dough were delivered to the different homes who had offered to bake. Mamma said the cookies were baked ahead, and Grandpa bought a lot of sugar cubes and cheese."

Helen Peters Epp recalls similar offers of help. "When Uncle John and Aunt Anna Hiebert Peters got married at our house, they built a lean-to onto the house. All the neighbors brought extra things. When my husband's sisters got married, the neighbors sent milk and butter."

In central Kansas weddings were held in the spring or fall. The wedding ceremony frequently took place on a Thursday afternoon. The schedule in the bride's family home went something like this: Monday was the day for butchering a beef or hog with neighbors and friends coming to help. Big washtubs were put to good use for mixing giant mounds of ground meat. Tuesday everyone was busy baking and cooking. Huge batches of *Zwieback* dough were mixed in the large washtubs on Wednesday. The bridal pair delivered billowing chunks of dough to friends for baking. Finishing touches were put on the bridal gown. Thursday morning the church was decorated and the cakes were cut in time for everyone to attend the ceremony.

Uncle Dan Jost remembers cakes baked for his wedding, April 22, 1920. "Before the wedding we baked cakes and cakes. My sister, Minnie (Jost Krause), and two others helped. We must have had thirty cakes — far more than we possibly could eat."

The Double Wedding

For some families the cost of inviting the entire congregation to a daughter's wedding was more than they could afford. A happy solution seemed to be the double wedding. Several young couples would decide to be married the same day. This way they could divide the cost of the feast among several families, not to mention the work of preparing the large quantities of food. The Huebert family of Henderson, Nebraska, had two daughters, Sara and Tena, and a son, John, all of whom were married on the same day in June, 1900. These couples celebrated their triple golden wedding anniversary together in 1950.

The Tent Wedding

When weddings were very large, few homes could accommodate the guests, so it became fashionable to have the reception and sometimes even the wedding ceremony in a large tent. In those days it was unthinkable to have a wedding without a wedding meal. Tents were popular from the 1890s to the mid-1930s. Usually set up with planks for seating and table boards for eating, the tents sometimes had a platform for the minister, the piano or organ and the wedding party.

For these occasions the whole farmyard — the barns, sheds and the house — had to be readied for the guests. Marie Berg again shares from her memories of family weddings. "When my parents were married, the whole church and all the relatives were invited. The church was too small to hold everyone, so Grandfather Wiebe rented the tent that was used for large festivals in the churches."

In Canada the wedding reception and sometimes the ceremony were held in a machine shed as had been done in Russia. "The unusual location affected neither the legality nor the gaiety of the occasion," comments Herb Neufeld in *Harvest Anthology of Mennonite Writing in Canada*. Eventually, fellowship halls and church buildings replaced the tent and barn receptions and ceremonies.

The *Polterabend (Pultaovend)*

In Canada weddings frequently took place on Sunday with the *Pultaovend* or bridal shower held on Saturday night. At Margaret Albrecht's wedding the young people arrived on Saturday bringing with them about six hayracks and several large pieces of binder canvas. The racks were lifted off the wheels and set on their sides against the south side of the house to construct a temporary shelter. Poles were lain across the top of the racks and the canvases placed over them. The inside was transformed with tree branch decorations, making an inviting, cozy room, heavy with the fragrance of the outdoors.

The *Pultaovend* was usually filled with fun, laughter, games and entertainment. No invitations were issued. Those who wished to could come. In Kansas games were sometimes played to the music of a mouth harp. Mariam Penner Schmidt says of this evening, "There was usually a serious program followed by hilarious poems, skits and songs."

The following is a copy of a printed program from a *Polterabend* held in Reesor, Ontario, in 1930. This program survived between the covers of a book and is a bit of a witness to the wedding entertainment of the past.[22]

Program for the *Polterabend*
of
Peter Dyck & Erna Töws
Reesor, Ontario, 1930

1. *Begrussungsgedicht* (Poetic Greeting)	Alice Töws
2. *Ein Konditor* (A Confectioner)	Frieda Töws
3. *Die Zigeunerin* (The Gypsy)	Olga Töws
4. *Das Lied von der Glocke* (Song of the Bell) by Friedrich Schiller	
(Read by a narrator and depicted in five tableaux vivants)	Amateur Group
5. *Mädchen mit Blumenstrauss* (Girl with Bouquet)	Hilda Fast
6. *Der Bäckerjunge* (The Baker Boy)	Alice Töws
7. *Der kleine Schwäger* (The Little Brother-in-Law)	Peter Töws
8. *Käti mit dem Besen* (Katie with the Broom)	Käti Töws
9. *Die zwei Kohlerkinder* (Two Innocent Children)	Alice and Frieda Töws
10. *Nante Strumpf*	D. Fast and H. and J. Bergen
11. *Ein Ehepaar aus alter Zeit*	Olga Töws and
(A Married Couple from Olden Times)	Hilda Fast

Wedding Fashions

In the days before the automobile, it was customary for a young couple to ride to their wedding in a new carriage drawn by a spirited, well-groomed team of horses. The couple sat in the back seat while the driver, a friend of the groom, handled the horses. The carriage had been decorated with ribbons, flowers and tassels.

Upon arrival at the church, the bridal couple were preceded down the aisle by the ministers. There were no attendants and no rings.

Wedding dresses in the early pioneering days were black, made of wool or cashmere, according to what the bride's parents could afford. The dresses were floor length with a gathered skirt, a ruffle at the hemline and long sleeves trimmed with lace. Later a bit of white was added to the bodice. This progressed to royal blue but in the very same style. There were no veils, only the myrtle wreath crown. Flower decorations, too, were frowned upon.

"In the Bruderthal church, Hillsboro, Kansas, the first white silk wedding dress with a veil was worn in 1898 (almost a quarter century after the Mennonites arrived). The last black dress was worn by a bride in 1907 in the same congregation."[23]

Uncle Dan Jost remembers his 1920 wedding to Bena Goertz. My bride "made her own wedding gown, a plain white dress trimmed with lace. I wore a blue serge suit which would cost a pretty penny today. I think I had my first haircut and shave by a real barber for the occasion."

The day after the wedding, "I got the lumberwagon from the place where I batched, hooked up the horses and went over to the Goertzes. Bena had things that belonged to her. We took along the gifts from her mother, blankets and what have you. We loaded up our stuff and took it to the place where I lived, and we were ready to settle down."

An American Custom—The Shivaree

Festivities for the newly married couple sometimes ended with a shivaree. This custom, new to the Mennonites, was added to the traditions among families who lived in the midwestern United States. A week or ten days after the wedding, a group of friends came to serenade the newlyweds with the din of clanging pots, pans and kettles outside their bedroom window. A special noisemaker called a "horse fiddle," a homemade instrument made of disc blades and a cog wheel, made such a clatter it often brought a reluctant couple out of the house. They were expected to invite the merrymakers in for treats of candy, cookies and other refreshments. Following is an account of such an occasion in western Kansas in 1932.

Marie Loewen Franz: We were enjoying an evening all to ourselves when suddenly all thunder broke loose. It was a shivaree. Naturally we were expecting it, but we didn't know when. Every newlywed couple had one. If our friends had failed to do this for us, we would most certainly have felt neglected or slighted. It was just the thing to do those days, and it was lots of fun.

There must have been about twenty young people in the group each bringing the loudest noisemaker they could find. They approached the house very quietly and then suddenly "let go." At times shotguns were used, of course, only for the sake of extra noise. It was like Halloween without costumes and masks. Then as soon as refreshments of sweets and punch were served, the noise stopped, as well as the tricks. For a few of the tricks, they draped a spare tire over the tail of the windmill, also a pair of Herb's overalls on the very top. After refreshments there was much visiting and laughter. We were complimented for being good sports. Shivarees? We loved 'em.[24]

The *Nach-Hochzeit* or After Wedding

A very old custom practiced among some of the Mennonites from the days in the Vistula Delta was the *Nach-Hochzeit,* German for "after-wedding," which was held eight days after the ceremony. This custom was common in some Canadian Mennonite circles until World War II. A description of the event comes from the book, *Mia,* by Mary M. Enns. The event followed the wedding of Abe and Mia Reimer DeFehr on August 17, 1940.

"On the following day, Sunday, [a week after the wedding] they all celebrated, as was traditional in most Mennonite marriages, the "after wedding" or *Nach-Hochzeit.* Mia wore her wedding gown once more and the Nystrom sisters took movies in the garden. After another festive supper the young couple left for a honeymoon at Granite Lake near Kenora." [25]

*   *   *

Russian Mennonite weddings in North America have gone through many transitions. Today they are often very similar to weddings among other groups. Still there is an emphasis on simplicity and good stewardship. Bridal couples often have attendants and flowers, and the ceremony and vows are sometimes specially written by the bridal couple for the occasion. There is a lot of music. Receptions vary greatly from a simple coffee table with cake and punch to a full buffet meal, depending on the circumstances of the parents. During a 1950s wedding when very simple tea tables were fashionable, an elderly gentleman, accustomed to the old-style Mennonite reception, commented, "Why, it hardly paid to come."

A Canadian Mennonite Wedding Supper, 1940s
Roast Beef
Baked Homemade Sausage
Baked Home-cured Ham
Potato salad
Pickles
Zwieback and Fresh Bread
Plümemooss
Coffee Cakes & *Plauts*
Cakes & Cookies
Coffee, Postum, Milk

The Seasons

The frost comes later, on tiptoes. It slowly moves over the steppe when the wind is still and the moon shines brightly. One doesn't notice it during a walk in the evening until the walls of granaries and feedsheds crack, startling the wanderer.[1]

—Arnold Dyck

To everything there is a season and a time to every purpose under the heaven.

—Ecclesiastes 3:1

The Seasons

In central California where I live seasons are subtle. Snow is rare. The climate is fairly mild and picnics at the beach are possible year round. My memories take me back to the prairies of my childhood, to a time and place when weather, temperature and time of year dictated the work and pleasure of the day. As each season emerged, there came with it a new rhythm and pattern of life.

Winter

Winter provided a wonderful respite from the intensity of summer for the Russian Mennonites. There were small jobs to be done outdoors by the farmer. House, barn and implement repairs needed taking care of. With the first, sharp, cold days there came hog butchering with its lovely fresh pork sausage and crisp cracklings to make a real winter breakfast.

Outdoors the garden and orchard took a well-deserved rest. Flower beds were bare and gardens empty with not a leaf on the fruit trees. The only growing plants were pots of geraniums and parsley on the kitchen windowsill. At Christmas Mother's cactus, suddenly a cascade of bright pink blossoms, was brought downstairs to spread its glory in the bay window. The parlor, as it was then called, was closed off during the week to save heat and opened only on Sunday. On weekdays it seemed forlorn and uninviting.

Winter meant keeping the house warm by stoking the furnace at night or keeping a pot-bellied, living room stove going all day. Evenings provided a welcome time for handwork, mending, eating apples and popping corn. The first snowfall of the season was for sledding and making snow ice cream. And what a great day if school was declared closed due to drifts too high or temperatures too frigid.

In my father's family the pond provided skating for the boys and townsfolk throughout December and January. December, of course, brought the greatest excitement of the year — the celebration of Christmas with a tree and ornaments, program practices at church, family secrets and presents.

In January winter set in with a vengeance. Coping with the cold on the prairies was a challenge. Herbert V. Neufeld says, "A prairie house on a hill may be a subject for art or poetry in summer, but in January it made life a battle for survival. Without storm windows and insulation, the winter wind seemed to blow through with scarcely a pause." My husband, Alden, remembers waking up on winter mornings with snow having drifted through cracks onto the wool comforter. The inevitable sharing of bedrooms with brothers and sisters became desirable in winter.

When the drifted roads cleared and the sun shone, people found time to go visiting. Neighbors and relatives used weekday afternoons to call on each other. They talked about the old country, the farm, the church and sometimes even the relatives. A Canadian friend remembers his parents having long discussions about the Russian Revolution with their friends. Usually,

Several young women from the village of Rosenthal in 1911.

A group of Russian Mennonite young people on an outing in 1895. Complete with samovar and wine bottles.

guests stayed for supper. In spite of the cold and boredom, winter provided its own beauty and calm.

Winter Memories from Russia

Mary Dirks Janzen: The tile oven is heated, the house cozy and warm, the sun is melting into a vast sea of white snow. It is too early for supper. Too early to light the kerosene lamp. We sit and visit and at times sing. Jacob plays guitar or mandolin. It is pleasant to sit around the large table with father at the head and have a simple supper of barley soup cooked with sour milk, rye bread, liver sausage, onions and vinegar.

Anna von Kampen Funk: In the winter evenings we did our spinning and knitting while eating sunflower and pumpkin seeds. We ate sour pickles and apples while telling Indian stories.

Helen Pankratz Siemens: In the evening the family sat around the table by gas light. We sewed in the daytime and made buttonholes at night.

Mary Dirks Janzen: Going to bed was a task. Our trundle-type beds had lids, which were opened and leaned back with pillows and featherbeds. On winter nights the howling of the icy wind was heard outside and watchdogs kept guard. Even the cattle on the other side of the thick kitchen wall were comfortable and warm. About 9 p.m. the animals would receive their last feeding.

N.J. (Nick) Kroeker: (Chortitza, 1901) At times we went to the nearby pond. It was a pleasure to see girls in shortened skirts dressed in snugly fitting jackets with fur collars and muffs and wearing fur caps to match. They were able to do figures on ice. The teachers at the school never fussed nor forbade skating. All they would do is remind us in class not to forget our homework.[2]

Fuel Shortage, Chortitza, 1919

N.J. (Nick) Kroeker: Because the heating systems in most homes were specially designed so that straw, wood, or dried manure bricks could be used for fuel, every family had seen to it that enough fuel had been garnered for the winter. Where straw was lacking because so many fields had been abandoned due to the acute shortage of horses, there grew thousands of acres of tall weeds. Just about every family saw to it that they chopped down the weeds and dried them for fuel. Fetching them home in two-wheeled carts (one man pulling and another pushing) they brought home their fuel for the winter.[3]

Winter Memories in North America

Minnie Jost Krause: On cold mornings Dad built a big fire in the heating stove and then called us. We snuggled down in the featherbed a few minutes longer before dashing down to the stove to dress where it was warm.

On long winter evenings in Kansas we played harmonica. Dad had an accordion and we sang. We ate a lot of sunflower seeds and played checkers with corn and buttons.

Ted G. Jost: Some of my happiest memories of farm life when I was a kid were in the wintertime. A typical winter's evening scene might have Dad rocking a couple of the kids or playing the harmonica. Mother might be writing a letter or sewing. Sometimes the kids would be playing Rook, or maybe studying.

Marie Loewen Franz: Evenings were spent together as a family, each doing his or her own thing, much of it around the table with a gas lamp in the center. There were no electric lights. Evenings like this were especially cozy on cold winter nights, near the pot-bellied heating stove. Even the baby's cradle was brought into the large family room, and all evening, while Mother either crocheted or read, she rocked the cradle with her foot. At bedtime the cradle was moved back into the bedroom and the rest of us scampered off to bed as fast as we could before we froze. You see, we slept in the attic under the shingled roof, and it was cold! We'd say our prayers while kneeling beside our beds, nearly freezing our toes on the wood floor.[4]

Tina Harder Peters: On long winter evenings in our home in Manitoba, we children played games around the table. My father sometimes read aloud while Mom was sitting and spinning. The boys played cards. Mother used to read German stories to herself. Books were passed around in those days. They sometimes came in sets of ten. In order to pass my English exam, I often read the newspaper aloud to my father. He, in turn, reported to the neighbors the news I had read to him from the paper. We would have *Brockemalkj* (bread soaked in warm milk) before going to bed.

Dan G. Jost: As children and teenagers we didn't have the privilege of galavanting all over the country. A five-mile radius was the limit. We were less exposed to the many temptations of today.

My father was a person who loved to have a pond on the place. We lived about a mile and a quarter from Hillsboro and many of the townsfolk came to skate. We boys didn't have skates because we couldn't afford them. So we kept a fire going for the women who got cold feet or had a skate come off. We got pretty good pay, usually about a dime for the whole evening, and we thought we were doing real well.

Bertha Fast Harder: Winter evenings in our home were special. My father was a friend to all our neighbors, even the Norwegians with whom few other people had social contact. They were not included in our threshing or butchering rings; those were almost always Mennonites who knew how to butcher and thresh like we did. On a cold, clear winter night, however, he would call the Norwegian neighbors and ask, "How about coming over and playing cards?" He'd invite as many as six men. And then we would watch for them, crunching across the snowy fields in their big boots, swinging their kerosene lanterns. They would sit around the dining room table playing cards and eating sunflower seeds. Mother didn't seem to mind that they spit out their shells. Later she would serve something special she had baked. As a little girl I liked to stand behind them, watching. I appreciate that our parents helped us learn to know people from other cultures.

Herbert V. Neufeld: Evening togetherness around the kitchen stove came naturally since this was the only reliable warm place. The trouble with this togetherness was that if one of us caught the flu or the croup or chicken pox, we'd all get it, which meant it was around the house for quite a while.

OKLAHOMA FRONTIER YEAST BISCUITS

The Oklahoma frontier opened for settlement at noon April 22, 1889. A few years later John C. Peters, a Kansas farm lad, set out in horse and buggy to file a claim and build a shack. He returned to Kansas to marry his sweetheart Anna Hiebert on April 23, 1906. John honored his new bride with a train ride to Tyrone while a friend drove his horse and buggy back to Oklahoma.

This is one of Anna's receipts, stirred up at night and baked fresh in the morning. Hot biscuits must have been especially appealing on cold winter mornings when the wind blew across the prairie and howled around their little house.

Soak 1 cake yeast, 3 tsp. sugar in ½ cup water overnight. Mix with a little flour in the morning. Let rise a little. Then add 1 cup sugar, 2 eggs, lard the size of an egg, 1 pint milk. Mix in yeast and enough flour. Salt to taste.

— From Martha Taeves' Academy Notebook, 1916
—Anna Hiebert Peters
— Helen Peters Epp

OVERNIGHT FRENCH TOAST
(*Arme Ritter*)

6 eggs
2 Tbsp. flour
1 Tbsp. sugar
1 tsp. cinnamon
1 tsp. salt

1 tsp. baking powder
⅛ tsp. nutmeg
2 cups milk
1 tsp. vanilla

Beat eggs with wire whisk. Add flour, sugar, cinnamon, salt, baking powder, nutmeg and beat well.

Add milk and vanilla and mix well.

Slice bread in thick slices. Soak in egg mixture overnight, squeezing pieces close together. Ten minutes before cooking turn slices to finish soaking.

Sauté slices in butter in a large frying pan until golden brown on both sides. Serve with sprinkled powdered sugar, syrup or jam.

SΆUERKRAUT *BORSCHT*
(*Süakommstborscht*)

Canadian Mennonite cooks add parsley root to sauerkraut *Borscht*. Both parsley root and celery root are common soup ingredients in the Ukraine. This practice probably dates to the time when fresh parsley and celery were not available during the winter season. Parsley root gives a richer flavor than the parsley sprigs. Sauerkraut *Borscht* is often ladled over boiled jacket potatoes cut up in individual serving bowls.

1 ham or pork hock	1 parsley root*
2 quarts water	Salt to taste and ¼ tsp. pepper
2 potatoes, cubed, or 1 small potato per serving	1 quart sauerkraut
1 medium onion, chopped	½ – 1 cup sour cream

* When parsley root is not available, use ½ bunch of parsley while cooking. Reserve ½ bunch to add during the last minute of boiling before serving.

In a soup kettle cook ham hock until tender. Remove and cut meat from the bone. Set aside. Strain broth through a fine sieve or cheesecloth to clarify liquid. Remove fat. Add enough water to make 2 quarts.

Add potatoes, onion, shredded or cubed parsley root and seasonings and cook until potatoes are done. (When serving potatoes separately, boil small size potatoes with skins — new, tender potatoes are best — until soft. Before serving, place potatoes in individual soup bowls and ladle finished soup over them.) Add sauerkraut (drained if desired) and boil ½ hour. Add sour cream just before serving and do not reboil. Makes approximately 10 1-cup servings.

BEEF BROTH WITH NOODLES
(Kjielkjesupp)

Mariam Penner Schmidt: Grandmother Penner often made a *Kjielkjesupp*. When she had a hot boiling broth, she would make a thick *Kjielkje* dough with flour, egg and milk. She put the piece of dough on a little board and cut off little pieces into the broth and cooked it until the *Kjielkje* were done. I think she added a little sour cream and vinegar. She called it *Kjielkjesupp* and it was good.

Pick and Choose Soup

An old-fashioned, village-style way of serving soup was to place potatoes in one serving dish, rice in another and the meat and carrots on a platter. Each person could choose from the ingredients to create a soup of his or her own liking. This was often done with variations of *Rintsupp*.

HOMEMADE NOODLES FOR SOUP

Agnes Rempel Braun: Chicken soup should have very fine noodles.

Marie Harms Berg: My grandmother, Sarah Voth Wiebe, made a lot of noodles in one day. She would make the dough, roll it out real thin and hang the slabs to dry. Then she rolled them up tightly, and whom did she call to do the cutting? Grandpa. She said nobody could even come close to cutting noodles as fine as Grandpa. Grandpa was the preacher, Peter A. Wiebe, an elder in the Springfield KMB church, Lehigh, Kansas. He supervised the building of the church and did a lot of the carpenter work himself.

6 eggs	6 Tbsp. water
2 tsp. salt	4 cups all-purpose flour

Mix eggs, salt and water. Add flour gradually to make a stiff dough. Knead thoroughly. Divide into 2 or 3 pieces. Form into balls. Roll out these balls into very thin sheets.

Spread sheets of dough out on a table to dry. Dough should not be allowed to get brittle. Roll sheets of dough and cut into strips for very fine noodles. Toss gently so they don't stick together. Cook in salted boiling water until done. Put through colander and drain. Rinse quickly with cold water and return to pot. Add 2 Tbsp. butter and stir to prevent sticking.

ℬEET BORSCHT
(*Beetaborscht*)

Although Mennonites traditionally preferred *Kommstborscht,* there were still those, like Agatha Martens, who "always used beets. We used two or three and seasoned the *Borscht* with dill and *Päpaschoote.* It could be quite hot."

Agatha Schroeder Fast's mother added beets for color. In this *Borscht* you have a pleasant sweet-sour flavor. The sweetness of the beets contrasts with the sourness of the tomatoes.

"We had a regular menu every week as did many families. We always had *Borscht* on Tuesday," remembers Helen Pankratz Siemens. Another regular was *Bulkje.* "We always had *Bulkje* [crusty white bread baked in the Russian oven] with *Borscht.*"

2 lbs. soup bones	1½ Tbsp. parsley, chopped
2 quarts water	Few fresh sprigs dill weed
1 medium head cabbage, chopped fine	8 peppercorns
2 medium potatoes, cubed	1 cup cooked beets, diced
1 medium onion, minced	1 *Päpaschoot* (small red pepper)
2–3 carrots, sliced	2 tsp. salt
1–1½ cups tomatoes (fresh), cut in pieces, or substitute 2½ cups canned tomatoes	⅔ cup sour cream

Boil soup bones in water in soup kettle. Skim to clear. Remove bones and clear meat stock. Trim off beef and set aside to serve separately.

Add cabbage, potatoes, onion and carrots. Simmer until vegetables are done.

Add tomatoes and bring to a boil. Add parsley, peppercorns (in spice container) and dill weed. To retain the color, add the cooked beets and red pepper during the last 10 minutes of cooking. Correct seasoning with salt. Immediately before serving, add sour cream. Do not reboil. Makes approximately 10 1-cup servings.

Tip: Beets cooked too long or reheated too often take on a brown or pale color. To give brownish *Borscht* a good red color, grate a fresh raw beet into it and simmer the soup 10 minutes. One cookbook suggests baking the beets beforehand, adding most of them shredded during the cooking and reserving 1 baked beet, shredded and sprinkled with lemon juice, to add about 10 minutes before serving.

Sour Cream

Sour Cream (*Smetana*) is a staple in Slavic cooking. Fresh homemade sour cream is a rich, thick, sweet cream, despite its name. There are a few dishes that sour cream will not improve. In Russia it contributes to the meal from soup through the dessert.

ℋOMEMADE COTTAGE CHEESE FOR *VARENIKJE*
(*Glomms*)

1 gallon whole raw milk	1 tsp. salt
1 cup sour milk	1 gallon water

Combine whole raw milk and the sour milk in a stone jar or other container and set in a warm place until it separates and turns to clabber. Stir several times so milk warms evenly. This same process may be accomplished by heating clabbered milk gently over low heat.

When the clabber separates from the whey, pour through a cheesecloth or cloth bag and hang to drain. Whey, a watery liquid, will drain off, leaving the soft curds in the bag. Sprinkle with salt.

Pour water over cheese and wash well. Drain again. The cheese may be mixed or refined with a mixer or potato masher.

Glommsbiedels

Rivalry and clannishness were strong among the youth from different villages in South Russia. At social gatherings they eyed each other cautiously, often hurling colorful and insulting nicknames. According to Gerhard Wiens, the villagers of Neu Halbstadt were known as *Glommsbiedels* or cottage cheese bags!

𝒫ASTRY *PERIESCHKJE* FILLED WITH MEAT

½ tsp. salt	1 egg yolk
½ cup plus 2 Tbsp. butter	5 – 6 Tbsp. ice water

Cut butter or shortening into sifted flour and salt until mixture resembles coarse meal. Combine slightly beaten egg yolk with water. Sprinkle liquid over flour and mix lightly until dough forms a ball. Chill thoroughly.

Roll ¼ inch thick and cut into 4″ inch squares. Place a portion of filling in center of each square. Bring edges together and seal tightly. Place, sealed side up, on a greased baking sheet. Brush with 1 egg beaten with 1 Tbsp. water or milk. Bake at 400°F. for 15 – 20 minutes.

Chicken Filling

1½ cups cooked chicken, cut in
small pieces
⅓ cup diced celery
2 Tbsp. diced green pepper

1 Tbsp. chopped onion
1 Tbsp. chopped parsley

Sauté celery, pepper and onion for 10 minutes. Add parsley and combine with chicken. Simmer together for 10 minutes. Cool.

$\mathscr{M}$EAT BALLS
(*Klopps* or *Kloppsküake*)

Klopps denote anything made with meat, flour, bread crumbs, liquid and egg. *Klopps* is a German word.

1½ lbs. ground round steak
Salt and pepper
1 egg

2 Tbsp. flour
½ onion, chopped
½ cup sour cream

Combine ground meat, seasonings, egg, flour, onion and cream. Form into balls and brown in hot oil in skillet. Brown on all sides and cook until done.

$\mathscr{S}$TEWED CABBAGE
(*Schmuakommst*)

Schmua in Low German means to simmer or stew. A long, slow simmering of cabbage or beans gives an excellent flavor. This method of preparing cabbage was common in West Prussia.

Edna Friesen Reimer: I grew up on this recipe. It is *very* good.

½ head cabbage	1 Tbsp. vinegar
Salt	1 Tbsp. sugar
2 Tbsp. lard, butter or margarine	Dash pepper

Cut cabbage in half and cut up rather coarsely. Cook cabbage in large saucepan covered with water and salt. Drain. Add lard, vinegar, sugar and dash of pepper. Mix well and simmer slowly for 15 – 20 minutes.

Spring

Finally, in March, there came those longed for signs of change. The ice on the pond at Grandfather Jost's farm began to break, the ground felt soft under our shoes and country roads turned into a nightmare of mud. Women's talk turned to early gardens, planting new peas and radishes. Days grew longer. When it seemed safe, sprouting potatoes were planted. Trees swelled with buds. Then there came a day so warm we girls dared to roll up our long, winter underwear and roll down the long, tan stockings that had hidden our legs all winter. For this spring ceremony we stayed well out of our mother's sight.

In April our mother sewed and fussed over new Easter outfits for us girls. And one Saturday night we convinced our father of the urgency of buying the new pairs of white, patent leather sandals in the window at Schaeffler's store. These shiny, magic slippers were placed on a bedside table, waiting for Easter and summer freedom. They would be worn on Easter, regardless of sun, rain or snow. In the snapshots we appear gangling and silly, trying desperately to look warm while refusing to hide new outfits under the old winter coats.

If flowers were on schedule, there were peonies in bloom for Mother's Day or Decoration Day. We made a yearly pilgrimage with Mother to the family graves on Decoration Day. Relatives met at the cemetery and stopped to visit amid tombstones and fruit jar bouquets in the warm spring sun. Although an unlikely spot, it seemed there should be a picnic in the tender new-mown grass.

One warm, bright morning, just meant for jumping rope and playing "jacks," Mother declared war on the winter dirt and launched her annual spring cleaning. We literally tore the house apart. Floppy mattresses were dragged down the stairs to air in the sun while rugs draped the wash lines to be beaten with a broom. Lace curtains dried in the back yard on wooden stretcher frames. Storm windows came down, screens went up and winter cobwebs were swept away until everything sparkled. Dry cleaning was expensive, so winter clothes were washed in "naptha gas" before being stored for the summer. Woolen sweaters and blankets were layered in moth balls in Mom's red cedar chest until fall.

What a weary, wonderful feeling it was to go to bed that night. The whole house smelled fresh and clean.

The Russian Mennonite Villages in Spring

Mary Dirks Janzen: (Gnadenfeld) On our way back from school we could watch the changes which occurred with the return of warmer days. The school path and our garden path would become softer and softer, until our feet would sink in and get our rubber shoes muddy. When spring had come, our gates were closed and all the horses were let out for some exercise. Oh, this was delightful to observe. After being tied up in the barn all winter, they were able to be free for a few hours and move and run as they pleased. They frolicked and played around in the front yard like a group of children.

Arnold Dyck: (Hochfeld) It is completely spring now. The big oven isn't being heated any more. The inner living rooms lie deserted. The upper half of the rear house door stands open the whole day. There is no one in the house all day. The barn is empty too. The cattle are at pasture, the horses in the field. Olga digs up the vegetable garden. When he [Hanschen] has seen the first swallow, he doesn't put on a sock any more.[5]

N.J. (Nick) Kroeker: (Chortitza) The children were particularly fond of riding the hay wagons. They'd sit sideways, putting their legs between the bars and letting their feet dangle. This always seemed to be a picnic highlight.

The tower clock of the *Zentralschule* could tell about beautiful spring days when fruit and chestnut trees were in bloom and the scent of pear and apple and *Kruschkje* [small round wild pears grown in Russia] was heavy upon the air. It could tell of music and singing issuing through the open windows of one of the other teacher's quarters. It could tell of the boys waiting at the large gate for the girls from the *Mädchenschule* to come by, two by two. Then the boys would range themselves behind them also two by two. And so they walked down the street and the birds were singing and the girls were laughing and the grownups would smile knowingly. The clock looked down upon the children swinging on Froese's double swing that would seat two or three children at a time, or the game of skittles going on under the *Kruschkje* trees at Penners. And in the evening a horn blew in the distance and the cows came home from the pasture raising a cloud of dust, and even on the schoolyard the milk pails clattered as the women went to milk the cows in the pen behind the barn.[6]

Spring in Kansas

Frieda Pankratz Suderman: Life in Moundridge in the early 1900s was beautiful and peaceful. Many of the streets were shaded on both sides by maple and elm trees. There were no power mowers; wild flowers bloomed in the ditches of the curbless street. There were what we called buttercups, black-eyed Susans, snake flowers and some dandelions. The dandelions were not as plentiful as they are now though the city park was sometimes yellow with them. Across the street to the west of our house, the sidewalk was a cinder path. Tall lilac bushes stood so near that after a heavy rain one became wet walking along the cinder path.

Some Low German Sayings and a Poem about Spring

Räajen, Räajen, groote Dreppe,
Daut däm Foarma de Scheeskje weepe.

Rain, rain large drops.
It rains so hard the farmer's coattails flutter.

* * *

Aprell, Aprell, ekj kaun die heije aus ekj well.

April, April, I can tease you as much as I want.

* * *

Mei, Mei,
jeff dee Koo en Wesch Hei.

May, May,
Give the cow a bundle of hay.

* * *

Daut Farjoa Kjemmt
Wann woam Wint fomm siede kjemmt,
Onn de Schnee fomm Laund wajch nemmt,
Dann woat dee Foarma froo jeschtemmt
Onn sajcht, "Daut Farjoa kjemmt."

Wann kloa de Sonn von Himmel schient,
Onn't nijch mea so ielent nemmt,
Dann sajcht dee Leara enne School,
"Kjinja, daut Farjoa kjemmt."

Onn wann em Fluss daut Iess oppbrakjt,
Onn de Krauj äa Leet aunschtemmt,
Dann weet een jiedra gauns bestemmt
Daut nü daut Farjoa kjemmt.
—*Author Unknown*

Spring Is Coming
When a warm wind blows from the south,
And the snow melts on the land,
Then the farmer is glad
And says, "Spring is coming."

When the sun shines clear in the heavens,
And things aren't quite so hurried,
Then the teacher in school says,
"Children, spring is coming."

And when the river ice begins to break,
And the crow begins her song,
Then everyone knows for certain
That now spring is coming.

*B*ARLEY-BUTTERMILK *MOOSS*
(*Joashtnejrett or Jrettemalkj*)

This *Mooss* makes a refreshing evening meal on a hot day. Cooked slowly in the buttermilk and cooled, it was eaten with cold milk. Some prefer it plain, others with a little sugar.

4 cups buttermilk   ¾ cup pearl barley

Soak barley in 2 cups water overnight. In a double boiler combine buttermilk and barley. Cook slowly over simmering water for several hours. Stir often. Cool and serve with cold milk.

*H*OMEMADE CLABBERED MILK FOR *SCHMAUNT SUPP*
(*Dikje Malkj*)

Place 1 quart raw milk in a warm place at room temperature. Cover and let stand for 20 – 24 hours until milk is well set. A little sour cream (½ cup) added to the milk hastens the clabbering process. Chill well before serving. Serve plain with a little sugar

Ukrainian Cultural Connection: *Kholodnyk*

Ukrainians have a dish similar to our *Schmauntsupp*. They combine sour milk and sour cream and add diced cucumber, diced cooked beets, chopped green onion and dill. Hard-cooked eggs are added as well. This is served chilled as a summer soup.

ℳOCK SORREL BORSCHT
(Blinje Süarompsborscht)

In the absence of sorrel, this soup becomes *Blinje Süarompsborscht*. Here rhubarb substitutes and adds the tart flavor. *Blinje* is Low German for blind, or in this case "mock."

1 ham bone	½ cup young beet leaves, chopped
2 quarts water	Several sprigs parsley
6 new potatoes, diced	2–3 stalks rhubarb, chopped
1 cup chopped onion tops	1 cup fresh dill, chopped
1 cup spinach, chopped	Salt and pepper
3 cups lettuce leaves, chopped	½ cup cream

Cover ham bone with water in large soup kettle and simmer gently until cooked. Remove bone and skim excess fat.

Add potatoes to ham stock and cook until tender. Add all greens and boil slightly. Season to taste and add cream. Do not boil, but heat through.

Summer

If ever a season was made for children, it was summer. No school. Warm days for going barefoot. Swimming. Long evenings when the neighborhood children gathered to play games. For us, the one hindrance to all this freedom was German school. Oh the punishment of having to give up those first free days to sit as German scholars conjugating verbs. Our generation was quickly becoming Anglicized, and Mother decided we must learn the language of our grandparents. So off we marched each morning to read about Hans and Erika. Now we are grateful.

Summer was a busy time for mothers, especially on the farm. There were gardens to tend, clothes to wash, hired hands to cook for and children to keep busy. There were anxious days when the wheat was ripening. Too little or too much rain, too little or too much wind, it seemed a gamble until the trucks and wagons rolled up to the elevator with the heavy loads of harvested grain.

Summer also meant harvest in the garden. Our large spreading apricot tree bore endless fruit. There were bushels of peaches to peel and apples to dry. Canning meant working against time, before the birds took over. When we lived in town, bargain hunter Dad couldn't pass up a "hot buy" late Saturday night. Just before the grocery store closed, they reduced the price of peaches or tomatoes by the bushel. Because they were dead ripe, they had to be canned that very evening.

Most summer Saturday nights were a social event. Farmers came to town "to do their trading." Mother remembered last minute grocery shopping. Dad went downtown to visit. He was sure to find a cousin or a friend standing at the bank corner. They might sit in a car and talk.

Girls strolled the sidewalks, sometimes with hair in curlers, and boys cruised the streets in old cars. The "in" drink at Penner's soda fountain was cherry coke.

All work stopped on Sunday. Stores closed. The local cafe pulled the front shade. Saturday at sundown the church windows were opened to let the breeze "draw through." Even so the church was hot on August Sundays and women fanned with paper fans from Goertz Mortuary. Fancy women brought their own special Japanese fans.

There were Sunday afternoons with "nothing to do" that seemed an eternity while parents took a nap. Other summer Sundays there were late afternoon watermelon feeds with huge roaster pans heaped with *Rollküake*. A family birthday called for a big freezer of homemade ice cream and saltine crackers. For us cousins there were early evening games of tag or catching fireflies in the dark out in the pasture. Often there was swimming in Grandfather's slightly muddy pond.

Late summer brought "dog days," the hottest time of the year. Upstairs bedrooms in our two-story, white frame house held heat like an oven. Mother sprinkled down the beds with cool water. It evaporated immediately. Dad moved a cot out under the apricot tree and camped there until the nights cooled. We girls joined him often, lying there in the quiet of the night, listening to crickets and bullfrogs, feeling very safe.

Summer ended when pasture flowers withered. Milkweed pods burst and sent a shower of shimmering, silky threads into the wind. Goldenrod and asters heralded the coming of fall. It was time for new shoes and schoolbooks. We were ready.

The Russian Mennonite Village in Summer

Mia Reimer DeFehr: We would sit outside in the warm evening air and listen to the singing of the Russian workers, this folk song now deep and melancholy, now bright and gay. And in between they danced on the threshing floor to the delight of their audience. One of the fellows sang with such power he could be heard a half mile away.[8]

Anna von Kampen Funk: On warm evenings we would sit in the hay in the yard, watching the moon and listening to the nightingale.

Helen Pankratz Siemens: We girls liked to walk together in the pasture and look at the beautiful flowers. The neighbor girls came across the pasture to our house.

Mary Dirks Janzen: In our village there were small flowers in the grass. The mulberry hedge was rich with delicious mulberries. We would watch the clouds in the sky change their shape. On a quiet day we could hear nothing but the humming of a bee or the distant voices of neighbors as they were occupied with their work.

There were three huge walnut trees, giving us the needed shade on hot summer days. Between two of these, right near the cistern, was an ideal spot to have our large dining table, which would seat about twelve people. This is where we ate all our meals during the summer. It was a most beautiful spot to sit awhile, rest and enjoy *Rollkuchen* and watermelon, chicken *Borscht* or fried potatoes and *Kirschen Mooss*.

Anna von Kampen Funk: We had fruit *Perieschkje*, baked individually or in long strips. Everyone in our village made fruit pancakes, fruit fritters and had *Rollkuchen* with watermelon.

Helen Pankratz Siemens: Mother would serve fresh cucumber pickles in a bowl with a big loaf of fresh white bread for *Faspa* outside under the tree.

Chortitza in the Summer of 1919

Mennonites, caught in the midst of a civil war, had difficult times in the villages. Transient armies ransacked homes and farms whenever they passed through. Animals had been confiscated; there were not enough horses to work the land. But people teamed up. That year the fields, gardens and orchards yielded a blessed abundance.

N.J. (Nick) Kroeker: The branches of the cherry, apricot, apple, pear and plum trees were bending low yielding as never before. They cut the fruit, baked it in the oven and then spread it out on a screen to dry. There was enough sunlight and the screens were carried outside into the open air for the day and in at night. After the fruit had dried for some three or four days, it was bagged and the bags hung up in a dry place.[9]

Summertime in North America

Frieda Pankratz Suderman: If I could choose a day to go back to, I would like to go back to a certain summer Sunday morning that remains vividly clear in my memory. It was a beautiful, clear morning after a recent rain. The only sounds in our world were the songs of birds and the ringing of the church bells, each bell a different pitch. Near the back porch on the wooden sidewalk Papa was just finishing the ice cream he had made in the hand freezer. We girls were dressed in starched, white Sunday dresses. Our hair was neatly braided and tied with wide, brightly colored, silk ribbons. So many times in the last sixty years the picture of that Sunday morning has returned to my mind that I wonder if I knew it was special even then.[10]

Mary Pankratz: Father would lie outside in the shade to rest and take a short nap after dinner. He put his hat over his face to keep the sun out of his eyes. Then at one o'clock he'd jump up and say, "Well, gotta go to work."

Minnie Jost Krause: On summer nights we liked to lie on a blanket in the pasture and look up at the stars. It was fun to run through the cool grass catching fireflies.

Mary Pankratz: Our summer kitchen was very much a part of the summer season. This was a little, squarish frame house with windows and a door where we had the milk separator and the big *Miagrope*. When the weather warmed up, Mother moved all her cooking utensils out to the *Sommakjäakj*. Dad set up the old drop leaf table and chairs, and we children carried out the dishes to fill the cupboard. Mom hung the clock, calendar and plain, crisp, white curtains. We were in business. To us children it seemed like a big play house. And we liked being close to things going on out in the yard.

During threshing season Mom and my aunts cooked huge meals and did all the baking out there. We carried the food indoors to the cool dining room where it was comfortable to eat and relax. On their way to wash up under the tree, the threshers would peek inside and take a good deep whiff of the meat and potatoes and fresh pies on the ledge. "Sure smells good, Mam," they'd say. We often ate *Faspa* out there too. Mom wasn't as fussy about things as she was in the house.

When the days began to get cooler, Mom moved all the things back to their regular place in the kitchen, and the summer kitchen would be used only on washdays and for butchering.

Little by little the clutter of things we didn't need in the house began to accumulate out there.

We have very fond memories of that little place. With air conditioning and fans we no longer need a summer kitchen. I rather miss it. It was a cozy, pleasant place in summer.

Marie Loewen Franz: As a teenager and the oldest girl, I helped Dad by driving tractor. I was never bored doing this for him because many things happened throughout the day, like baby rabbits running along the furrow just ahead of the tractor. On some days there were beautiful fleecy white clouds up against the pure blue sky, taking on many different shapes. One day I was caught in a sudden rain storm. On nice quiet days there were those small, narrow, very tall, harmless twisters, moving along in almost any direction.

When the sun began to sink in the western sky, creating a beautiful golden glow, I'd always get my second wind and could have made several more rounds but it was quitting time. Time to go home, take a bath in the old tin washtub, have supper and then soon retire for the night. And oh, how good it felt to slip between those cool, clean sheets for a good refreshing night's sleep.[11]

Frieda Pankratz Suderman: Life was pleasant on the farm at the turn of the twentieth century. I remember a rainbow stretching from north to south after a thunderstorm; all the world had an amber glow and looked clean and washed. I remember hoards of yellow butterflies over purple blooming alfalfa and a new orchard in radiant bloom south of the house. Papa carefully tended two arborvitae trees by the east door.[12]

*　　*　　*

Not all was idyllic and perfect in summer. For the farmer, especially the new immigrant settler, everything depended on harvesting his crop. David V. Wiebe, in his book *Grace Meadow*, takes us back more than a century and tells of one of the dreaded crop disasters near Hillsboro, Kansas, in the summer of 1874.

David V. Wiebe: On the 6th day of August on a bright summer afternoon the sun became strangely hazy and speedily darkened so that chickens hurriedly took to their roosts. Yet there was no sign of rain or of a dust storm. Men cultivating their fields stopped their oxen or teams and looked into the skies with apprehension. Women in their pioneer shanties noticed the strange shadows and wondered where the clouds had suddenly come from. They heard a whirring noise in the sky, which grew louder as the shadows increased, and soon there was a pelting on the roof and ground as of hail falling. But this was not hail — these were living creatures, green and brown, two and three inches long, that planted themselves on corn stalks, grain, trees and even on persons who ventured out.

At first the people were too stunned to grasp the extent of the terrible calamity, but when they saw that there were millions of these creatures that kept restlessly milling about, a great fear struck their hearts. This enemy was invincible. They quickly learned that it was grasshoppers, 300 billion at least, that had descended. They devoured everything. Not a green plant was left. Thousands of pioneer farmers became destitute and lost all their crop in a few short hours.[13]

Herbert V. Neufeld: With a few exceptions each growing season was spoiled by some calamity. If it wasn't drought, it was frost or grasshoppers or no market. One time we shipped beef to Winnipeg and found that the price didn't cover the freight costs. In any case, the memories of the Revolution in Russia made every other condition or prospect look good.[14]

* * *

Harvest was the most important time of the summer for the farm woman. Everything was marked by it. "We'll do it before harvest," or "It will have to wait until after harvest." Up to the last day there was a concerned sense of uncertainty. Would it be too hot or too rainy, too windy or too dry?

When the time was right and the wheat was ready, other events took second place. The crop must be brought in. Most farm women helped drive the tractor or the grain truck. They ran countless errands for repairs or parts. Everyone was indispensable.

My sister-in-law, Minnie Schmidt Voth, helped her husband in every harvest until one summer she lay sick in a city hospital with cancer. To ease her mind, she begged her husband not to visit her during the harvest days. "Stay with the combining. Don't make the trip here into the city late in the evening." The night he returned to her room he reported that all was well, the last truckload was in the elevator. She sighed deeply and said, "Now I can rest in peace."

ROLLKUCHEN

I use no soda, no baking powder, no cream in my *Rollkuchen.* I like to fry mine in deep fat. When I was a child, watermelon was always served with Grandma's good, crisp *Rollkuchen*—a perfect complement.

2 eggs
½ cup melted shortening
2 tsp. salt

½ cup milk
2½ cups all-purpose flour

Beat eggs until light and lemon-colored. Add the shortening and salt. Add the milk alternately with the flour until you have a soft dough. Turn out onto floured board.

Roll out small amounts very thin. Cut dough into 3″ × 6″ strips. Cut a slit down the center. Twist one end through the slit or leave plain. Fry in deep fat at 375°F. Drain on paper towels. Place in low temperature in oven to keep warm.

— *Mariam Penner Schmidt*

CLABBERED MILK WITH NOODLES — A SOUP SALAD
(*Schmauntsupp* or *Kjielkjesalaut*)

Betty Fehr Ens: We ate this in summer with a spoon, thick with cream-clabbered milk. We also ate it with white, cooked beans.

Anna Derksen Rosenfeld: Perhaps it was called salad because it was eaten cold.

Agnes Rempel Braun: The name may seem strange, but we also call potatoes and macaroni combined with cream a salad.

Kjielkje
1 quart clabbered milk
½ cup sour cream

Salt and pepper to taste
1 tsp. vinegar

Cook and rinse the *Kjielkje* in cold water. Whip the clabbered milk with a whisk or beater. Add sour cream, vinegar, salt and pepper. Pour over *Kjielkje* and eat with a spoon.

CLABBERED MILK DESSERT

1 quart pasteurized or raw milk
1 cup fresh sour cream

Mix together. Cover and let stand in a warm place at room temperature for 20–24 hours or until the milk is well set and thick. Chill thoroughly. Serve in ways similar to yogurt.

REAREI FOR TWO

4 fresh country eggs
2 Tbsp. half-and-half
2 tsp. flour

Salt and pepper
Margarine or butter

Break eggs into a bowl or blender, add half-and-half, flour, salt and pepper and beat well. Pour eggs into warm, lightly buttered skillet. Cook over medium-low flame, pushing the eggs aside with a spoon as they solidify until all is solid but still moist. Remove eggs from pan while still soft. Eggs have a tendency to dry out very quickly.

Fall

Autumn was lovely on the prairies. In October the sun was mellow and mild. Trees stood like splashes of gold and crimson against a watercolor blue sky. Lazy, fluffy clouds posed no threat of rain. Pastures had turned brown and corn shocks stood straight and tall in the fields.

Indian summer, the prized time of year, brought deceptively warm days. Children had returned to school. New shoes were well broken in and by now somewhat scuffed. The frantic pace of summer had come to a halt, and we welcomed the first crisp evenings.

Cooler weather meant cooking apple butter and making the last grape jelly. On the night of the first frost warning, we gathered in the last tomatoes. The garden was spent and deserted, but green tomatoes made a fine pie or pickles. There were nippy mornings when Mother made hot biscuits for breakfast. Cellar shelves, lined with rows and rows of jars filled with summer's fruits, vegetables, pickles and jellies, brought reminders of days of work.

Fall, too, was the season for hunting. Dad would join several brothers tramping the fields with the dog. Hunting was an adventure back into boyhood days when they had trapped and hunted to add variety to the menu and to earn a little spending money. It belonged to fall.

Now that the heat had passed and the busy days were done, there were weddings. In summer farmers were too busy to take time out for big celebrations. In November there were also evangelistic meetings and harvest festivals, a time set aside to give thanks to God for the bounty of the land, the good harvest and the abundance of food.

The earth had come full cycle and as the year rounded out there was a touch of melancholy mixed with gratitude.

Wheat Harvest from the Steppes to the Plains

He who gathers crops in summer is a wise son,
but he who sleeps during harvest is a
disgraceful son.   — *Proverbs 10:5*

Pray for a good harvest, but keep on hoeing.
                        — *Slovenian Proverb*

Wan't emm Winta kracht
Can buschelt't emm Somma em Sack.

When you hear the cold in winter crack,
The summer harvest will fill the sack.
                        — *Low German Maxim*

Wan't ne stelle Loft aum Johannes jeft
Hafft de Korn ne good steft.

A gentle breeze on St. Johannes Day
Brings good corn at harvest.
                        — *Old Vistula Delta Saying*

Wheat Farming on the Steppes of South Russia

Mennonites came to Russia from West Prussia in 1789 with quite primitive farming equipment. Wagons, plows, harrows, flails and forks were about all they had. Most farming was done on a very small scale. Mennonites raised a variety of crops — rye, oats, barley, potatoes and vegetables. Wheat was only one of many crops. As late as 1850 only about one-third of the land was plowed, and wheat accounted for only one-third of the crops grown on this land.

Through the wise instruction of Johann Cornies, a Molotschna agricultural specialist and head of the Agricultural Association, land was allowed to lie fallow which increased productivity and helped to overcome the drought. The growth of larger cities in the area, Russia's penetration into the Crimea and the opening of ports along the Black Sea made wheat a desired commodity. It was both exported and shipped into the interior.[1]

Wheat production increased. The Mennonites took the lead in selecting varieties best suited to their land and climate. Gradually, winter wheat became more prominent. Mennonites also began producing and exporting some of the finest flour available at the time.

The wheat favored by Mennonite steppe farmers was Turkey Red. This variety suited the land and climate in which they lived and was also raised by other local farmers. Because of the high quality of flour it produced, this wheat gathered appreciation on the London market. It was also exported to regions around the Mediterranean for making macaroni.

Demand for wheat changed the agricultural and economic picture for the Mennonites. They went into large-scale wheat farming and into manufacturing farm and milling equipment as well as building and operating mills themselves. According to Cornelius Krahn, "The birth of Mennonite industry, in line with big-scale wheat raising, took place when Peter Lepp of Chortitza built the first threshing machine in 1853."

*   *   *

Wheat harvest has been a significant part of our Mennonite history. The Bible and the plow are symbolic of the early economic, cultural and spiritual life of our people.

Wheat harvest included not only the men, but also the women and young girls who not only provided abundant food during a time of strenuous work, but also joined the men and boys in the field to help bring in the precious grain.

Wheat Harvest in Russia

"Harvest was done with many people, many horses and many wagons," says Mary Dirks Janzen, remembering her childhood in the Mennonite village of Gnadenfeld.

Before the time of threshing machines, grain grown in the colonies was cut with a scythe which had a cradle attached. After several strokes, the cradle would fill with wheat. It was then dumped into a neat pile on the ground. Men gathered these bunches of grain and bound them into sheaves (bundles). Using a scythe and cradle a man could cut about two acres a day.

When the bundles were dry, they brought them home by *Ladawoage* (hayracks) to be stacked in the backyard of the farmstead. Later, when the field work eased and the farmer had more time, he threshed the grain. The bundles were pitched down from the stacks. One by one, they were opened and laid out evenly on the threshing floor with the heads all pointing one way.[2] When the floor was filled, a team of horses hitched to the notched threshing stone was driven in circles while the grain was threshed. The team was taken off the floor while the threshers turned the stems over with the heads going in the other direction, again making an even layer. Once again the team was driven in circles until the task was completed.

The workers gathered the straw in their arms, shook it out for stray kernels which still clung to it and began building a straw stack. After the straw was removed, the wheat on the floor was shoveled together and thrown into the wind until it was cleaned of all chaff or straw. Then it was shoveled into grain sacks, tied shut and carried up a ladder into the house loft for storage. The entire process was repeated with each batch of wheat until the harvest was finished.

Eventually, threshing machines came into use and phases of the operation changed considerably. N.J. Kroeker recalls how he, as a young boy of twelve, was employed as a harvest hand by a neighbor who paid him 50 kopeks a day.

"My jobs were simple but varied," he says. "At six in the morning we hitched the teams of horses to the hay wagon and drove to the fields to pick up our loads of grain. The Russian workman loaded the grain with a large fork and I stamped it with my feet to form a full load. The workman then drove the team while I lay on the load and looked up at the clouds.

"Driving into the yard, we took the load right up to the threshing machine where we hitched eight horses to the 'Merry-go-round.' I then mounted the platform and made the horses walk continuously around in an even gait. This set the threshing machine in motion. Usually the head of the household fed the grain into the threshing machine by pushing each bundle carefully into the threshing separator after the twine surrounding the sheaf was cut."[3]

A lasher drum knocked out the kernels. The straw that belched forth from the threshing machine was removed and transported in a net to the place where another worker added it to the straw stack.

Finally, grain was separated from the chaff, cleaned and stored in special bins in the attic. Mennonite farmhouses were usually one story with solid, thick walls and steep roofs with ample space for grain. Here the wheat remained warm and dry and helped provide insulation in the winter. Carrying the grain up the ladder to the attic was no easy task. When a boy could shoulder such a load, he "became a man."

In the village of Osterwick, when the last load of wheat left the field, the driver would place a sheaf of wheat on his pitchfork and stick it upright into the top of the load, announcing to the whole village that his fields had been cleared. Among the native Ukrainians it was customary to decorate this last bundle with flowers and later use it in a prominent place in the *Obyinka* festival, a celebration of the end of the harvest.

Henry B. Tiessen remembers the cleared fields: "During harvest I was struck by a nostalgic feeling. The big grain fields that we had observed for months were suddenly gone and replaced by stook upon stook of grain, as far as the eye could see. The whole surrounding countryside had changed. This sudden change was accompanied by the pleasant aroma of newly cut grain."[4]

Mary Dirks Janzen also remembers: "Gnadenfeld had forty full farms, each about 160 American acres. In addition there were twice as many small farmers with about one-fourth as much land. It was a busy and noisy time when forty neighbors were threshing at the same time. The three weeks of harvesting in the hot sun seemed like three long months to us children."

The Russians, Harvest and Song

On Sundays during harvest (and often at other times of the year) there was a festive mood among the Russian workers. In the afternoon they gathered in the village square to visit and sing. They often dressed in their native costumes, promenading up and down the street or sitting on the benches along the side. They sang in four-part harmony, singing folk songs, patriotic songs, hymns and choruses. Often a high tenor led the singing with the group echoing the chorus. "They kept their listeners spellbound," remarks N.J. Kroeker.

Good Food for the Harvest Hands

Henry B. Tiessen: It was always a relief for men and animals when lunch time rolled around. In the case of faraway fields, we always took our day's supply of food along. But in the case of nearby fields mother, with my younger brothers and sister, would bring the food to the field. She would usually come on the two-wheeler pulled by one horse. Since at this time the cherries were ripe, she often would bring cherry pancakes and cherry *Mooss*. Since this was also the beginning of the watermelon season, she often came along with cool ripe watermelons and *Rollkuchen* [crullers]. In addition to this there were large containers of coffee, cold milk and cold water. It was truly a big feast, and, refreshed, we proceeded with our work.[5]

Mary Dirks Janzen: It was a good thing there was a noon break. Our family ate at a large table under the walnut trees near the cistern. The hired peasants ate on the other side of the kitchen on the porch, which had a brick floor and steps with Virginia Creeper climbing all around the railing, reaching up to the roof. Here was a table large enough for about five boys and four girls. They ate the same food as we did only they used fewer plates, forks and knives. For example, if there was *Borscht* and chicken noodle soup, there would be one or two large bowls in the middle of the table, from which the peasants would spoon the soup with Russian wooden spoons. They were good bread eaters and didn't mind if it was sliced thick. They would eat all they wanted, and drink all the milk they wanted. When watermelons were ripe, the whole gang, at both tables, would eat watermelon for dessert. Milk and watermelon were the only dessert we had in Gnadenfeld.

The Harvest Celebration

Most Mennonite churches celebrated the bounties of harvest with a festival called *Ernte*

Dank Fest at the end of summer. Mary Dirks Janzen remembers the first time the church caretaker in Gnadenfeld, a Mrs. Unruh, made beautiful wreaths of woven wheat and hung them from the railings in the balconies. She also brought vegetables and placed them before the pulpit.

Mia Reimer DeFehr, who grew up in the Kuban, also recalls the church of her childhood decorated with bouquets of flowers with fruits and vegetables placed in front of the altar. The Kuban churches added to the celebration with a dinner outdoors under the shade trees in the churchyard.

*   *   *

In the Vistula Delta where the Mennonites lived before moving to Russia, it was customary to bind up the master of the house with rope or straw bands after the last grain had been tied into bundles in the field. Only through gifts of money could he "buy" his freedom. After he was free, the last sheaf, the maidservants and the farmhands were seated in the harvest wagon and doused with water. At the end of the harvest a wheat wreath was raised and a harvest festival with food and dance celebrated the occasion.[6]

The Santa Fe Railroad, the Immigrants and Turkey Red Wheat

In the summer of 1873 several scouting parties of Mennonites arrived in the United States and Canada from South Russia to seek new homes for fellow Mennonites who wished to leave that country.

The Mennonites had come to Russia in 1789 at the invitation of Catherine the Great, czarina of Russia, who was looking for hard-working, prosperous farmers to develop the unsettled areas of her country. Mennonites from West Prussia, along with Germans of other religious faiths, fit the need and responded to the call. To these new colonists, Catherine guaranteed special rights and privileges which protected their religious and cultural freedoms and exempted them from military service. However, in 1870 there was a dramatic change in government policy and many of these privileges were revoked.

Village leaders throughout the colonies, alarmed at these new developments and the possibility of general military conscription, gathered to discuss future plans — how best to follow their conscience, where to move and how to explore emigration possibilities. They agreed to send delegations of church leaders to investigate the economic and religious opportunities in North America. Cornelius Janzen, a Russian Mennonite serving the Prussian Consul in Berdyansk, gathered information regarding immigration from Mennonite leaders in the United States and Canada.

Meanwhile, significant events which would attract the Russian Mennonites were transpiring on the western side of the Atlantic Ocean. In 1863 the United States Congress had passed a bill making possible the construction of railroads across the vast stretches of virgin prairie. This grant gave the Santa Fe Railroad three million acres of fertile, unoccupied grassland in Kansas. In 1869 the first locomotive reached Topeka. In 1871 the line extended to Newton. By the end of 1872 the railroad had been completed from Missouri to the Colorado border. As the railroad pushed westward, thousands of fertile acres awaited new settlers.[7]

The railroads decided to appoint agents whose duty it was to search for industrious farmers to occupy these lands. The Atchison, Topeka and Santa Fe Railroad engaged a dapper young German-speaking man, C.B. Schmidt, from Dresden, Germany, as a representative to make contacts with prospective settlers. "This man probably did more than anyone else to bring the Mennonites to Kansas," said David V. Wiebe.

A few Mennonites from Pennsylvania had already purchased land from the Santa Fe and settled in Kansas. Through contacts with them, the Santa Fe Railroad became aware of the events in Europe — the possibility of a large number of Mennonite emigrants leaving Russia in search of religious freedom. Word had also gotten to the agents that the Mennonites of Russia were good farmers, thrifty and honest — ideal for settling the Kansas prairie country.

In 1872 Bernhard Warkentin and three friends came to the United States to explore settlement possibilities. His letters back to Russia were circulated in the Molotschna Colony and beyond. At the same time United States Mennonites, led by John F. Funk, editor of *Herald of Truth* based in Elkhart, Indiana, encouraged and invited concerned Mennonites in Russia to send deputies to investigate the possibility of relocating in the United States.

In the summer of 1873 more than a dozen delegates from various churches in Russia arrived by ship to inspect the land for colonization. Among them were my husband's great-great-grandparents, schoolteacher Johannes W. and Elisabeth Isaac Fast, representing the Krimmer (Crimean) Mennonite Brethren church in the village of Annenfeld, located in the Crimea.[8] Arriving on the same ship were two brothers also from the Crimea, Peter and Jacob Funk, who were the first to actually purchase land in Kansas and settled in what later became the Bruderthal area.

In October, 1873, Johannes Fast and son-in-law Heinrich A. Flaming along with C.E. Krehbiel and a group from Illinois arrived in Kansas. There they met with Santa Fe agent C.B. Schmidt. After much consideration Fast reserved a plot of land in Risley Township, Marion County, where the land and climate reminded him of his homeland in South Russia. In February, 1874, Great-Great-Grandfather Johannes Fast wrote to his children remaining in Russia. Following is an excerpt from that letter.

Most dearly beloved children,

We can say that at the beginning of a new home we have never felt so glad as we feel here now. What I have seen here in Kansas has been inviting to me, and regarding the law of nature Kansas ranked first for me. The climate here is considered healthy and the winter is shorter and milder than farther north, and consequently the summer is longer. Everything depends on God's blessings, but blessings can only be expected where it does not contradict the laws of nature. May the blessings of the Lord rest upon the land here.

We advise you, dear children, to come here. Gladly we would also have the whole congregation here. I do know that with prayer and supplication and much sorrow, I have searched and selected here in the hope that the Lord has heard my pleas and led my choice.

My plea is not only for a good home but also to build God's kingdom and then to eat our bread.
Your parents who both love you,
The Fasts

This was a time of keen competition among railroads and land agents who were wooing good colonists. In Canada government officials enticed Mennonite delegates by offering any new settler twenty-one years of age and over a free homestead of 160 acres of land in Manitoba with additional options at $1 per acre. Religious freedoms and practically all the other privileges originally granted by Catherine in Russia were also promised by the Canadians.

Santa Fe Railroad agents were also well aware of the Mennonite concern for religious freedom and exemption from military service. Aided by state immigration, they secured passage of a law exempting future colonists from the Kansas state militia.[9]

Many Mennonite immigrants reaped the benefits of this competition which stretched across the western prairies.

Vast stretches of railroad land in Kansas were offered from $2.50 to $5 per acre. A Sante Fe brochure advertised: "Nothing down for four years, eleven years credit, seven per cent interest. Contact C.B. Schmidt, German agent, Topeka, Kansas."

Influential men among the immigrants and members of various committees were granted free tickets for travel. The Santa Fe even chartered a Red Star ocean steamer to bring a shipload of household goods — chests, crated wagons, plows and a hundred Russian threshing stones free of charge.[10] Later the Santa Fe Railroad also erected five immense, immigrant houses for settlers until such time as they could build their own homes.

In February 1875, this Moses of the Mennonites, C.B. Schmidt, made a trip to Russia. Armed with more than a hundred letters from satisfied settlers in the Kansas villages of Gnadenau and Hoffnungstal, he traveled from village to village, preaching the gospel of immigration. He visited a total of fifty-six villages, sometimes speaking two and three times a day, urging the Mennonites to resettle in Kansas. The Russian government, now trying to stem the tide of emigration, made Schmidt's visit so precarious that he strung the Gnadenau letters on a tape and tied them around his body under his clothes. "If they had been discovered," says Schmidt, "my mission would have been nipped in the bud." The Santa Fe had told Schmidt, "Bring the Mennonites at any cost."[11]

Through God's leading, the keen interest of the railroads, the tireless efforts and encouragement of John F. Funk and the support of eastern Mennonite churches, the way had been prepared for Mennonites of Russia to come to America. And they came. In the summer of 1874 more than 2000 Mennonites arrived in Kansas including some thirty Krimmer Mennonite Brethren families from Johannes Fast's congregation in Annenfeld.

On a hot, windy summer afternoon, August 10, 1874, under a spreading cottonwood tree, Elder Jacob A. Wiebe and Franz Janzen of the Annenfeld church signed a contract with Agent Schmidt for twelve sections (7,680 acres) of Santa Fe land along the South Cottonwood River near what is now Hillsboro, Kansas. Here this group built grass thatched huts and mud adobe houses. They dug wells, forming the European-style villages of Gnadenau (Grace Meadow), home of the Fasts and Flamings, Hoffnungstal (Hope Valley) and Alexanderfeld (Alexander's Field), where my own grandparents lived.

According to tradition, these Annenfeld farmers are credited with introducing Turkey Red hard winter wheat to Kansas.[12] They had consistently sown this variety of wheat in the Crimea because their summers were too hot and dry for spring wheat. It had grown natively along the Black Sea and the coast of Azov and was raised by Cossacks, Ukrainians, Turks, Greeks, Bulgarians, Germans and the Dutch-Low German Mennonites.

When the Mennonite immigrants of Dutch-Low German ancestry arrived at the Peabody depot by Santa Fe train early Sunday morning, August 16, many carried bags of precious Turkey Red wheat seed in their handmade chests along with apple, cherry, peach, wild olive and mulberry seeds from their orchards in Russia. In a family letter Johannes Fast too had urged his children in Russia, "Do bring seeds. And do bring winter wheat. That, if only several pounds per family."

In the Crimean group was a young girl, Anna Barkman (Wolgemuth), who in later years recalled in an interview that she, as a child, had helped her parents, Peter M. and Anna Goosen Barkman, prepare for the trip by filling a cloth sack with the very best kernels of wheat she could find. Her mother then placed the sack in a round, old-fashioned hat box in her parents' trunk. Anna Barkman Wolgemuth remembered that other families also brought kernels of wheat to America.[13]

Andreas Flaming (brother of Heinrich A.), a schoolteacher in the early Gnadenau village school, reported that he brought a peck of grain in a trunk and planted it one and a half miles west of Florence, Kansas. From that peck he reaped two and a half bushels of wheat.[14] Joseph Harder, Moundridge, also spoke of a family trunk from Russia packed with household goods and hard winter wheat seed.[15] The two Funk brothers, who arrived in 1873, planted 150 acres of this hard winter wheat in 1874.[16] Their neighbor, Elder Wilhelm Ewert of Bruderthal, planted 35 acres. On March 22, 1874, Johannes Fast again wrote to his children in Russia:

> Now, dear children, we have received your letter yesterday afternoon in Marion Centre, where we bought a plow for 18 dollars. It goes very well behind two horses and plows four acres a day. We have already plowed 16 acres for wheat and want to plow 13 for barley and 16 for oats and then 35 more for corn. We expect our dear Annenfelders to help with the harvest, for if the Lord helps us with all of our undertaking, we will have at least 130 acres to work. Of winter wheat we have 44 acres and of that we get half of the harvest. On March 12 we started to plow. If the Lord helps, we can already make our living for the coming year.

Again in a letter dated June 18, 1874, Fast wrote:

> Peace and grace to all who read these lines as our welcome to the country which shall be their place of refuge in order to live according to their faith! Dear Children!
>
> Now children, I now know more. I can say to them [Annenfeld emigrants] in good conscience: Come and choose Kansas, for now we know that it is not against the order of our dear heavenly Father to bless with bread in fullness. *For we have now already raised very good wheat!* It is standing very good so that when I pass by our wheat I am moved to tears about the providence of our heavenly Lord. The other grain is also standing very well. The

meadows, or so-called prairies, are just beautiful. In places our cattle walk in the grass up to their knees.
Your parents, J. Fasts

Turkey Red proved very hardy and yielded prolifically. An observer at the time wrote: "Day after day, through all the fall and winter, the Mennonites came in with wheat. The native American stands on the corner and complains but the Mennonites come in with the wheat." After experimenting with different varieties other local farmers realized that the hard Turkey Red was best suited to the climate and conditions of Kansas. It was quickly adopted and eventually revolutionized the wheat industry in Kansas.

Bernhard Warkentin, whose father had been a miller in the Ukraine, became a great promoter of Turkey Red. Warkentin established a gristmill along the banks of the Little Arkansas River in Halstead before the first immigrants arrived. In 1885 and 1886 he imported the first large shipment of Turkey Red from the Crimea for distribution in Kansas and also established one of the leading milling companies of the Midwest, the Newton Milling and Elevator Company. In 1900 at the request of the Kansas State Miller's Association and the Kansas Grain Dealer's Association, Warkentin imported a shipment of fifteen thousand bushels of seed wheat from the Ukraine for distribution to Kansas farmers. The pioneering Russian Mennonites had helped turn the grassland prairies of Kansas into one of the greatest breadbaskets of the world.

The original Turkey Red variety has given way to newer, better varieties, now basically hybrids. But Turkey Red is one of the strains from which more than thirty varieties of hard winter wheat have been developed. Wheat remains the state's major crop and central Kansas is the nation's principal wheat producer.

Threshing Turkey Red on the Midwestern Prairies

On the day of the arrival of the Crimean immigrants at Peabody, Kansas, Elder Jacob A. Wiebe, his wife, Justina Friesen Wiebe, and their family rode from Peabody by wagon to the land they had purchased from the Santa Fe Railroad a week earlier.

"I had loaded some lumber, utensils and my family on top," he wrote. "We rode in the deep grass to the little stake that marked the spot I had chosen. When we reached the same, I stopped. My wife asked me, 'Why do you stop?' I said, 'We are to live here.' Then she began to weep."[18]

It was barren flat prairie, covered with grass three feet tall. There were no roads, no trees, no houses — only a fringe of green along the creekbank. There were no familiar sounds. Hot wind blew across the parched grass. Only a short time before a scourge of grasshoppers had stripped every green leaf and blade of grass in sight. Sick at heart, Justina Wiebe and other Annenfeld women wept for the fine homes and stately acacia trees of the Crimea and wondered what lay ahead.

It took great courage to make such a beginning. For the women it was particularly difficult. Settlement was complicated by the absence of stone, timber and fuel. There were no immigrant houses. Some families stayed with neighbors. Fourteen families lived for a time in the barn on the Peter Funk farm. Others put up tents. Some used inverted wagon boxes as part of their huts. Their first dwellings were crude shanties — A-shaped houses with no side walls and roofs reaching to the ground. Sides were held up by poles and thatched with reed grass. With borrowed money they bought cows, chickens and everything necessary to begin this new life.

By pooling their labor, horses and oxen the men broke the tough virgin prairie with "sod buster plows" — a most difficult task. They worked feverishly, knowing that winter would soon be upon them. When the ground was ready, they sowed their wheat seed, so carefully brought from the Crimea. David V. Wiebe later wrote, "Perhaps the most outstanding character trait of these people was their concept of the dignity of work. They accepted as unalterable the biblical injunction: 'In the sweat of thy brow shalt thou eat thy bread.' Work, to them, was a blessing in disguise."[19]

In the summer of 1875 Peter Barkman and Andreas Flaming of Gnadenau and Elder Ewert and the Funk brothers of Bruderthal (Valley of Brothers) cut their wheat with hand scythes — the first Turkey Red wheat grown in Kansas.[20] "The first sown wheat brought a bountiful harvest. We had not sowed much but the little brought much and that gave us courage," wrote Elder Jacob Wiebe of that first harvest.

The wheat was threshed by rolling a heavy, Russian threshing stone, turned by horses, across the cut wheat to beat the grain out of the heads — just as had been done in Russia. However, the use of threshing stones continued only a short while. A few farmers had even manufactured a number of threshing stones for fellow Mennonites, but the power thresher soon rendered this primitive method obsolete. The 100 Russian-style threshing stones shipped by Red Star and the Santa Fe in 1874 were never used.[21]

In the summer of 1875 Noble L. Prentis, a Kansas historian, visited Gnadenau and other farms in the area. He wrote of the harvest. "At the home of Bishop Buller [possibly Elder Jacob Buller of Alexanderwohl] saw evidence of progress. One of the stone rollers which was procured to thresh grain was lying in the yard while a short distance away was an American threshing machine in full blast." At the home of Abraham Reimer near Hochfeld "was a house with two large barns and at the rear of it numerous stacks of grain arranged in a circle. A stout boy and girl were engaged near by in stacking hay, the young lady officiating on the top of the stack."[22]

On March 16, 1876, the *Peabody Gazette* reported that "a gristmill [in Gnadenau] is running day and night."[23]

In 1878 C.L. Bernay wrote in the June 10 edition of *Zur Heimat,* "They [the Mennonites] have been so successful with their choice [of location to settle] that the leaders of the Mennonite churches whom we visited yesterday assured us that all the damage they had suffered through loss of time and money for the long journey had already been compensated for after their third harvest.

"We find these simple but well-disciplined German Russian Mennonites engaged in extensive farming — forty, eighty, one hundred and even thousand acre fields are sown of wheat. The Mennonites use plows, drills, mowers and threshing machines for their cultivation. Upon their arrival they had clumsy threshing stones with notches which, seen from the top, had the shape of a star. They had used such threshing stones in Russia but realized very soon that the use of this crude threshing stone in the large wheat harvests would set them far behind their neighbors who were using American threshing machines. They bought new machinery, and these stones, which had to be dragged by horses over the scattered grain, are now lying in the farmyards as reminders of the first years.

"We drove for many miles with many Mennonite homes in sight and the most promising orchards and immense fields of greenest wheat. I have never elsewhere seen such a picture of agricultural prosperity."[24]

For anyone who has grown up in wheat country there is a deep appreciation of harvest. From the time the wheat is planted there is constant awareness of its growth and development and constant concern for the weather. "But wheat, like a cat," says Uncle John Toevs, "has nine lives and survives much. It is a tough plant."

When the days lengthen and the fields of ripening golden grain wave in the wind, there is added sense of excitement and watchfulness as harvest draws near. Uncle Dan G. Jost sums it up well. "The day for threshing was perhaps the highlight of the farm experience. In essence it was the farmer's pay day. Many things depended on it — food for the family, paying the taxes and bills of every sort waited for this day. Two giant words hung over every farm — words we feared and respected — mortgage and interest. If you couldn't pay off the mortgage after wheat harvest, at least you tried to pay the interest."

Harvest was also a time of extraordinary activity. Only the necessary chores were tended to. So critical was this time in every farm household that all other tasks were postponed until the wheat was in the bin. It began with the cutting of the grain using a binder or header.

When the binder was used, the grain was cut and tied with twine into bundles. This process was called cutting and binding. Next came the hard work of picking up the bundles from the ground and standing them up one against the other to make a shock. Grain heads always stood upright in the shock to help prevent possible rain damage before harvest. It took twelve to sixteen bundles to make a shock.

Threshing was usually done by a group of farmers who formed a threshing ring. "My father would be part of such a ring," says Bertha Fast Harder. "They would start at one place and then go on to the next." Sometimes additional itinerant farm workers were hired. These workers followed the harvest from the Gulf of Mexico on up to Kansas. Most of the workers, however, were friends and neighbors.

On an appointed day a tractor pulling the threshing machine, a huge metal monster, belched and puffed down the road at the incredible speed of two and a half miles an hour. For children threshing time was probably comparable in entertainment to a circus or state fair. Following is an account of the excitement this generated among the children.

Bertha Fast Harder: We kids would be so excited. We would go down our lane and watch out by the road and all of a sudden we would hear "chug, chug, chug." Here came that old tractor pulling the threshing machine, followed by wagons or trucks into which the grain would be put and behind them came the bundle wagons pulled by the horses. On each bundle wagon would be the man who owned it. These wagons would go out into the field and the men would load them full of sheaves. It was important that the sheaves were carefully arranged so that the wagon wouldn't be too heavy on one side and tip over. There were some men who always prided themselves in stacking the best bundle wagon. These bundles of straw and grain were then fed into the big threshing machine.

*   *   *

The threshing process is also described by my uncle Dan G. Jost. He speaks about the years 1915 – 1918 when he was a young man at home helping with the harvest.

Dan G. Jost: The engineer usually got up at 4 a.m. to stoke the boiler and get the steam to the point where it would be the right pressure for threshing. His was a job that everyone envied. He sometimes put in as many as fifteen or sixteen hours of work a day because the day went from sunrise to sunset. Next to the engineer was the water monkey. He hauled the water for the boiler while the fireman tended the boilers which produced the steam. It took about six tanks of water a day. The water came from a creek, dam or a big tank. Sometimes the water monkey had to go quite a distance for water. When the engineer whistled four long whistles, he was on his toes. He stopped drawing water immediately and drove in as fast as he could in order to supply that steamer with water.

The separator man was a master mechanic. His job was looking out for trouble and keeping the machine running. With an oil can in one hand, he was constantly dabbing oil on the moving parts of that big machine.

An alternative form of running the harvest was picking up the bundles in the field with the bundle rack, driving them to the farmstead where bundles were artfully placed in layers, creating a huge wheat stack usually about twenty-five feet high. Later when farm work eased in the fall, the threshing machine was pulled up beside this huge stack and the bundles were fed into the machine from this stack.

One fellow pitched bundles into the machine while another fed him bundles from the far side of the stack. The grain was separated with the chaff and straw blowing out from a large pipe and forming a huge straw stack in back of the machine. The beautiful, threshed grain was channeled into a grain wagon.

*   *   *

Often it was the task of younger family members to help distribute the wheat from the blower into the corners of a wagon or truck. Even the young participated.

Bertha Fast Harder: There were years when it was my job to shovel grain. I would have a shovel and stand near where the grain was coming out of the shoot and I would push the grain into the front of the truck until the truck was almost loaded. Then the driver would take over and take it away to the farmyard where they would put it in an elevator. During these fifteen or twenty minute breaks I could just sit out in the shade.

*   *   *

The threshing machine engineer conducted the whole operation with blasts of the whistle. If a grain wagon was needed, the engineer would sound out several short blasts. He called his

191

water monkey with four long blasts. Certain blasts also signaled the crew to stop for three meals and lunch at mid-morning and mid-afternoon. The threshers quit around 7:00 or 7:30 p.m. Horses were unharnessed and fed and other chores were done. After this supper was served. Then farmers who lived nearby went home for the night while others spent the night in the barn. Finishing the job took three days on most farms.

A good day of threshing might bring around 1500 bushels of grain. The grain remained in the farmer's granary and was sold later when the price was right. Fifteen to twenty bushels to the acre were considered good, according to Dan G. Jost. The selling price at that time was around $1.25 a bushel. It sometimes took fifteen to twenty men to bring in the harvest.

Remembering wages, Dan Jost says pay for an engineer and separator tender was $4 a day while the man who pitched bundles into the machine earned $2. The farmer for whom the crew worked would feed them three full meals plus lunches. "The crew usually brought their own bedrolls and bedded down on haystacks or in the barn loft or right on the ground outdoors. When they retired, all the pranks they knew were played."

Older people who remember those days of hard work sometimes even say, "What a grand time it was. The sun was hot and the sweat ran. The chaff made your body itch and the soot and cinders got into your eyes, but we loved every minute of it. Tensions were eased by many a practical joke. Lunches and bountiful dinners when the cooks put forth their best made everyone feel refreshed and provided something different to talk about."

Those were the good old days—long, hot, hard, but satisfying. "There was a sense of community," Dan Jost adds with a smile. Threshing was indeed the highlight of the summer.

*   *   *

Aunn, spaun aun;
Trien, hool de Lien;
Mitsch, hool de Pitsch;
Soa, set opp onn foa!

Ann, harness up;
Kate, hold the lines;
Marie, fetch the whip;
Sarah, get on and drive!
—*Low German Nursery Rhyme*

Members of the first and oldest Mennonite church in Russia stand before their building in the village of Chortitza.

Three Mennonite women pose in the photographer's studio in 1913.

GRANDMA'S DARK MOLASSES DROPS

This is an updated version of an old recipe, one which molasses lovers will enjoy. Grandmother's was a deep, richly flavored cookie using dark molasses and a little coffee to dissolve the soda. Light molasses makes a milder version.

1 cup butter or margarine	½ tsp. salt
1 cup sugar	1 tsp. instant coffee powder
1 large egg	2 tsp. cinnamon
1 cup dark molasses	1 tsp. ginger
4 cups sifted all-purpose flour	½ tsp. cloves
3 tsp. baking soda	¾ cup sweet or sour half-and-half

Beat butter until light. Gradually add sugar and beat until fluffy. Beat in egg and blend thoroughly. Add molasses. In separate bowl stir together flour, baking soda, salt, coffee powder and spices. Add alternately with half-and-half to the batter.

Drop dough by heaping teaspoonful onto greased cookie sheet about 2 inches apart. Bake at 375°F. about 12–15 minutes or until done.

GRANDMA FUNK'S BUSHEL COOKIES

Ruth Hiebert Penner: Every year at harvest time my husband's grandmother Maria Funk busied herself making sour cream cookies for her children's families. Threshing days were busy times for her sons and daughters, for they were farmers living in the Bruderthal area near Hillsboro, Kansas.

When the cookies had cooled, she placed them in muslin flour sacks and packed them into bushel baskets. Into the car went the baskets and off she drove, from farm to farm, delivering cookies. Her grandchildren still call them "Grandma Maria's Bushel Cookies." When Grandma Funk made a smaller amount they were "Half Bushel Cookies." Here is her recipe, just as she baked it during wheat harvest time back in the 1920s and '30s.

1 cup melted fresh homemade butter	2 tsp. vanilla
2½ cups sugar	½ tsp. each salt and nutmeg
3 eggs, beaten	1 tsp. each baking soda and baking
1 cup farmer's sour (or dairy) cream	powder
	4½ – 5 cups sifted all-purpose flour

Melt butter and cool. Mix sugar and butter. Add well-beaten eggs to sugar. Add sour cream. Add vanilla. In a separate bowl combine sifted flour, salt, leavening and nutmeg. Gradually add flour to batter. (Sometimes 4½ cups flour is sufficient.)

Drop by spoonful onto lightly greased baking sheet. Bake at 350°F. for 10 – 15 minutes, depending on how brown you like your cookies. Cool. Store in airtight tins.

— Maria Funk Funk
— Ruth Hiebert Penner

$\mathscr{R}$EMPEL FAMILY SYRUP COOKIES

Mary Pankratz Rempel: My husband's family brought this recipe from the village of Einlage in the Chortitza Colony.

2 glasses sugar	2 tsp. baking soda dissolved in
1 glass lard	1½ glasses boiling water
1 glass watermelon syrup	Flour to make a soft dough that can
2 tsp. vanilla	be rolled out

Cream lard and sugar. Add watermelon syrup or substitute dark corn syrup and molasses. Add vanilla. Dissolve baking soda in hot water and add to batter. Add sifted flour to make a dough that can be rolled out.

Cut with cookie cutter. Place on greased baking sheet and bake at 375°F. for 7 – 9 minutes or until cookies are lightly browned. Do not overbake. Cool. Store in airtight container.

— Maria Schultz Rempel
— Mary Pankratz Rempel

Rempel Family Watermelon Syrup Cookies *by Mary Pankratz Rempel*

A large section of the Rempel family vegetable garden on the outskirts of the small, southern Manitoba town of Oak Lake was devoted to watermelons. Most of the melons were only six to eight inches in diameter, just large enough for an after school snack. My husband, Dick, and his two older brothers would each pick one, cut off the top and eat the sweet inside, scooping it out with a spoon.

Since the growing season was short, many of the melons never totally ripened. But they were excellent for making syrup. The rinds were cut away and the centers, cut into large chunks, were put into a clean flour sack. An old printing press, cleaned thoroughly, was set into a tub. The sack of watermelon was put under the 12″ × 18″ steel plate which was then screwed down to press out the juice. There would be gallons of it. It was first boiled in a cauldron outdoors. When enough water had evaporated, it was transferred to a kettle and set on the back of the wood burning kitchen stove. Here the juice would simmer for several days until it had boiled down to about a glass of precious syrup. This was used to make the Rempel Family Syrup Cookies.

*F*RUIT *MOOSS*
(*Obstmooss*)

1 cup dried apples
1 cup dried prunes
1 cup raisins
½ cup dried peaches
½ cup dried apricots
8 cups water

1–2 Tbsp. cornstarch
¾ cup sugar
½ tsp. powdered cinnamon or 2 sticks cinnamon
½ tsp. salt
2 cups milk

Wash fruit and place in kettle with water. Cook until almost tender.

Prepare thickening of cornstarch, sugar, cinnamon and salt. Add a little water. Stir into the *Mooss*. Cook 5 minutes.

Cool *Mooss*. Add milk.

Hint: If using stick cinnamon, add before the last boiling. Also, adding 2 Tbsp. vinegar enhances the flavor.

*V*ILLAGE MUSEUM FRUIT *PLAUTS*

The Mennonite Village Museum Restaurant (Steinbach, Manitoba) serves only authentic Low German fare — tasty stoneground wheat bread, steaming hot *Borscht, Zwieback, Varenikje* and for dessert there is *Plauts*. In summer the rhubarb *Plauts* is outstanding. Kaethe (Mrs. D.D.) Warkentin, who grew up in the Crimea, shares her recipe. It is served to museum visitors daily.

Dough

1 cup sifted all-purpose flour
1 tsp. baking powder
2 Tbsp. margarine

1 egg, slightly beaten
5 Tbsp. milk

Combine sifted flour and baking powder in a bowl. Add the margarine and mix, rubbing between the fingers until fine crumbs appear. Beat the egg slightly. Combine with milk and add gradually to the dry ingredients.

Knead until the dough forms a ball. With your hands spread the dough into a 9″ × 9″ baking pan. Press the dough up around the sides of the pan. Pat evenly.

Fruit

cherries
plums
apples

rhubarb
apricots
other fruits in season

Slice or halve the fruit of your choice, and place a layer of fruit on the dough.

For very sour or juicy fruit mix 2 Tbsp. flour and ½ cup sugar and sprinkle this over the fruit before adding the *Streusel* topping.

Streusel Topping

¾ cup sifted all-purpose flour
¾ cup sugar

½ cup margarine

Combine all three topping ingredients and rub together between your fingers until the mixture turns to fine crumbs. Sprinkle over the fruit. Bake at 375 – 400°F. until the fruit is done and the crumbs are golden brown, about 45 minutes to 1 hour. May be served warm or cold.

— *Kaethe (Mrs. D.D.) Warkentin*

QUICK AND EASY *PERIESCHKJE*

Mariam Penner Schmidt: For *Perieschkje* I use a rich pie crust dough. Roll it out into 4″- or 6″-squares. Top each square with any type of fruit — cherries, gooseberries, apples or other fruits. Sprinkle with sugar. Bring all four corners together in the center and press together. Bake at 350°F. until done and golden brown.

TIPS FOR OLD-FASHIONED FRIED CHICKEN

Chicken is best fried in a thick, black frying pan or cast-iron skillet. Women used to use pure lard. Roll the chicken pieces in flour, have the grease hot enough to fry chicken when you put it in. Let one side brown, turn pieces over and brown the other. Cover with a lid. A chicken cooks in about an hour, fried on medium heat. The chicken won't be tender if you brown it too fast.

When frying chicken in lard, add three tablespoons butter to make it brown well. Cook on a low temperature for thirty minutes. Be careful not to burn meat. After thirty minutes take the lid off and remove the top pieces which have not been submerged in the grease. Turn the heat up to medium and fry until remaining pieces get crispy. Drain on paper towel.

Women and the Harvest

"When the engine whistle blew three long blasts, it was time for dinner," says Minnie Jost Krause of threshing days. At that moment the most appreciated people on the farmstead were the cooks. Mealtime broke the monotony of work, brought respite from the heat and dirt and provided an opportunity to savor the finest food the women of the house could produce. Women's reputations were on the line. "They always liked to come to our house because Mother made all sorts of special things. She saved the best for the threshers," adds Minnie Krause. "Every woman in the ring tried to outdo the woman before her."

It was customary to cook meals for threshers in the summer kitchen so the house and dining room remained cool. In some areas the threshing rig traveled with a cook shack, a kitchen on wheels, and two young women did all the cooking. Wherever food was prepared, it was always a welcome sight to the weary, hard-working field hands, morning, noon and night.

"When word came that the threshing ring would be arriving, the women of the house went into high gear," says Dan G. Jost.

Bertha Fast Harder adds, "When my dad said to my mother, 'Anna, tomorrow we'll come here after dinner [the noon meal] and probably we'll be here for [afternoon] lunch,' my mother knew she would have to start baking right away so she'd have enough food for all those men."

Neighborhood women, sisters, aunts or grandmothers came to the rescue and helped with preparations. The work of peeling potatoes and baking bread, cakes and pies began early in the morning. Butter had to be churned and cream hauled from the well or cave where it cooled. Apples and peaches were picked from the orchard, tomatoes and beans came from the garden. Chickens would be butchered. Some families even butchered a hog the day before.

A home-cured ham might be fetched from the smokehouse and scrubbed and trimmed so it could be baked or boiled the following day. There were many details to organize so meals could be served on time. Summer days were long and if the weather was good, threshing continued into the evening, making five meals to prepare and serve during the day.

It must be remembered, too, there were no electric or gas stoves, no electric mixers, refrigerators, freezers or other conveniences. All food was prepared by hand and from scratch.

Sometimes women got up as early as 3 a.m. if some of the men had to be in the field by dawn. Those threshers who had stayed overnight were served first since they had to stoke the boiler fire early. The farmer, too, had to tend his chores, feed the chickens and livestock, milk the cows and harness the horses — all before joining the threshing crew in the field.

Younger children had assigned tasks — bringing in the wood, gathering garden vegetables, running errands, setting the table, taking lunch to the field or making a place for the men to wash their hands.

Bertha Fast Harder: One of the jobs for us girls was to put up a low bench by a tree or the kitchen door. On it we put a pail of water, a dish of soap, basin, combs and mirror and on a nail we hung a long roller towel so when the men came in from threshing, they could wash their hands. While they waited for the others to wash up, they sat under the trees and chatted with each other. When everyone was ready, my father said, "*Kommt nen*" [Come in], and they filed through the back door into the kitchen and on into the dining room and sat around that long dining room table. Everybody stopped for prayer, then began eating.

*   *   *

Memories of preparing for threshing days are shared by two of my family members, Bena Goertz Jost and Minnie Jost Krause, who as young girls were much involved in cooking for threshers. In spite of the hard work, there was reason for young women to look forward to harvest time. Wheat harvest was not without its romantic side. Some of the hired hands might be young unmarried neighbor boys and there would be opportunity for fun and teasing. Minnie Krause and Bena Jost vividly recall the hard work as well as the rewards of those earlier days. Their accounts, which follow, take us back to a different era in the family kitchen.

Bena Goertz Jost: When threshers came to our house, we started about 4 o'clock in the morning. It was a busy, busy day. We got up early so that the first ones who came for breakfast could eat. There was baking to do. We'd get the stove heated up and set the table. We had baked the day before.

Mother often made *Rearei* [scrambled eggs] for the men for breakfast. She would have the oven hot and bake it in the oven. Sometimes we had eight to ten extra men for breakfast. If we did stack threshing, all the pitchers would stay there for the night.

Soon after breakfast we had to start getting the lunch ready. We packed homemade rolls, *Portselkje,* fresh buns and sandwiches in a big dishpan. Mother often made crullers. We usually had coffee and sometimes lemonade. Sometimes we'd carry it out. Other times we sent it along with a wagon to the field.

For dinner there were pies to be baked. One day we'd have sausage, one day chicken, and one day noodle soup. Boy, did we cook noodle soup! We made all the noodles by hand. Everybody helped with the dishes.

Minnie Jost Krause: Sometimes when the crew finished a neighbor's threshing late the day before, we would have them for breakfast. They moved the machinery onto the yard during the night and slept in the barn. They had their own things with them and slept on the hay. If it was warm, they slept outside.

For the noon meal Mother would have a big roast, cooked ham or baked chicken. Once in a while we had *Jreene Schaubelsupp* (green bean soup) which she made like a stew with lots of fresh beans from the garden. There would be mashed potatoes or parsley potatoes with cream, cucumbers, sliced tomatoes, stewed apples, pickles and lots of cole slaw. Dad liked pie, so there was pie for dessert. We also had *Mooss* on the table.

When they were through with all the threshing, the bunch of men came together to settle up their work (some had worked longer than others). We generally served a big freezer of homemade ice cream.

Sometimes women also helped in the field. After a long day outdoors, the women would still have to feed the hungry workers. Unless there were young girls old enough to help, they would cook the meal, do the dishes and put the children to bed. If they were expected in the field the next day, there was more preparation so they could be outdoors again. My Grandmother Jost regularly helped make the stacks for threshing.

Dan G. Jost: Dad wasn't the best stacker. There were times when my mother would make the stacks. Her babies came regularly, and she always had a little one. Often her baby would be nearby in the shade of another stack and she would stop to nurse it in between time. Dad would throw the bundles up to her and we kids would load the wagon and bring it up to where the stacks were.

Alden Voth: At our house, too, Mother was the stacker. Dad said he didn't like stacking and did not do it well. So he pitched the bundles to her. All of this was done out in the field, under the hot July sun. It was steady, hard work. Then at the end of the day she would come in and cook the meal.

The Cook Shack

The cook shack was set on wheels and was pulled from field to field as the harvest progressed. This mobile kitchen featured stove, tables and benches. Ventilation was limited and when the sun beat down, accompanied by the heat generated by the stove, the cookhouse was more like a hothouse. Usually two women operated the cook shack and did the cooking. They were hardy souls and put in as many hours as the men.

Marie Harms Berg: When the time came for threshing, we were on the lookout. At last we heard the engineer blow the whistle and our excitement increased by the minute.

A cook shack came with the outfit. They parked under our large maple trees. At one end was the stove, at first heated with wood, but later the Perfection oil stoves came in. There were tables along each side of the shack. Benches ran along the inside with hinged lids where numerous items were stored.

When night came, the weary cooks pulled out folding cots and slept in the middle aisle. There were no real windows, only screens and wooden shutters to let down when wind and rain came up.

Very early the engineer went to fire up the engine. He was sent a breakfast when the crew went out to the field. Rainy weather was always dreaded since the crew had to be fed even if they were just sitting around.

When the dusty crew came from the field, they found a bench with pans of water and soap and also towels hanging on the branches of a tree. There were several extra men for Mother to feed, since men had to be hired to haul away the wheat.

After the cook shack pulled out, we always went to see what they had left. There was a pile of empty tin cans from the fruits and vegetables they had cooked. They had such pretty pictures of pears, peaches, cherries, beets and pickles. We stripped the labels off and cut out the pictures to paste in our books. Mother canned everything in glass jars with no labels. We thought then that the fruit was much more appealing in the tin cans.

Threshing was over. Papa paid the boss and we settled back into our regular routine.

The Celebration of Butchering

Aules haft en Enj,
Bloss ne Worscht nijch.
Dee haft twee Enja.

Everything has an end
except a sausage.
It has two ends.
— *Low German Saying*

Doa schlachte see Schwien;
Doa drinkje see Wien;
Doa daunst de Müss;
Doa fiddelt de Lüss;
Doa flijcht de Kuckuck
Üt'm Fensta rüt.

There they butcher the hog;
There they drink the wine;
There dances the mouse;
There fiddles the louse;
There flies the cuckoo
Out the window.
— *Old Low German Nursery Game*

The Celebration of Butchering

In Russia butchering was a big
event — the biggest celebration. It
was almost like a wedding.
— *Ann DeFehr Dueck*

With three generations of Russian Mennonites in America, traditions have changed. Far from the celebration it was in the Russian village, hog butchering is almost unheard of today.

Our family lived in a small Kansas town and Mother bought her meat at Funk's Market. Ted Funk did all his own butchering and made his own sausage just the way Mother liked it.

Even though we didn't butcher, there were some years when we helped Grandfather Toevs on that day. My dad, a hunter from teenage years, had the job of killing the pig. My job was to stay out of the way, which was no problem. The safest refuge was under the kitchen table, crouched against the wall, ears stuffed with cotton or fingers, awaiting the dreaded blast of the gun.

A vivid memory I have of butchering is feasting on fresh, wonderfully seasoned pork. In those days we could enjoy spareribs, cracklings and sausage without feeling pangs of guilt about fat. We ate and enjoyed.

Grandfather was the true pork lover. He sat at the oilcloth covered table, napkin tucked under his white beard, and ceremoniously presided over a good-sized length of raw, smoked sausage, a bowlful of thinly sliced onions marinated in sugar and vinegar and a chunk of Mother's dark rye bread spread before him. There he feasted, savoring every bite, occasionally dabbing his beard for vinegar dribblings.

Another winter dish that followed butchering was *Bobbat,* a batter yeast bread baked with chunks of sausage. It was heavenly, but so filling you wanted only to head for the couch and hibernate the rest of the afternoon rather than return to school for a United States history lesson.

*   *   *

The importance of hog butchering goes back to the Mennonite days in Polish Prussia in the 16th century. There in the Vistula Delta they developed their love for pork. The true West Prussian farmer indulged in ham, homemade sausage, pork belly, cracklings and ribs with great delight. So popular was pork in the Polish Prussian diet that Napoleon's French soldiers who quartered there called the Vistula Delta the "lard pot" or "grease pot."

Hog butchering and a love for pork continued after the Mennonites arrived in Russia in 1789. It survived in North America as late as the generation of my parents. As with other traditions, the memories are fading. It is mainly the older people who remember. Following are butchering day accounts, related with some pride and gentle humor, by the men and women who participated in this unique event, this celebration of fellowship, shared work and feasting.

Memories of Butchering Day

Mary Dirks Janzen: In our village of Gnadenfeld we invited those people to help in butchering who knew what to do. They wore white aprons and came for breakfast. It was quite an honor to be invited. Even the preacher came to help.

Dan G. Jost: Butchering and threshing in our Kansas community were family affairs. Uncles, aunts, brothers and sisters got up early and each tried to beat the others to the farm where the butchering was to be done.

Peter D. Zacharias: Several days of food preparation preceded this event in the village of Reinland, Manitoba. The day before hog-slaughtering was one of feverish activity. Equipment was borrowed from the neighbors, if necessary. The ropes and blocks, vats [*Miagrope*] for boiling cracklings and lard, a trough for scalding, the sausage machine, ladders, tubs and other necessaries were set ready. In the evening the men inspected their *Schlachtmesser* [butchering knives].

A popular figure at these gatherings was the *Ütnäme,* a person skilled in the art of evisceration. An *Ütnäme* of repute generally received many invitations to hog-slaughtering bees.[1]

Herbert V. Neufeld: We [children] tried our best to stay out of school by being helpful. The trick was to stay out of the way until it was too late to get to school on time.[2]

Mariam Penner Schmidt: On butchering day my cousins Albert and Elsie and I would race back to Grandma's at dinner time, thinking of the wonderful chicken dinner she would have for the workers. After school we tried to outrun each other to Grandma's, to watch the casings being cleaned, the sausage made and the spareribs and cracklings being cooked in the big cauldron. It was an exciting day for us children.

It Took a Lot of Meat and Lard

A successful butchering was gauged by the number of hams put away and the gallons of lard cooked and poured into the big crocks. The women stood counting with pride and satisfaction —5, 12, 14, 16, 21. Twenty-one gallons of clear, sweet smelling lard and two gallons of dark, flavorful crackling lard! A fruitful day!

Herbert V. Neufeld: A fat pig was considered most valuable. I can see why because the lard from it provided crackling, grease for the frying pan and sandwich spread.[3]

Ann DeFehr Dueck: In Russia some butchered eighteen hogs. Five or six neighbors would come to help.

Mia Reimer DeFehr: In the Kuban cows, pigs and fowl were necessary to our large household which included many farm workers, carpenters and leather workers. We would slaughter up to nine large pigs in one operation in order to meet these needs. During the Revolution everything had to be kept under lock and key.[4]

Pork or Beef

Mennonites were great pork eaters. In Russia and the early pioneering days in North America many hogs were butchered, but rarely beef cattle.

Gerhard Lohrenz: Pork was economical. Beef was more expensive. Hogs could be raised more quickly.

Frieda Pankratz Suderman: More pork than beef was used, probably because it was easier to keep since it could be cured. I think it was also because we liked it better. In fall Papa usually bought a pig or two to fatten for butchering.[5]

Stella and Orpha Schrag: Formerly, no beef cattle were killed. Hogs matured more quickly and cattle were scarce since cows were used to supply milk and steers were trained as oxen.[6]

Helen Voth Schmidt: Beef was not as popular as ham and pork sausage; it had to be canned to preserve it.

The Ceremonial Sip of Wine

Peter D. Zacharias: When light appeared in the eastern sky and the stars faded away, it was time to go outside for the shooting. A glass of wine, on occasion, preceded this event.[7]

Arnold Dyck: On butchering day in Russia the master of the house would make the rounds with a bottle of brandy and a small glass from time to time, in order to strengthen his neighbors. This strengthening went on all day, frequently enough to keep everybody strong and in a good mood. In their high spirits and good humor they fooled each other and did such things as hanging pigtails on each other. The boys, who died laughing at the old men, so awfully respectable at other times, caught their happy mood.[8]

Henry B. Tiessen: At the supper liver sausage and choice pieces of meat became part of the evening fare. Occasionally the men would sip a little wine or fruit juice to take the bitter taste away, as they would say.[9]

Frieda Lehn Neufeld: My mother said her Grandfather Bartel [in Russia] always served wine on butchering day. Grandmother Bartel was opposed to it, but Grandpa said the men had worked hard. I wonder if they served it to the women also?

Sharing the Bounty

Hog butchering took place as soon as the days were cool enough and "as soon as nature's freezer was reliable," says Herbert V. Neufeld. The day began before dawn so that by evening everyone could share in the bounty. Often there were fresh cooked spareribs and liverwurst for supper along with generous portions of fried potatoes and *Plümemooss*. There were those who ate too much fresh pork and became ill during the night. But the lesson was never remembered. The next year the same thing happened. Those who had accepted the invitation to share in the work were rewarded with a gift of fresh pork to take home.

Dan G. Jost: It was a time of visiting and fellowship and everyone went home with a generous supply of pork.

Mariam Penner Schmidt: Everyone was given a portion of the spareribs, cracklings and liver sausage to take home.

Henry B. Tiessen: Before parting, the woman of the house would present each one of the guests with a bag of cookies and a nice, plump, freshly cooked liverwurst.[10]

Butchering Bees at Reesor, Ontario *by John H. Enns*

One of the time-honored traditions that brought neighbors together for work and a good time was continued in our settlement of Reesor, Ontario. This was pig-killing time in late October or early November.

In their villages in the Ukraine farmers had always provided the entire meat supply from their own stock and every farmer was an experienced butcher, sausage maker and curer of hams. Pigs were usually killed when they were full-grown and fat, for the farm larder required a good deal of lard, as well as meat.

The invited helpers would arrive very early, a good while before dawn. Large cauldrons were filled with water and brought to a boil. By the time the water boiled the men had stuck the pigs and put them into special wooden troughs for scalding. The boiling water was poured over the dead animal to soften the bristles.

From the troughs the pigs were put on trestled tables for shaving, which was done with well-honed butcher knives. When the shaving was done, the animal was strung up for drawing. Great care was taken not to cut the gall bladder and to collect all the viscera undamaged and intact, for almost every part of the animal found a use.

The stomach was cleaned and used as a bag to hold a special chopped meat mixture that was later smoked in the sewn-up bag. The small intestines were cleaned in a lengthy and laborious process to become casings for red-meat sausages; the large intestines were prepared in a similar way to encase the liver sausages.

Hams had to be trimmed and salted away to prepare them for later smoking. The two- or three-inch layers of fat had to be cut up into half-inch cubes for rendering, meat had to be ground for sausages, salted and seasoned with ground pepper, and stuffed into the casings with a special machine. Certain meat portions had to be boiled for headcheese and liver sausage and the pigs' feet had to be prepared for pickling.

Everyone had his task and if the work was to be done by nightfall, there could be no idling away of precious time. Yet people talked and joked while they worked and found some time for practical jokes. One favorite lark was to hang the pig's tail onto some busy worker so that he would not notice and provide merriment for the assemblage by wearing it unknowingly. Snickers and amused countenances would follow him wherever he went until he finally became suspicious and turned to see whether some wag had perchance decorated him with the almost universal adornment that nature had denied the human species. If he found that he had indeed been the butt of the general merriment, he would quickly detach the ignominious appendage and hide, only to repeat the mirthful outrage on someone else after a lull in the general vigilance that followed each discovery.

For repetition of the lark was, of course, expected and, all day long each outbreak of hilarity, no matter what the cause, would result in a sudden flurry of backward glances to see whether it was one's own posterior that had caused it. To see their usually sedate elders disport themselves in this manner was the source of immense amusement for the children of the family. It was almost impossible for the parents to deny them their fervent entreaties to be allowed to stay home from school for the day.

Thus pig-killing day became a school holiday to the children of the household involved, except in the few cases where the illegality of it caused concern to the father. Most people, however, felt that their connivance was rendered less culpable by the rational implication that the children's help was needed on so busy a day. To ease their own consciences and the children's return to school on the following day an appetizing fresh liver sausage was often sent along for the teacher.

This poor man had to accept the gift in good grace as a token of friendship and appreciation, since its role as bribe or appeaser could only be suspected, never proven.

When all the meat and fat was finally disposed of and all the greasy utensils were washed and put away, the weary company sat down to a sumptuous supper, made up largely of the fresh food they had just prepared. When the visitors left in the dark of late evening, they took a gift of fresh meat with them.[11]

Pigs-Killing Time in Manitoba (*Schwienschlachtstiet*) *by Herman Rempel*

Sometimes butchering day was also called *Schwienskjast,* a crude term literally translated as a "Pig's Wedding." It generally took place toward the end of October [in Canada] or up to the middle of November and was a one-day occasion where about four to six couples were invited. A family of ten slaughtered up to five hogs, weighing between 400 and 600 pounds each. It was not admitted by anyone, but there was a kind of competition among neighbors as to who slaughtered the heaviest pig, or who rendered the most lard. Lard was a very important product for the family in those days.

Very often the same group got together to kill the pigs at each neighbor's place in turn. Being invited to a pigs-killing bee had its social implications. Not being invited could mean that the couple not invited had lost some of their social status in the community. It might also mean that the couple doing the pigs-killing was excluding certain people because they were miffed at something those people had said or done.

The pigs-killing bee was as much a social event as it was a necessary operation for the farmer's livelihood. It began about 6:30 or 7:00 o'clock in the morning when the invited guests would arrive for breakfast while it was still dark. There was much chatter and banter around the large breakfast table.

After breakfast the older folks, such as the middle-aged parents, retired to the living room to smoke, boast and tell jokes while waiting for daylight. The teenagers or the younger folks were responsible for preparations such as heating water in large cauldrons for scalding the pigs.

The young men were eager to get out to the pigpen. "Is it time yet?" they asked.

"In a few minutes," was the usual reply. The honor of shooting and stabbing the pig went to the oldest boy of the family where the event was taking place. This was an important moment for the boys who took pride in being able to shoot a pig with the first shot. Some of the older men were always around to supervise this initial step of the operation.

The back of the rear legs of the hog were then slit lengthwise, the tendons exposed and the hooks of a singletree attached to the tendons. A horse was hitched to the singletree and the pig was unceremoniously dragged to the scalding trough. It was rolled into the trough and boiling water was poured over the carcass. When it was sufficiently scalded so the bristles could be easily removed, it was raised by means of ropes and a ladder to make it more accessible for scraping (removing the bristles).

When the pig was properly scraped and the supervisor gave the OK, the singletree was re-inserted in the tendons of the hind legs, and the pig hoisted up to the beams of the barn by means of a wire-stretcher or some sort of hoisting device. One of the women brought a large pan of warm water and washed down the carcass carefully.

Each community had certain men who had the expertise to eviscerate (*ütnäme*) the pig. After the women had washed the pig, one such expert took over. Taking out the insides of a pig required the services of a specialist who knew where everything was, which part to cut and which part not to cut.

Two women held a large tub between the eviscerator and the hanging hog carcass. The eviscerator deposited the intestines into the tub as part of his *ütnäme* operation. Taking the tub to another location, the women then cleaned the intestines to use later for sausage casings. They began by turning a six- to ten-inch end of an intestine inside out. Pouring warm water down that part of the intestine caused the whole piece to turn inside out quickly. Next they placed the intestines into a brine solution and scraped the excess fat from them by drawing them between two knitting needles held somewhat like chopsticks. If the intestines were cleaned too well, they developed holes. If the operation was too short, however, they were not considered sufficiently clean. Cleaning these casings was an art and accomplished women rarely made mistakes. When the woman of the house felt they were clean enough, she put them in cool water and set them aside until the sausage meat was ground.

The head was removed while the pig hung upside down and one or two of the younger men were commissioned to clean it. They removed all the bristles from every part of the head so it would be clean enough to cut up. The lower jaw was called the *Hei-spodem* (hay-spade). Perhaps it was called this because it resembled the shape of a hay knife used for cutting a slice of hay from a haystack. The claws from the feet were removed with a claw hammer.

In the meantime the dissected carcass would be placed on the cutting table and cut into manageable chunks. About this time the owner or host brought out a bottle of wine, or on rare occasions liquor, and every adult male would take a swig out of the bottle according to the thickness of the pig's bacon. This was called *Spakj mäte* (or measuring the bacon).

The meat chunks consisted of spareribs, pork chops and ham. The heart, liver and sometimes the kidneys were removed and placed in a desalinating barrel (Nätatonn) full of water. This drew out the blood. Kidneys were not a popular food item, but many thought the pig's brain was a delicacy. I personally enjoyed pork brain fried with raisins a great deal.

Under the skin was the lard. The skin, together with the lard, was cut into manageable strips and the men laid these strips on the cutting table and pulled the skin through under their knives, separating the lard from the skin.

The lard was placed in large cauldrons and brought to a high heat. This process took several hours and the mixture had to be stirred continually. Suitably cut pieces of spareribs were added to the lard. This had to boil at just the right temperature. Women who were "in the know" claimed that if you stuck your finger into the boiling lard for a second, took it out quickly and felt no pain, the temperature was just right.

What was left after the lard had been dipped off and the boiled spareribs removed were the cracklings (*Jreewe*). When these dregs had settled, the gray lard left at the bottom of the cracklings was used as butter. We called it *Jreeweschmolt*.

While all this was going on the men trimmed the meat and the carcass, separating the lean from the fat meat. The lean meat was cut up into a hamburger-like mass with a meat grinder and the sausage stuffing began. When the sausages were stuffed, the boys took them to the smokehouse where the smoking would begin right away. Another group worked on stuffing the liver sausage.

Lunch was served early and the teenage girls shone. They reveled in being able to feed the big gang of workers. Most often the menu was roast chicken with *Bobbat*.

Five pigs yielded 20 hams, 10 front and 10 back. About half of them would be salted down in a pork barrel while the other half would be smoked.

Head cheese was another delicacy made from the meat of the pig's head and the skin of the pig. This was put through the meat grinder and boiled in a large cauldron. When it had jelled, it was cut into smaller pieces. This was often pickled in the whey of milk, which added flavor as well as acting as a preserving agent.

Children were often excused from school so they could participate in the gala affair. Many an unsuspecting, dignified elder found himself walking around with a pig's tail attached to the back of his overalls. The kids usually knew whom they could tease without too many repercussions. As soon as the pigs' bladders were available, the children would blow one up with a bicycle pump and play football.

The guests usually left around 3:00 or 3:30 after *Faspa* had been served, leaving the cleaning and chores to the owner and his family unless a young volunteer or two stayed to help. Ah yes! Those were the days.

℘ORK LOIN ROAST

Use a lightly smoked 3-pound center-cut pork roast. Score fatty outer part of roast and place in pan with fatty side up. Place in preheated 325°F oven and roast until browned and nearly done, about 1–1½ hours.

Add 1 cup water, 1 small onion and 1 tomato (cut in pieces). Continue roasting for about 15 minutes. Remove roast from pan and make a gravy.

℘ORK LOIN GRAVY

Thicken the liquid from pork roast with 2 tsp. cornstarch which has been blended with a little water. Bring to a boil and cook a few minutes. Add 5 Tbsp. sour cream or canned milk. Serve with pork roast and sauerkraut. In the Vistula Delta this would have been served with a pureé of peas.

ℬOILED HAM

Scrub ham in warm water with a stiff brush and wash it well. Place the ham in a deep kettle and pour enough boiling water over to barely cover. Cover kettle and simmer until meat is tender, 25–30 minutes per pound. Remove from water, strip off the skin and place in baking pan.

Mix 1 cup brown sugar, 2 tsp. dry mustard and 1 Tbsp. horseradish. Cover top and sides with mixture. Stud with whole cloves. Bake ham in 400°F to 425°F oven for 20–30 minutes until the sugar is melted and delicately browned.

Baste several times with fruit juice. In the Ukraine old country cooks use the syrup of any pickled fruit for an interesting flavor. Serve with horseradish sauce or homemade mustard.

ℛOAST CHICKEN OR DUCK WITH *BOBBAT* DRESSING

Bobbat dressing with raisins or dried fruit is the favorite Russian Mennonite stuffing for fowl. This was typically served on Sundays or holidays. Follow directions for roasting chicken or duck. When the fowl is half-roasted, spoon *Bobbat* dressing into cavity and continue roasting at 325°F. until done. See *Bobbat* recipe on page 73.

ℛAISIN POTATO BREAD
(*Rasienenstretsel*)

This bread has a wonderful fragrance. It makes a lovely light, moist loaf that is delicious warm from the oven.

1 cup boiled mashed potato	½ cup lukewarm water
2 – 2½ cups raisins, plumped	2 Tbsp. active dry yeast
2 cups milk	2 tsp. sugar
⅓ cup sugar	2 eggs
¼ cup margarine	1 Tbsp. grated orange rind
1 tsp. salt	7½ – 8 cups bread flour

Cook a large potato, drain and mash. Cool to lukewarm. Steam raisins and cool.

In a saucepan over medium heat combine milk, margarine, sugar and salt until margarine melts. Stir well and cool to lukewarm.

Sprinkle yeast and sugar over ½ cup lukewarm water and stir briskly. Allow to become bubbly.

In a mixing bowl beat eggs slightly. Add potato, milk and yeast mixtures and orange rind. Gradually add half the flour and beat with electric mixer for five minutes. Gradually add remaining flour, enough to make a stiff dough.

Turn dough out onto floured board and knead until smooth and elastic. If using dough hook, add enough flour until dough leaves sides of bowl. Knead until smooth and elastic. Work raisins into the dough. Place dough in greased bowl. Cover and set in warm place until doubled in bulk. Punch dough down. Divide into three pieces. Shape into oblong balls and place in greased bread pans.

Cover lightly and set in warm place to rise until doubled in size. Bake at 375° for 45 – 50 minutes or until bread is hollow-sounding when thumped on bottom. Cool on racks. This bread is good with the addition of a simple icing when served with coffee.

CANNED GOOSEBERRY MOOSS
(Kjressbäa or Stachelbäamooss)

Sara Zacharias Ens: Wie deede Kjressbäare ennbudle. [We canned the gooseberries in bottles.] If the berries were large, we used knitting needles and pushed them into the long, narrow-necked bottles. They were packed only in cold water and didn't spoil. Later we used them for *Mooss* and gooseberry *Varenikje.*

2 cups canned gooseberries	3 Tbsp. flour
1 cup water	1½ cups milk
1 cup sugar	½ cup cream

In a saucepan bring gooseberries and water to a boil. Add sugar and stir well. Combine flour, milk and cream in another saucepan, stirring until smooth. Bring to a boil and cook until bubbly.

Add gooseberries to cream and milk mixture. Bring to a boil, stirring constantly. Remove from heat. Additional sugar may be added if necessary.

Busy Days

Hooltje soage,
Woate droage,
Fia moake,
Kjielkje koake.
Kjinje nü komt äte.
Wan jie nijch fuats äte kome
Woa wie mett'm Plümesack schlone.

This little Low German nursery rhyme suggests a very busy day. There is wood to saw, water to draw, a fire to be made and *Kjielkje* to cook. The mother urges her children to come eat "right away!" If they tarry, she threatens to spank them with the plum sack.

The Good Old Days Were Not So Great

How easy it is to paint a nostalgic picture of village and farm life of bygone times. We are often tempted to think of it as a picturesque era of simplicity and enduring values. But we can be overly romantic about times past.

For the pioneer Mennonite women who immigrated in 1874 or the 1920s, there was great hardship and unrelenting work. A farm wife toiled, sometimes fourteen or more hours a day. "I remember mother actually running from one place to the other," recalls Marie Penner Klassen. "Slaving over a hot stove" was more than a clever phrase. It was an actuality.

"I remember my mother standing over the washboard crying. She had to make fire in the morning because the house was so cold. Sometimes with the old stove one had to stay up or get up at night to stoke the fire. She carried fire from one stove to another," says Betty Fehr Ens of early life in Manitoba.

There were no conveniences, especially in the beginning. For the pioneer woman getting the daily water supply was a regular part of household chores. It meant carrying rainwater from the cistern outside or drawing bucket after bucket from a nearby well. All the water for drinking, washing, cooking, dishes, laundry and bathing had to be brought in buckets to the house.

Gathering the family's fuel supply was another heavy chore. There were no forests or groves of trees in Kansas. Without a ready source of firewood or coal, the early settlers were forced to find alternatives for heating and cooking. Scouring the prairie for anything burnable, they fired their stoves with dried twigs, prairie grass, twisted hay, old corncobs and woody sunflower stalks. By far the most popular sources of fuel, however, were the abundant chunks of dried cow dung. In dry weather the housewife and her children roamed the pasture in search of cow chips. They were gathered in baskets or stored in old gunnysacks and stacked somewhere in a dry corner of the barn to be burned during the long winter months.

There were no convenience foods to give this woman an occasional break. She cooked everything from scratch on a wood-burning stove. She baked all of her own bread, often in an outdoor oven. She used her own dried, canned or stored products. Preparing meals took a large part of her working day.

Her hands were calloused from scrubbing clothes on a washboard. She and her daughters usually did all the milking, separating milk and churning butter. She planted, weeded and tended the garden. Often, she also shared in the farm work. The baby slept in the shade of a stack while she stacked wheat.

Babies came regularly. Says Louise Kornelsen, "My mother helped dig the foundation for our log cabin in Saskatchewan when she was eight months pregnant with me, her fourth child." A woman had to be as strong as a man. Sometimes stronger.

Along with regular farming and cooking chores, the housewife and her daughters devoted much of their time to sewing. Ready-made clothes were too expensive for the immigrants, so all the family's clothing was sewn at home. Hours were spent stitching new skirts and trousers, darning socks, knitting sweaters and embroidering the household linens. "Mother made all the boys' shirts, sewed all of our dresses and made our underwear from flour sacks," remembers

Aunt Minnie Jost Krause.

Thankfully, clothing was simple, designed for practicality and economy. Farm life provided few opportunities for silks and frills. Men wore denim overalls and blue cotton work shirts. Women wore simple cotton dresses and aprons.

In addition to clothing, women made all of their household linens, sheets, quilts and comforters. An occasional quilting party relieved the daily drudgery. Most women kept a few geese along with a flock of chickens for down feathers to stuff pillows.

In this busy life there was little time for rest and leisure. Even when women sat a few minutes, they busied themselves with stitchery. One of the few outlets for artistic instincts was embroidery. My own mother was scolded for too much *Poppa mola* (drawing dolls) as a grade school girl. Embroidering tea towels, on the other hand, was quite acceptable. Women channeled their need for beauty into colorfully embroidered table linens, pillow cases and dresser scarves. Artistry and design also emerged in the quilts they created, whether they were patchwork or delicately appliqued tulips and roses with tiny, barely visible stitches. Our family treasures the crocheted doilies, table scarves and dress trimmings, all with perfect even designs, which Mother and the aunts created during that era.

Nor did the endless drudgery and hard work always bless these women with prosperity. Poverty was a constant companion. The forces of nature, often hostile on the prairies, would bring sweltering heat and bitter cold.

There were times when the wheat crop in the field stood ripening in all its golden bounty and the hot winds came early and shriveled the wheat kernels in the heads. Tall and beautiful corn sometimes was burned to a crisp in the hot Kansas wind. Localized hailstorms could destroy a field in a matter of minutes. Cinch bugs and grasshoppers created havoc.

Dan G. Jost: When the ordeal was over, we farmers would go and investigate. Perhaps fields that were ready for harvest or in full bloom would be flattened to the ground, at times, a hundred per cent loss. There were years when there was too little or no rain at all.

Another aspect of pioneer life was loneliness, especially on the frontier — western Kansas, Oklahoma, Saskatchewan and Manitoba. Often there were no neighbors for miles. In some places the vast expanse of flat monotonous prairie stretched for miles without a single tree. Winter, in particular, added to the loneliness and difficulties. With children cooped up in a single, heated room, life was sometimes most trying.

Women also had to take responsibility for keeping the family healthy. Disease was a constant threat. Sometimes weakened by poor nutrition and substandard living conditions, the Mennonite pioneers were highly susceptible to various illnesses. Cleanliness was difficult living in a *Serrei* (Russian-style early Mennonite A-frame house) or a dugout. In summer it was simplest to go for a swim in the pond at bath time.

Doctors were scarce and at least as far away as the next town. In one frantic emergency, my family remembers Grandmother finding herself in the doctor's office with only one shoe on. She and Grandfather had raced to town by horse and buggy with an injured child.

Hospitals were virtually nonexistent. Actually, people were skeptical about going. Out of fourteen children in my father's family, only the last was born in a hospital. Grandmother's sister, Taunte Koop, was a midwife. She delivered many of the babies in the surrounding area.

Most of the time it was mothers who knew what to do for chills, how to calm fevers and how to treat a cough or an earache. They had learned it all from their mothers. Grandmother Jost treated most everything; her sons think she did as well as any doctor. When the women were sick, a friend or relative came to care for them. People looked after each other.

These were hardy women, our great-grandmothers. Over the years they learned to cope with the monotony and drudgery of daily life and did not expect life to be filled with pleasure. With grim determination, much hard work, faith in God and yes, many tears, they toughed it out. They developed an inner strength and fortitude which helped them overcome the hardships. The words of Helen Harder Peterson, whose family built an adobe house on the barren, western Kansas plains, are revealing, "We refused to be beat." Survive they did; these stalwart souls of another day.

*　　*　　*

It is difficult in this day of conveniences to fully comprehend the way these women lived. The following firsthand stories take us back to the monumental weekly task of doing the laundry, which usually occupied two days, one for washing clothes, the second for ironing. Some of the accounts also describe Saturday, which was a day of cleaning and preparation for the Sabbath.

Washday in Russia

Laundry days, as some of us remember, were tough and demanding. Laundry day in Russia, however, was probably the single most physically punishing of all the farm wife's routines. There were no machines and no miracle detergents. Women used muscle power and a scrub board to beat, rinse and wring every piece, from the large, heavy tablecloths and sheets to the everyday work clothes. The young wife needed a lot of stamina and fortitude to do the job.

Helen Pankratz Siemens: On Sunday evening we made soap water. We soaked all the sheets in large barrels. Laundry wasn't done in just one day; it took two or three days. We wrung the wash by hand after it had soaked in the soapy water. We had big tubs where two people rubbed on the washboard all day long. We put the wash into another batch of boiling soap water. Then we rinsed it twice. We did our ironing in the mangle house which was operated by two women. In summer we washed every three weeks.

Anna von Kampen Funk: During the "good old times" we washed two times a year, one week at a time. The wash was soaked, soaped, rolled up and put into a barrel to soak overnight. Then the washing was *gestuckt* [beaten], rinsed, washed on the washboard and put into ice cold water to soak overnight again. In the morning what needed to be starched and blued was done. Then it was hung up. Some white laundry was bleached by spreading it out on the grass during warm weather and on the snow during cold weather. In my time we had fewer clothes, so washing had to be done more often. We used homemade soap. It was a very hard week.

Ironing and Mangling

Regular items of clothing were pressed with irons which had been heated on hot plates or which had been filled with glowing hot coals.

In the days before electric dryers, one way of ironing large sheets, tablecloths and flat pieces was to put them through a mangle. This machine consisted of a stationary flat platform. On it was a large box filled with heavy stones. Wooden rollers about five inches in diameter and four feet long were placed between the platform and the box. Large items were pressed by wrapping them around the rollers and moving the heavy box back and forth.

Mangles were used both in our villages in Russia and in rural Mennonite communities in America. Often there was a neighborhood or community mangle. A few families had their own "ironing machine."

*L*AMB *BORSCHT*
(*Schops Borscht*)

Kaethe Kasdorf Warkentin: Lamb was the meat used in soup in the spring and summer. Mother made *Solankje* with lamb, onion, potatoes, seasoning and cream. In Osterwick we made *Borscht* only with lamb or chicken. I had never eaten beef *Borscht* until I came to America.

You may cook this similar to the directions for beef *Borscht,* substituting lamb. Then add cabbage, onion, perhaps 1 carrot and potatoes. In Russia we also used a thick tomato pureé (*Mors*) which we canned in bottles specifically for soup. Mother always garnished each bowl of *Borscht* with a teaspoon of sour cream.

BIEROCKS

Dough

2 Tbsp. active dry yeast
2 cups lukewarm water
½ cup sugar
1 tsp. salt
½ cup shortening, margarine or
butter (at room temperature)

2 eggs
6½ cups (about) unbleached or bread
flour
Ground beef and cabbage filling

Dissolve yeast in ¼ cup lukewarm water; let stand about 5 minutes until bubbly. In mixing bowl combine remaining water with sugar, salt, shortening and eggs. Add yeast and 2 cups of the flour. Beat with electric beater for about 5 minutes. Cover and let stand in warm place until mixture is bubbly, about 30–40 minutes.

Gradually, add 4 more cups flour. Turn dough out onto floured board. Knead until smooth and elastic, 5–8 minutes. If using dough hook, complete kneading according to mixer directions. Add extra flour, if necessary, so dough is not sticky. Place in greased bowl, turning to grease top of dough. Cover with plastic wrap and set in warm place until doubled in bulk (about 1–1½ hours). Prepare filling.

Filling

2 lbs. ground beef
2 large onions, chopped
2 cloves garlic, minced
6 cups chopped cabbage

½ cup water
1 beef bouillon cube
2 tsp. salt

In large skillet brown beef. When meat has started to brown, add onion and garlic. Add cabbage, water, salt and bouillon cube. Cover and steam until cabbage is tender and juices have cooked away. Cool.

Punch dough down and divide in half. Roll half of dough into a 12″ × 24″ rectangle. Cut into 8 squares. Repeat with remaining dough. Divide filling equally on the squares. Bring opposite corners of squares together. Pinch the edges together securely. Moisten them with water to seal. Place on greased baking sheets, 1 inch apart. (Cover lightly and let stand until light and puffy.) Bake at 375°F. for about 30 minutes or until golden brown. Brush tops with melted butter while still hot. Serve warm.

EASY BIEROCKS II

2 pkgs. crescent dinner rolls

Ground beef filling (Easy *Bierocks* I)

Prepare filling according to directions. Separate each package of 8 rolls into only 4 rectangular shapes and place on ungreased baking sheet. Pinch together perforations and place an equal amount of mixture on each piece of dough. Bring sides together, sealing edges tightly.

Place, seam side down, on ungreased baking sheet. Bake at 375°F. for about 10 minutes or until crust is light brown. Makes 8 *Bierocks.*

KJIELKJE

1 egg
½ cup milk
½ tsp. salt

Flour, enough to make medium-stiff dough

Beat egg, milk and salt. Gradually add flour and knead until it forms a firm dough. Some cooks simply cut off pieces of dough with a spoon and drop them into a kettle of boiling water. Boil 4 minutes. Drain.

My mother rolled the dough about ½ inch thick and cut it into 1-inch strips. She stacked two or three strips and cut them like noodles into ½-inch pieces. Drop in boiling water and cook until done. Drain, rinse and serve.

𝒫OTATO PANCAKES
(*Eatschockeplauts*)

Sylvia Unruh Abrahams: Mom says they used to make these for her eight brothers. They had to make several gallons at a time, and they ate them with syrup.

6 medium potatoes   1 Tbsp. flour
2 eggs   Salt and pepper

Peel potatoes. Hand grate or use blender. Add eggs, flour and seasonings. Fry in bacon drippings, like pancakes. Eat plain or with syrup.

—*Anna Unruh Bartel*

𝒫LAIN *PANKÜAKE*

In the Russian Mennonite Molotschna Colony the villagers of Pastwa were nicknamed *Panküake.*

1 cup sifted all-purpose flour   5 eggs
¼ tsp. salt   2¼ – 2½ cups milk

Mix flour and salt. Beat eggs and milk together. Add flour and mix well until you have a smooth batter.

Grease hot skillet with butter. Pour ⅓ cup batter into pan. Rotate to cover entire pan. Brown on both sides. Serve sprinkled with sugar or syrup.

—**Altona Women's Institute Cookbook**, 1954 edition

COTTAGE CHEESE CAKES
(Glommsküake)

3 eggs   ¼ cup flour
1 cup sieved cottage cheese   ¼ tsp. salt
2 Tbsp. salad oil

Beat eggs until light in color. Blend in cheese and oil. Sift together flour and salt. Stir in until just blended. Bake on hot griddle until brown on both sides.

BASIC WAFFLES
(Wofle)

1 cup all-purpose flour   2 eggs, separated
1 tsp. baking powder   1 cup milk
½ tsp. salt   2 Tbsp. butter, melted
1 Tbsp. sugar

Stir together flour, baking powder, salt and sugar in a bowl. In another bowl beat the egg yolks and mix in the milk and melted butter.

Stir in the flour mixture just until moistened. Do not beat.

Beat egg whites until they hold firm peaks and fold into the batter. Spoon batter into preheated waffle iron. Bake until golden brown and crispy. Makes 4 or 5 large waffles.

DOUBLE QUICK SWEET BREAD DOUGH

Jennie Jost Duerksen: I speed up mixing time in breadmaking by using powdered milk and instant yeast (SAF). This eliminates scalding time.

2 cups lukewarm tap water	½ cup (minus 2 Tbsp.) sugar
2 Tbsp. SAF instant or regular yeast	2 eggs, beaten
⅔ cup powdered milk	1 tsp. salt
2 Tbsp. sugar	4 Tbsp. dehydrated mashed potatoes
½ cup margarine or shortening	7 – 7½ cups bread flour

Place tap water, yeast, powdered milk and 2 Tbsp. sugar in mixing bowl and allow to become bubbly. Add margarine, ½ cup (minus 2 Tbsp.) sugar, eggs and salt to bowl and mix well. Add dehydrated mashed potatoes. Gradually add enough flour so dough is not sticky.

Turn out onto lightly floured board and knead about 5 minutes by hand. Place dough in greased bowl, turning to grease sides of dough. Cover with plastic wrap and set in warm place to rise until double in bulk. Punch down.

Divide dough into desired pieces. Place on greased pans. Bake at 350° for about 45 minutes.

Hint: Use just enough flour to make a barely workable dough. Keep it soft. Too much flour makes a tough loaf.

—Jennie Jost Duerksen

AMERICAN STORE BREAD

Marie Loewen Franz: Baking bread was a three-times-a-week major project. We never had bakery bread, except maybe once or twice a year when going to the city for the annual buying trip, or the County Fair, when we had sandwiches made of "boughten" bread. This was special.

All of us (children) were packed into the car for the "buying trip" and at noon for lunch Dad bought several loaves of unsliced bakery bread plus a whole, long stick of baloney. Dad cut off hunks of baloney with his pocket knife and we pulled hunks of bread by hand and ate the two together, and nothing else. This tasted so good. It was a special treat.

*　*　*

Busy Russian Mennonite housewives baked bread at home. Bakeries really did not make a difference in their lives. These pioneer women lived too far from towns. What is more, they were frugal. It was more economical to bake at home. To spend even 5¢ for a loaf of bread did not seem right.

Later, when women gradually allowed themselves the luxury of an occasional loaf of store bread, they discovered their children loved it. This bread was like cake. They liked the soft texture and the perfect, even slices. "Light bread," we called it, because it was lighter than homemade bread.

Store bread was especially popular eaten with rings of baloney or made into "sugar sandwiches" (buttered slices of store bread sprinkled with sugar). Anyone with store bread sandwiches in his school lunch pail was definitely the envy of the *Roggebroot* crowd.

Washday in Early Twentieth Century America

Washday in the early 1900s was a back-bending, back-breaking task. Water had to be drawn from the well or pumped from the cistern and carried indoors to the wash boiler or the cast-iron cauldron which was built into one end of the wash house. Marie Loewen Franz remembers the *Miagrope* filled with as much as sixty gallons of water.

Wood, too, was brought to the *Miagrope*. Often, on the prairie, cow chips were gathered either on Friday or Saturday because no one worked on Sunday. Heating the wash water might require four bushel baskets of fuel.

Monday morning women got up, preferably before daybreak, and worked to get through the many steps of scrubbing and boiling so they could have all the laundry dried and back in the house before the end of the day. Clothes had to be sorted into piles, according to fabric, treatment and color and according to how dirty they were. Work overalls were dirty! Most of the clothes were put to soak the night before to lessen the scrubbing task.

On Monday morning they were wrung out and placed in tubs of hot, soapy water from the boiler and scrubbed down, piece by piece, on the washboard and wrung out again. White items went into the boiler where they came to a boil and were stomped down with a clothes stick. Once more they were wrung out and put into a first rinse. A second rinse tub contained bluing, a kind of bleach. After the "bluing water" came a "starch water." Collars and cuffs of men's shirts had to be very stiff. They were dipped in a separate heavier starch. Dresses, shirts and linens were all starched in a lighter water. Finally they were hung on the line in orderly fashion. Women prided themselves on being the first in the neighborhood to hang clothes out on Monday morning. They took equal pride in a white wash.

Clothes were hung with care usually in a particular arrangement, such as sheets, towels, pillow cases and napkins all neatly lined up in the sunlight where a breeze might whip out the wrinkles. Colored clothes and flannels were hung in the shade to prevent colors from fading. Often a housewife was judged, even graded, by how early she hung out the clothes and how they looked. Once clothes were dry, they were not allowed to whip in the wind because edges might fray and hems give way.

On cold wintry days hands nearly froze while pinning clothes to the line. Clothes did freeze. Corners of the fabric, pinned underneath the clothespins, tore easily. Salt added to a rinse water helped somewhat.

Men's underwear (long johns) looked especially comical when frozen stiff. Marie Franz remembers bringing them indoors, standing them against the wall and watching them go limp. Clothes were draped over furniture or boards stretched between two sawhorses near the stove. The whole room smelled of the fresh outdoors while windows steamed with moisture as the clothes thawed. A large basement with a clothesline near a furnace was a luxury.

During a drought laundry day posed real problems. When water was in short supply, powdered alum added to the wash water caused the impurities and soap to sink to the bottom. Then the clear water was skimmed off and recycled.

Even in good times laundry water was never squandered or just "thrown out." It was used to scrub the kitchen floor, the back porch, the wash house, the summer kitchen or the outdoor toilet. The rest of the water was dutifully carried in buckets to the flower beds or young trees to do double duty. These women had never heard of ecology or saving natural resources. It was a way of life, thrift and economy, a respect and caring for God's gifts.

In those days everything had to be ironed — dresses, blouses, shirts, overalls, tablecloths, towels, pillow cases, handkerchiefs, even sheets. There were no drip-dry or wash-and-wear fabrics. Every piece to be ironed was sprinkled, rolled up tightly and placed in a tub or basket. Ironing was an all-day task with irons heated on the wood-burning range and rotated as they cooled. Later there were gas irons which gave off sickening fumes.

An early twentieth century book of household instructions lists the following utensils as necessities for washing:

wash boiler	**two or three pails**
wringer	**clothes stick**
washboard	**dipper**
washing machine	**large and small clothes basket**
three or four tubs	**starch pan**

Special Care

Clothes did not go to the dry cleaners in those days. Each housewife learned special treatment of colored clothes and calicoes. She learned how to "fix" colors so they wouldn't run, how to treat "laces and lawns," how to prepare laces to wash, how to care for black lace and how to wash and stretch curtains. Silks and satins, woolens and flannels, all needed special treatment. Home "dry cleaning" of certain unwashable fabrics was done by washing the garment outdoors in naphtha gas. (It was flammable.) The item was kept in the sun and wind until the odor disappeared.

Quick and Easy Washday Fare

In Russia washday was *Kjielkje* day in every village. The water in which the *Kjielkje* (noodles) were cooked provided a fine starch for the laundry. Women in America found that beans, slowly cooked, made a practical meal. Sometimes supper was a quick stirring together of fried potatoes and eggs.

Washday — How Could Anyone Forget?

Frieda Pankratz Suderman: Washing and ironing took an unbelievable amount of time before detergents or wash-and-wear clothes. Every Monday was washday. Before the big house was built we had no electricity and washing was done in a homemade, hand-operated machine that was brought into the kitchen from the back porch. Papa made the machine, which was considered a good washer, so he often made machines for others.

Mamma got up very early on Monday mornings so she could have the clothes ready for the line before it was time for us to go to school. And washing was not a simple once-over-lightly affair. First every batch was washed in fairly hot water. Next, the white batches were boiled. After that the whole wash was given another turn in very hot water. Usually everything was rinsed twice. Mamma's wash came out a cleaner white than people demand these days. No wonder she often had migraine headaches on Tuesdays.

There was not much in the wash that did not need ironing and we all learned to help. A beginner did pillow cases, handkerchiefs, underwear and Papa's work clothes. Midi-blouses were standard wearing apparel during high school days and they were not the easiest garments to care for.[1]

Minnie Jost Krause: We didn't change clothes like we do now. Washing was too big a job. The boys usually wore their overalls a whole week.

We always took the clean clothes to our neighbors, the Koops, to mangle. We always liked to go there. We took the wash in the buggy. It took us about a half an hour or an hour to mangle. They had the mangle in an outside shed built onto the barn. The mangle was a family heirloom and it stayed in one place.

Our "Sunday-go-meeting" clothes and the dresses were ironed at home with a sad iron. When the iron started to cool, we changed to a hot one. The handle got pretty hot sometimes. We had to keep the stove red hot to keep the irons warm.

Mariam Penner Schmidt: There was a trapdoor in the floor of the kitchen which led into the wash room. We always called it the *Loch* [hole]. The second room had the big mangle in it. All sheets, pillow cases and tablecloths were ironed on that.

The mangle room also had a large porcelain bathtub for our Saturday baths. There was a wash room in the basement with a "Stock" machine. On Mondays I had to move the lever of the machine up and down 500 times before I could go to school. How diligently I counted, but I am sure I often skipped several numbers.

Hog butchering time in the Chortitza Colony in 1913.

A Russian Mennonite mother with her children in 1910.

Homemade Soap by the Ton

A Moundridge, Kansas, couple, Herb J.T. and Edna Stucky, make old-fashioned lye soap in their garage to donate to Mennonite Central Committee relief projects. Persons donate the grease. Funds for the purchase of lye are provided by Edna Stucky's mission society at Eden Mennonite Church in rural Moundridge. They frequently make more than two tons of soap, averaging about 200 pounds a day. "Soapmaking is something to do," says Edna Stucky. "It's not hard, but sometimes it's tiring. But we feel it's for a good cause."

* * *

Krakjtijchkjeit es daut haulwe Läwe.
Kjinja, fäajt den Desch auf.

Cleanliness is half of life.
Children brush (the crumbs) off the table.
— *Old Low German Maxim*

ℋOMEMADE LAUNDRY SOAP

No extra frying fat, no sausage drippings, no tallow skimmed from soup and no deep frying fat was wasted. Fat was carefully strained, the liquid removed and stored until enough was saved for a batch or two of soap. Here is an old recipe for making soap.

1 can lye	¼ cup ammonia
4 cups water	1 tsp. salt
2 Tbsp. sugar	½ cup soft (rain) water
3 Tbsp. Borax	5 lbs. clean melted fat

Pour lye and water together. Allow to stand about seven hours. Add sugar, Borax, ammonia, salt and rain water to the clean melted fat. Pour lye water into the lukewarm grease, stirring with a wooden spoon until it is the consistency of honey. Cover.

The soap mold may be a wood or cardboard box lined with a dish towel or part of an old sheet. Citronella may be used for scent. You may also use oil of wintergreen, oil of cloves or other oils for scents. Mark in squares and cut before it is too hard.

Saturday, the Busiest Day of the Week

Sunday really began on Saturday. There was the house to clean, food to prepare for Sunday and all the weekly baking to do on this day.

"Am Abend werden die Faulen fleissig," Mother used to warn early Saturday morning. (In the evening the lazy ones get busy.) It was an unwritten rule: you worked and then played. A busy Saturday's tasks went something like this:

1) Help with milking and separating
2) Wash the milk separator after milking
3) Clean upstairs bedrooms
4) Clean the downstairs
5) Wipe pantry shelves and cellar steps
6) Wash and wax the kitchen floor
7) Trim the oil lamps and wash the chimneys
8) Butcher and clean chickens for Sunday dinner
9) Knead the *Zwieback* and bread dough
10) Bake the *Zwieback* and bread
11) Make Sunday's *Plümemooss*
12) Peel potatoes for Sunday
13) Cook the midday meal of *Kjielkje*
14) Rub the cutlery with ashes
15) Brush out the men's Sunday pants
16) Polish a row of Sunday shoes

After such a day, who had time to play? If there were several minutes at the end of the day, there was always the Sunday School lesson to read and study!

Memories of Busy Saturdays

Arnold Dyck: Every Saturday [in Russia] the floor is scrubbed with soap and water and strewn with fresh sand in beautiful winding ringlets and loops. Grandmother strews the sand, first mixing it with water. Once it has dried, it's snow white and gives the floor a pretty Sunday-like appearance. After that nobody is supposed to go into the great room before Sunday to avoid crushing the sand ringlets. Only Grandfather may, for he always stays in the great room and, besides, nobody may tell him anything.[2]

Anna von Kampen Funk: Knives and forks were polished every Saturday in Russia, either with brick dust, made by rubbing two bricks together, or ashes. Some people had Solingen steel cutlery.

Marie Harms Berg: We all had our cleaning jobs assigned on Saturday. Mamma did the baking. After all the dishes and utensils were washed, the lamps had to be cleaned and filled and polished. The buggy was cleaned inside and out — later the Model T Ford. Not much was left for Sunday morning.

Helen Jost Malin: Saturday was weekly cleaning day as well as weekly bath time and baking. My task was to clean the house, starting upstairs in the boys' room. I'd change the sheets and pillow cases, gather up the dirty laundry, sweep the floor and carry the lamps downstairs to be filled with kerosene and to have the glass chimneys cleaned. Next my bedroom would be cleaned and swept. Then I would begin downstairs. There was the parlor to clean. The parlor consisted of a soft green rug with large rose-colored flowers, lace curtains, an organ, two rocking chairs, overstuffed mohair chairs and a small center table with casters. After cleaning the parlor, I cleaned and dusted Mother and Dad's bedroom, then the dining room. It had a linoleum floor that had to be mopped with soapy water. The kitchen floor and porch had to be scrubbed on hands and knees. By the time I got to the kitchen floor it was late afternoon.

One Saturday my younger brother, Ted, came into the kitchen with dirty, muddy shoes and a bucket of milk which he set down on the floor. Angrily, I gave him a shove out the door. He fell backwards into a puddle of mud and let out a war whoop. I was reprimanded by my father. But Mother intervened, telling him how hard I had worked to clean up the house. Dad apologized. I was so impressed that my father would apologize to me.

Marie Loewen Franz: On Saturdays the heating stove was polished with a black liquid polish which gave it a nice shiny jet black appearance (my job). The whole house was spruced up for Sunday, floors were washed and waxed, furniture was dusted and polished, often front yards were swept around the house, especially around the front porch.[3]

Saturday Baking

Frieda Pankratz Suderman: Every Saturday was baking day. There were always *Zwieback* and coffee cake and sometimes bread and cake as well. Friday's potato water was saved and the sponge was started with yeast foam in the evening. Overnight the mixture had to be protected from chilling. In winter it was sometimes quite a problem. A fifty-pound sack of flour lasted three weeks. The by-products of the fifty-pound sacks were tea towels and diapers.[4]

Washing Dishes

Before the days of hot and cold running water, the sources of household water were often outdoor wells or cisterns. Some wells had hand pumps; many had pulleys which drew the water up in a bucket. Water was heated in the tea kettle or in the warming place in the stove and poured into the big, deep dishpan. Stacks of dirty dishes went into the hot water in the dishpan. With a dishcloth and a bar of homemade soap, each dish, one by one, was washed. Washed dishes went into another dishpan of scalding water where they were rinsed then hand dried.

Mom's Apron *by Marie Loewen Franz*

Rarely did we see our mother without her apron; it was just part of her. There were pretty ones and plain ones. They were wide enough to cover the front of her dress and long enough to meet the hem. She had many of them, one for each day of the week, sometimes more. Those for everyday were made out of an all-cotton material, either figured or striped, and always very washable.

When company came, she wore a pretty one in white, with lace or rickrack and with hand embroidered flowers. Always her apron had a pocket for a hankie to wipe the nose of a child. The apron was used for a quick wipe of the hands when the telephone rang or there was a knock on the door and no time to grab a towel. Mother put an apron on over her dress in the morning and sometimes removed it in the afternoon. For evening there was often another one, a clean one.

The apron came in handy for gathering vegetables in the garden. She just lifted it up at the lower edge, which formed a large pouch, and filled it with goodies. Sometimes she gathered eggs into it or little chicks as they hatched.

When Mom was busy at work in the hot kitchen, it was often used for a quick wipe of perspiration from her brow or to wrap around a youngster in cold weather. Often, without untying the string, she grabbed it at the lower edge and wrapped it around her head, like a shawl. At times little children hid behind Mom's apron to avoid looking at something or someone, maybe just to hide.

The apron was used to wipe away many a tear from a small child's eyes. It was a symbol of love and protection. It was like a uniform, such a memorable and special part of Mom.[5]

Saturday Baths

Mary Dirks Janzen: In our house in Gnadenfeld [Molotschna Colony] there was no bathroom, but father had a galvanized tin tub made, a fine roomy one, which was used during the colder months. It had to be brought in and set up in our kitchen. Since water for the bath had to be heated in kettles and pails, a tub would last for about three people. Then it was dipped out and carried outside, and fresh heated water was prepared for the next three people. We never saw a Turkish towel until we came to America; we had linen or damask towels. After the Revolution we did not even have fragrant bath soap, only homemade laundry soap.

Helen Peters Epp: Staying warm after the bath was a problem. In winter we shivered and shook. One of my sisters, trying to keep warm, crawled too close to Mother's Perfection oil stove and burned her stomach. When we wanted to make her mad we would just say, "Perfection!" and she'd come after us! It's funny now.

Marie Loewen Franz: I don't know how our mother managed, how she kept all of us clean and healthy. We had only one bath a week, on Saturday evening, in a galvanized wash tub placed in the center of the kitchen. The water was heated in tea kettles. All the laundry was done by hand on an old-fashioned rubbing board, and since washing was such hard work, towels for our baths were at a premium, so there were only two large towels for the whole family, one for the "head" and another for the "body." I always wanted to be one of the first ones to take a bath because the last ones had a towel that was already so wet it wouldn't dry anyone off too well. Naturally, we never "filled" the tub with warm water, and always several of us had to use the same water.[6]

Frieda Pankratz Suderman: On wintry Saturday evenings the family room became a steamy bathroom. Water was heated in a large kettle on the wood-burning stove, the round laundry tub was brought in from the wash kitchen, and bathing proceeded, beginning with the smallest child. The water became deeper for the later bathers because hot water needed to be added to keep the temperature right. Mamma warmed large pieces of flannel blanket behind the stove. When we were bathed, we were wrapped in warm blankets and set on chairs to wait until she had time to help us with our long nighties. It was wondrously cozy and comfortable. The time came when one night Mamma said to Papa that since we were getting a little older, she thought he should stop taking a bath so openly. From then on a large blanket was hung so as to hide him from our view. It made no sense at all to me![7]

Saturday Night Shopper's Special

In some families the week's work came to an end with a trip to town on Saturday night. In earlier years stores in small rural towns often stayed open quite late so the farmers could "do their trading." A trip to town on Saturday night was a social event for farm and small-town families.

*   *   *

Bertha Fast Harder: There came a time when we would go to town every Saturday night. Mother would stay home. I think she enjoyed that. It was kind of restful. We would ask, "Dad, can we go along to town tonight?" And most of the time we could. Once in a while, if we hadn't been diligent or had shirked some responsibility, we would not be able to go. That was a big punishment. We loved going to town.

In the center of our town [Mountain Lake, Minnesota] there was a park where we would meet our friends, sit on the park benches and visit. That's where the boys would come and talk to us. Once in a while a boy would say, "Bert, do you want to go for a walk?" Then we would walk around town. At ten o'clock, though, we had to leave for Grandma's where our car was parked. If we missed that ten o'clock, the next Saturday night we would very likely not go to town. When we came home, there on the kitchen table would be *Zwieback,* cold ham and cold sausage. That would be our late night supper.

Helen Jost Malin: Saturday night the older boys took the car to town. I would get a quarter from Dad to spend and sometimes the boys would take me along. That was very special. All the stores were open. People stood on the street corners visiting. Young girls marched up and down the streets, often followed by boys. Sometimes they took the girls for a joy ride in a car. The ice cream parlor and the soda fountain were places where young people gathered.

Pioneer Women in Paraguay

Frieda Siemens Kaethler: Sixty years ago our parents came as refugees to this wilderness and built their lives under most difficult situations — isolation, drought and grasshoppers, along with typhoid and malaria epidemics. As a five-year-old, I experienced the pioneering in Fernheim. I remember hardships and privations, but I did not feel them so keenly, for a child does not bear the responsibility. Much later I realized how hard the battle had been.

Just to take care of a home in those days would have been a big enough job for the pioneer woman. But she also had to go out into the bush and camp to help her husband. Often with the baby in her arms she had to help saw lumber, cut grass for the roof, make bricks, tame wild cows and oxen, build the house, plow and plant.

There was little time to play, even for small children. We could play over the noon hour and on Sunday. We had sores on our legs from insect bites. We cried with pain as we treaded the mass of mud and straw to make the bricks for the house. In the evening Mother tried to clean our wounds, but there wasn't enough water and there were no bandages. But the next day the work continued.

Our widows had the hardest lot. One of our neighbors, who was left with two little boys, had to tie them at times at home when she went into the fields.

In spite of poverty and illness, babies were born. When the time came for delivery, the woman could not go to a clean hospital with doctors and nurses. The other children had to be sent to the neighbors, and the baby was born in a poor hut, in a tent or, occasionally, even under a tree.

The midwives deserve an honorable mention. They did their best under the primitive circumstances. But when there were complications and accidents, they could not always help. At times I still hear the cries of a woman in labor until she becomes weaker and weaker and finally stops. A doctor might have been able to save the mother and child.

I remember, too, how mothers sat by the light of a lantern or oil saucer and sewed. For Christmas our mother sewed a ball of some remnants filled with cotton. She had to sew, patch and work until late at night or early morning. In the morning she had to milk, chop wood, hoe in the garden, make meals and many other things.

We would ask her today how she managed all that without despairing. The courage at times got low. Here is her answer: "God gave the strength for each day. To God belongs the honor."

We saw her calloused hands folded in prayer. In those early days we did much singing as a family. We have a rhyme in German which says, "God has given us songs to soothe our pain and sorrow." The pioneer women in Paraguay were valiant with the help and strength of God.

Orchards and Gardens

Kjemmt Tiet, kjemmt Rot.
Kjemmt Sodeltiet, kjemmt Sot.

Given time, a solution will come.
Come seeding time, seed will be on hand.
                    —*Low German Maxim*

Mennonite Orchards and Gardens

Grandmother's Garden

Grandmother's garden was a place of joy, a model of neatness and order. Across the driveway, near the house, Grandfather had built a fence with a sturdy gate to protect her vegetables and flowers from a straying pig or scratching chickens that might dig up the tender young plants. Her garden was large, row after arrow-straight row of vegetables and flowers.

Grandmother was not an educated woman, but she knew a lot about plants — which ones grew best in certain kinds of soil. She knew all about seeds, when to plant, when to hoe and when to harvest. She knew how to keep them healthy without the magic of commercial fertilizers and fancy gardening books. Prize tomatoes and tender sweet corn thrived on manure from the barn and chicken house. Sometimes she sprinkled ashes from the furnace as well. She knew about drying herbs and beans and making sauerkraut from cabbage.

Despite her wisdom, she was occasionally seduced to plant peas and potatoes in the first early warm days of March, only to find them covered, several weeks later, with a late spring snow.

At the end of summer Grandmother carefully saved seeds from her prize flowers. She sorted, separated and lovingly wrapped them in bits of brown paper. Some she tied in a white cloth and others she stored in canning jars. Each package or jar was marked and labeled and put away until spring.

Grandmother never owned a fine painting or had time to try her hand at watercolors. But she knew how to make a flower garden as beautiful as any museum painting — rows of feathery cosmos, saucy zinnias and pale pinks lined the path in a blend of color and artistry. I can still see her there, in her long dark dress and striped apron, hair pulled back in a tight bun, tending the flowers. I think she felt the nearness of God in her garden and there drew peace of mind. It was the bright spot in the midst of days of drabness and demanding work. She took humble pride in sharing a task with the Master Gardener.

*　　*　　*

Raising flowers and vegetables has always been important in the lives of Mennonite women. In the Vistula Delta back in the sixteenth and seventeenth centuries, Mennonite settlements were known for their fine gardens.[1] Even to the last days of those villages during World War II, one could identify where a Mennonite lived by looking at the garden.

In Russia, too, flower gardens added beauty to the entire village. Shade trees surrounded the yards. Every family had its own orchard and vegetable garden as well. Tulip beds testified to the Dutch heritage and background of the settlers.

The Werder Flower Garden

We have no descriptions from Mennonite women detailing their gardens in the Vistula Delta. However, Werder chronicler Siegfried Rosenberg describes the flowers of those meticulously manicured gardens and allows us a glimpse of their beauty. In addition to seasonal perennials which bloomed throughout the spring and summer — early crocuses, snowdrops, bluebells, lilacs, tulips, narcissus, many varieties of roses, Easter lilies, gladiolus and chrysanthemums — the women planted from the following:

pansies	petunias
snapdragons	zinnias
forget-me-nots	bachelor's buttons
Canterbury bells	impatiens
lupine	asters
verbena	poppies
marigolds	sunflowers

A Touch of Color and Beauty — Flower Gardens in Russia

We are fortunate to have women among us who still remember their youthful days in Russia. Mary Dirks Janzen provides a vivid description of her family's garden.

Mary Dirks Janzen: Along the street in the village of Gnadenfeld were about four rows of tulips and one row of skunk lilies. Not far from the cherry trees were a few plants of hyssop and some violets. I loved the hyssop. It resembled myrtle and could be used for playing wedding or funeral. We did this frequently since we attended all weddings and all funerals in our church from the time we learned to walk.

There were rose bushes in a number of places in our yard and orchard. We had lots of roses, but only one bush of snowballs. We had lilac bushes on the right hand side of the path leading to the *Schulensteg* [school path]. There was a garden bench where we liked to sit and enjoy the beauty of the orchard. It seems that nowhere on earth are there lilacs like those two or three bushes in Gnadenfeld. The clusters were enormous and the fragrance potent.

Mia Reimer DeFehr grew up on the large Reimer estate in the Kuban. Their home was surrounded by a lovely garden. A row of linden and chestnut trees bordered the picket fence near the main street. The front garden was often a riot of color with some twenty varieties of roses, tulips, lilies, narcissus, red and yellow begonias, forget-me-nots, larkspur, buttercups and poppies. Tiny border flowers lined the many pathways and there were numerous ornamental shrubs.

My husband Alden Voth's great-great grandparents, Johannes A. and Elisabeth Isaac Fast, arrived in Kansas in 1873 from Annenfeld, Crimea. In a letter to the Fasts' children still in Russia, Johannes Fast urges his children to bring many things with them, among them seeds.

There are all kinds of flowers here which we do not know, but similar to our wild roses and a kind of aster, and many more. And now, dear daughter, when you come, bring seeds for carnations, a few tulip bulbs, and if possible, a small rose bush. The latter may be difficult.

Tiep Heenatjes (Little chickens)

Tiep Hee-na-tjes, tiep Hee-na-tjes, Waut doo jie opp däm Hoff? Jie ple-kje aul dee Bloom-tjes auf, Jie moa-ke daut too groff. Dee Ma-me woat junt schel-le, Dee Pa-pa woat junt schlo-ne. Tiep Hee-na-tje, tiep Hee-na-tje, Woo woat et die dan go-ne?

Translation

Little chickens, little chickens,
What are you doing on our yard?
You are picking all the flowers,
And throwing them into the dust.
Mother will scold you,
Father will hit/spank you.
Little chickens, little chickens,
How will you feel then?

Vegetable Gardening in Russia

The Ukraine, where the Mennonites settled in the eighteenth century, is blessed with rich, deep, black soil, abundant rain and a mild climate. It is one of the most fertile croplands in the world. For centuries the Ukraine was called "the breadbasket of Europe." Plowing, sowing and reaping set the rhythm of life in every home. In the following sections Mennonite women share the joy and love their mothers and grandmothers found in their gardens and orchards.

A Gnadenfeld Garden

Mary Dirks Janzen: In the village of Gnadenfeld there were two fields just beyond the windbreak that we alternately used as vegetable gardens for such large items as watermelon, cantaloupe, potatoes, cucumbers and, on occasion, corn, milo or millet. We had a Russian name for this garden or field, *Baschtan.* It was huge and took a crew to keep the weeds out. There were long rows of potatoes and watermelon. Since it rained at least every two weeks, the weeds came faster than the tender plants, so we had to work on hands and knees to separate the watermelon sprouts from the weeds.

My sister Agatha was the baker at our house. The rest of us, plus a number of peasant boys and girls, did the hoeing. We enjoyed working, visiting, teasing and, of course, singing. At noon we packed our hoes on our shoulders and walked home for lunch. An old Russian peasant man was our watchman. He lived in a little thatched shelter in an adjoining field. We would bring him one hot meal and supply him with bread and *Salo* [salt pork] for the rest of his meals. Surely he must have recognized nature's beauty as a gift from God. How else could he have been so content in his little thatched hut?

Helen Pankratz Siemens: In the Ukraine we usually planted the garden about the beginning of April. By early or middle May some vegetables were ready to eat. Gardens were usually behind the houses. When we worked in the garden with the Russian servants, we talked Russian with them and sang all the Russian songs.

Johann Cornies (1789–1848)

Johann Cornies, the master farmer from the Molotschna Colony, and chairman of the influential Agricultural Society (a lifelong government appointment), wielded tremendous influence in shaping the life of the entire Molotschna region and unifying agricultural methods on the various Mennonite farms.

Cornies, an ambitious young man, determined to make the colony a success. He operated a model farm, eventually cultivating 25,000 acres in addition to raising and breeding horses, cattle and sheep. He also had a large nursery from which he furnished the surrounding colonists with seedling trees. On his own land he planted a forest which numbered in a short time 68,000 trees.

In 1845 over half a million fruit and forest trees were found in the Molotschna alone. Six years later there were over five million trees in forty-seven Molotschna villages plus 300,000 mulberry trees.[2] Alleys of trees were planted along roads and between villages. Every farmer had to plant a certain number of fruit trees each year.

The powerful Cornies worked tirelessly to improve Molotschna agricultural methods. In addition he advised farmers on gardening and orchard practices. Every colonist was required to maintain a prescribed orchard. Katharine Nickel in her book, *Seed from the Ukraine,* relates an incident of one colonist who concentrated on growing cherries in his orchard. Cornies insisted he pull some of the trees and plant a variety in their stead—apples, apricots, plums, pears and gooseberries. His children were not to go begging of the neighbors for these other fruits. It was Cornies' plan that each villager raise all the different kinds of fruit in his own orchard and take good care of them.[3]

Russian Orchards

Women who lived in the Chortitza and Molotschna colonies speak with a near-reverence of the damson *(Kjräkjle)* plums grown there. *Kjräkjle* make jams and jellies second to none. Their deep blue color and intense flavor turn ordinary *Plauts* dough into a summer feast and make elegant Christmas *Perieschkje* and filling for cookies.

The bright red sour cherries which grew in the Mennonite orchards were likely morello. They grow in Central Russia and in the Ukraine.[4] In fact, the correct translation for Anton Chekhov's *The Cherry Orchard* is *The Morello Cherry Orchard*. Juicy morellos made coffee cake fit for the czar and fresh cherry *Perieschkje* impossible to resist. In America morellos grow only in the northern United States and Canada.

Anna von Kampen Funk: There were hazelnuts, walnuts and mulberries on every farm. Each yard had a few trees. There were grapes on some places as well as sour cherries, apples, apricots and flowering bushes. There were damson plums, white plums and Italian plums.

Mary Dirks Janzen: There was a huge pear tree along with several cherry trees in our orchard in Gnadenfeld. Small pigs running free came to eat the cherries and crack the pits with their teeth. The piglets were like pets. We also had young apple trees.

Estate orchards rarely had the trees lined up as do commercial orchards. The fruit trees blended with chestnut and linden trees, flower beds and little sanded paths. Mia Reimer DeFehr, who grew up on a large estate in the Kuban, describes the orchard.

Mia Reimer DeFehr: Behind our house was a large vegetable garden surrounded by a hedge. Back of this flourished a vineyard of purple and white grapes as well as strawberries, raspberries, gooseberries and currants. Lining all this was a small forest of poplar and walnut trees. Benches had been placed there for rest and pleasure. An avenue of ash trees led to the old cherry orchard. This was a favorite trysting place for the children and young people. How quickly they climbed the enormous old trees and picked from their choice of different varieties of cherries and filled their baskets to the brim. So many cherries were popped into eager mouths that they scarcely found room for the picnic lunch they had brought.[5]

Remembering the Chortitza Summer of 1919

N.J. Kroeker: Summer and fall of the year 1919 ushered in with the biggest promise in crops that was ever seen. It was evident that God's grace was showered upon us. Abundant rainfall and sunshine descended making the gardens and fields produce crops almost beyond dreams. Every Mennonite household stocked up from the gardens which were annually dug by spading and our cellars began to fill up. Not only the fields yielded abundance but also the gardens and orchards. The branches of the cherry, apricot, apple, pear and plum trees were bending low, yielding as never before.[6]

*   *   *

1919 had another side to the coin. It was a time of civil war following World War I. In September of that year an army of bandits led by a former peasant worker, Nestor Makhno, moved into the Chortitza, plundering homes and destroying furniture. Men were shot without warning. The bounty of the harvest, dried fruits and long shelves with jars of honey, was smashed. The army took over barns and storage sheds. It was not long until the carefully stored abundant harvest had been depleted. Food supplies, demanded by the army, ran out and famine set in.

Gardens and Orchards of Early North American Mennonites

**When the baby's born and
the garden's planted, spring has arrived.[7]**
-Alma Barkman

In the summer of 1874 Mennonite families arrived by train in the new settlements in Kansas, Nebraska and Minnesota. When the last snow finally melted the next spring and the sun gently warmed the newly plowed prairie, the women brought out their little bags with flower seeds, carefully sorted, perhaps along with tears, from their gardens in the Ukraine. In the summer of 1875 flowers from these seeds bloomed outside the adobe houses in many of the settlements.

In August of that year a curious reporter from the Topeka, Kansas, newspaper, *The Commonwealth,* visited the Mennonite settlements and wrote: "That the Mennonite female is not destitute of an eye for the beautiful was shown by a well-kept flower garden at the south end of the house. It is true the flowers were arranged in straight rows, and there were such oldtimers as pinks, marigolds, four-o'clocks, and the like, but, after all, Solomon in all his glory was not arrayed like one of these."

A visiting writer for the *Marion Record* on August 11, 1876, reported: "When the settlers arrived the first thing they planted were flower seeds — and their yards are immense bouquets — putting American towns to shame."

Marie Harms Berg: Mamma had a large flower garden. She loved lilacs and had many kinds of posies — irises, peonies and tulips. There was a sand walk from the house to the road. She planted rows of flowers on each side. This walk had to be swept for Sundays. Mamma would take her guests to look at the flowers. We also had to sweep around the house.

Mariam Penner Schmidt: At Grandmother Penner's we had a back porch out of the kitchen, leading to the barn. Between the house and barn Grandma had a fairly large spot — all her own — which was her flower garden. As the daughters grew older and could take over the housework, she spent more and more of her day in that garden among her flowers.

Vegetable Gardening

Mariam Penner Schmidt: The diet of the early settlers was limited and monotonous, especially in winter. To add flavor and variety to the everyday foods, women grew a variety of herbs and spices. Every garden had a bed of dill, parsley and summer savory to be used in soups. Anise and caraway were planted for their seeds which were used in cooking and baking. My grandparents always had a wonderful garden. Grandpa Penner raised hops along the fence for Grandma's yeast. She always had enough to supply neighbors with yeast.

Helen Pankratz Siemens: We enjoyed gardening. First we harvested the lettuce and radishes and how much fun it was to pull the first onions. The onion greens and beet leaves were used to make *Krutborscht* [a spring soup made with greens]. Then we needed fresh potatoes so we would sneak a few from several plants for our soup. During wheat harvest we dug potatoes. The dill was used for making cucumbers [pickles]. We planted cantaloupe in the same spot where the potatoes had grown. The raw tomatoes were delicious at noon and evening meals.

Marie Loewen Franz: One forenoon on a quiet warm day on our farm near Ingalls, Kansas, Mother and several of us children were hoeing weeds in the potato patch when suddenly a large snake entangled with Mother's legs around the ankles. Of course she was frantic and so were we. At the moment we didn't know that it was a harmless one. With our help and the hoe she had in her hands, we soon eliminated the snake. But Mother was so shaken, she had to quit and go to the house.[8]

Moon Planting

A modern scientific gardener might scoff at the idea of planting during certain phases of the moon. According to ancient lore, those crops which mature underground — beets, potatoes, carrots, turnips — thrive when the seeds are planted in the "dark of the moon" or the waning phase, especially during the third quarter.

Crops which mature above the soil surface — beans, lettuce, corn, cucumbers — should be planted in the "light of the moon," the period between new moon and full moon or the waxing phase.

Considered superstition by many, some early Mennonite gardeners adhered faithfully to this philosophy. After all, it didn't hurt to be on the safe side, did it?

Plow the Dew Under

Marie Harms Berg: My mother, Anna Wiebe Harms, planted garden as early in spring as it seemed safe. My sister had a book called *Plow the Dew Under.* Mother insisted that we get up early and heap the dewy earth around the bean and cabbage plants. Next we packed hay and straw around the plants. Potatoes done this way never needed tending till they were dug. Tomatoes, peas and cabbage had to be hoed often since we had no irrigation.

Atchison Champion, May 4, 1882: The Mennonite settlers believed in "ploughing the dew under" in the morning and did not stop till the dew fell in the evening.

A Summer Treat — Roasting Ears

The Mennonites in Russia raised corn, but it was not considered fit for human consumption. However, in the New World, they rapidly adopted it, learning from their American neighbors.

Minnie Jost Krause: Roasting ears were a regular summer treat. Everyone loved a good mess of corn straight from the garden or field. It made a wonderful dinner with fried chicken, mashed potatoes and gravy. For about a week during the summer, corn was at its peak and Mother fixed it almost daily. Later when the kernels were more mature, Mother cut the corn off the cob and fried it in butter.

Grandmother's Berry Patch

Mariam Penner Schmidt: We had a big strawberry patch and lots of raspberry, gooseberry and currant bushes. How often I had to pick berries, under protest, when I would so much rather have been playing. I remember in the raspberry and strawberry season being awakened early, before the day became too hot, to pick berries. Aunt Helen would dress me in a long-sleeved dress. Because of the morning dew there were so many mosquitoes and this dress afforded good protection from them. I wore a bonnet, *Schlenta Hoot,* on my head which also protected my neck. I never did learn to enjoy the berrying season, though I loved eating the berries. In the winter we had lots of lovely jam for our *Zwieback* and bread.

From Prairie Grass to Fruit Orchards

In May of 1882, seven years after the immigrants arrived in Kansas, a reporter for the Atchison, Kansas, *Champion,* again visited the Mennonite settlements. "Another source of pride was the apricots. The seed was brought from Russia, and the trees bore plentifully last year and the Mennonites, taking them to Newton as a lunch, were agreeably surprised by an offer of $3 a bushel for them. Peter Schmidt showed us all his arboreal treasures; apples, cherries, peaches, apricots, pears, all in bearing, where seven years ago the wind in passing found only waving prairie grass."

At the time of the 1885 Marion County Agricultural Census, the 1874 immigrants' orchards were thriving. My husband's Great-Grandfather Flaming had forty bearing cherry trees, plus numerous others. On the farm of Elder Wilhelm Ewert near Bruderthal there were thirty peach trees, four pear trees, thirty apple trees, ten cherry trees and two plum trees. But the Peter Funk farm may have topped them all with a 200-tree peach orchard along with twelve apple trees, four pear trees and two cherry trees. The Funks maintained a one-third-acre vineyard while the Ewerts had one-eighth of an acre in grapes.[9]

Uncle Dan G. Jost recalls his own grandfather's orchard — not the number of trees, but the way it looked, the taste of the apples and the singing of the birds.

Grandfather's Orchard *by Dan G. Jost*

My grandparents, the Peter Josts, came from the village of Pragenau in the Molotschna and settled in the tiny, pioneering village of Alexanderfeld, near Hillsboro, Kansas. Grandfather Jost built a regular Mennonite-style house from adobe bricks. He and his family planted a large garden and an orchard with a great variety of trees, as did every homestead. They also planted numerous mulberry trees and used the branches and leaves to feed the silkworms. The cocoons were sold to a place in Peabody.

I remember many of the fruits from the orchard. The early June apple, when ripe, was quite tart; usually red stripes covered part of it. There was a summer apple, which tasted somewhat like the yellow delicious. Another tree was a cross between a pear and an apple — very flavorful. There was a special apple tree which was used for dried apples, and a crab apple for pickling. Still another apple tree gave fruit with a cinnamon flavor. When ripe it was yellow, juicy and tasty. There were winter apples (Keefer) which had to be put away and there was a Winesap tree. Ben Davis, the late apples, were stored in the basement or in a cave covered with straw where they stayed fresh and juicy till midwinter.

The garden was a paradise for birds in summer — mockingbird, brown thrush, king bird, hoot owl, wren, killdeer, cardinal, bluejay, yellow bird and pigeon hawk. On the pond there were wild doves, mud hens and a flock of other birds too numerous to mention. Yes, there were large walnut and cottonwood trees with the chatter of squirrels and the barking of coons at night.

Other Orchard Memories

Mary Pankratz: In late summer we collected countless bushels of apples and pears, which were carefully stored in straw or wheat in the barn. The fruity fragrance from the barn, full of stored memories, is an intoxicating memory.

Minnie Jost Krause: Dad had a big orchard right east of the house with apples, plums, peaches and pears. Sometimes we couldn't wait for the peaches to ripen and we would eat them green and have stomach ache that night. Mother also had a long row of gooseberries. We would make gallons of gooseberry jelly. We would pick mulberries and have mulberry and gooseberry pie. We had lots of apples, early and late. Some of the early apples were ripe about threshing time. They were called *Schopsnäs* [sheep's nose in Low German]. Grandfather Peter Jost probably brought the seeds from Russia. We often had fresh apple dumplings or pie for the threshers from this apple. We had at least six varieties of apples.

Whatever Happened to Those Old Apple Varieties?

During the first three hundred years of European settlement of North America, immigrants brought with them their favorite apple varieties and steadily spread them across the length and breadth of the land. All of Europe's best apples were brought to America, where they thrived, apparently almost as well as the immigrants themselves.

By the early 1900s several dozen European and American varieties had become highly regarded and established in both private and large farm orchards.

Then commercialization of the fruit industry took over and the wide variety of available apples began declining. Many older varieties "with unique flowers and unpretentious skins were abandoned for large, pretty, but often far less tasty varieties," says Dr. Tom Lloyd, who started the Preservation Apple Tree Company of Mt. Gretna, PA. Dr. Lloyd has developed dwarf apples from some of the old favorite varieties. His trees are supplied to nurseries all over the country or directly to the customer. For information write to Preservation Apple Tree Company, PO Box 279, Mount Gretna, PA. 17064. I wonder if he carries *Schopsnäs*.

A VERY GOOD *VARENIKJE* DOUGH RECIPE

The day after Thanksgiving the younger cousins in our Jost family gather at the farm home of Clint and Diana Jost at Burdick, Kansas, for an old-fashioned Low German meal. The men and boys roam the fields and rolling hills hunting quail. In the spacious old-fashioned kitchen the women and girls busily roll out huge batches of *Varenikje* dough, filling dozens of *Varenikje* pockets with cottage cheese.

At noon thirty to forty grownups and children from as far away as Texas, California and Wisconsin feast on the foods of our grandparents. Some prefer *Varenikje* boiled, others are adamant they should be boiled and fried, while a few request theirs just plain fried. However they are prepared, everyone loves *Varenikje* accompanied by hefty portions of country sausage. Diana Jost, a home economics teacher, provided this recipe. It may be doubled and tripled.

2 cups all-purpose flour	2 eggs
½ tsp. baking powder	1 cup heavy whipping cream
1 tsp. salt	

Combine flour, baking powder and salt and stir together. Beat eggs lightly. Combine with cream. Gradually work in the flour mixture. Allow dough to stand, covered, for an hour or more before using. Roll dough out quite thin and cut into 3-inch circles.

Place a heaping teaspoon of Cottage Cheese Filling on each circle. Fold over and pinch edges together tightly.

Drop *Varenikje* into a large kettle of boiling, salted water. Boil 5–8 minutes. Drain in a colander and brown in a heavy skillet.

Serve with gravy and country sausage.

COTTAGE CHEESE FILLING

2–2½ cups dry curd cottage cheese
2–3 egg yolks
Salt and pepper to taste.

Mix all ingredients together. Use as a filling for *Varenikje*.

CREAM GRAVY

There are many variations of this gravy. Melt 2–3 Tbsp. butter in frying pan and allow to cook until slightly browned. Add 1 cup heavy sour cream (preferably farm-style) and a dash of salt and heat through. Fried ham or sausage drippings add a good flavor.

SUMMER FRUIT VARENIKJE
(Obst Varenikje)

One of summer's pleasures is fruit-filled *Varenikje*. A variety of fruits — strawberries, blueberries, cherries or plums combined with a flour and sugar mixture — make good fillings. Prepare as for cottage cheese *Varenikje,* substituting a fruit filling. Serve sprinkled with sugar and a dollop of sour cream.

ℋELENA PETERS' FRENCH STEAK

Mix together about ½ cup flour, ½ tsp. salt and ⅛ tsp. pepper. Cut 2 lbs. of round steak into serving pieces. If desired, you may pound the steak with a steak hammer or the edge of a heavy plate, dredging until most of the flour is absorbed.

Melt a little lard or butter in a heavy cast-iron skillet and brown meat well on both sides. Add small, peeled onions and cover with water.

Cover tightly and simmer in oven about 2 hours at 275° to 300°F, or until done. Add 1 cup sour cream or sweet cream with buttermilk added. Do not boil. Just heat through. Serve gravy over jacket potatoes. This meal is even better when warmed over two or three times.

—Helen Peters Epp

Food Preservation

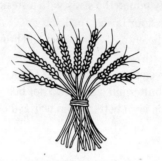

One year we put up seven
hundred quarts of food from
the garden and orchard.
We had ten or twelve gallons
of sauerkraut in big crocks.
— *Minnie Jost Krause*

Food Preservation

Summer in the Russian Mennonite home was one busy round of preparing food for the winter. Much of it was dried. Much more was canned. The attic and cellar literally bulged with food. The farm wife relied on her own little supermarket right there at home. Every farmstead was a very self-sufficient place.

The Bountiful Attic in Russia

Arnold Dyck: The farmhouse is like a fortress, prepared for a long siege. Its loft holds the most precious commodity, the newly-harvested grain. Three-foot-high board walls divide the whole floorspace into partitions filled with grain — above all, wheat. The whole year's crop lies here in a three-foot layer, weighting the stout floor beams down so much that they bend and must be supported by emergency props to keep them from bursting.

On the thick planks of a special scaffold in the loft lies the wheaten flour in heavy five-*pood* sacks [16.38 kg = 1 *pood* or 36.11 lbs = 5 *poods*]. There may not be fewer than five. From these sacks come many a delicious roll, many a fluffy loaf, pancakes, rolled cakes, waffles, biscuits, *Varenikje,* peppernuts for Christmas and *Portselkje* for New Year.

The contents of the big smoke room, connected with the chimney, are fatter and richer food. Sixteen to twenty hams and countless numbers of sausages, all round and heavy, make quite a show. It is necessary to send a John or a Hal when a new ham must be transported from the smoke room to the pantry. One must admit that the loft is chuck full of all kinds of goods and supplies.

In the roomy cellar under the pantry one must be especially careful where one sets one's foot. First there are potatoes, red and white. Oh yes, the potatoes. That there has been a time when a farmhouse had no potatoes is unthinkable for a Hochfeld housewife. Down in the cellar stand the pickled meat barrels, the little brine barrels with salted meat, big and small barrels of pickled watermelons and dill pickles, countless jam jars and syrup jars and the cabinet with fresh fruit. Also here are the watermelons left over after the best are buried in heaps of wheat in the house loft, where they remain fresh, sometimes until Christmas.[1]

My Mother's Cellar in Kansas *by Helen Jost Malin*

To get into Mother's cellar you had to go through a door in the pantry floor. The cellar door was made of boards and had a leather pull latch. As you walked down the steps, you passed a long row of canned goods on the right side. There were so many jars of fruit on those shelves, that they bent and sagged. Mother always canned the fruit in two-quart jars. Underneath the fruit shelves would be barrels with *Päakjelfleesch* [port in salt brine] and *Siltfleesch* [head cheese].

In one corner on the smooth dirt floor were potatoes. In the other corner were apples. Strings suspended from the ceiling held a bar across which we hung our sausages.

We kept a hundred-pound sack of sugar and a hundred-pound sack of raisins. Uncle Peter

Golbek always sent a big gunnysack full of raisins and prunes from California. There would also be stone crocks of lard and *Jreeweschmolt* [crackling lard]. A flour sack stood on the stairway. There was always at least one extra fifty-pound sack of flour on a shelf. Often six sacks of flour were lined in a row. Dad would take a load of wheat to town and have it ground.

There were hams, too, but most of them were stored in the oat bins in the barn. Bacon hung in strips. Apple butter was usually stored in a crock. We always had a long shelf of jelly stored in fruit jars.

When Mother made pickles in the summer, she put them in a crock. Later we canned them. We also kept big jars of sauerkraut in the cellar. And we always had a supply of small, pickled watermelons.

I loved the smell of my Mother's cellar. It was always fun to go down there.

Other Ways Food was Preserved

Frieda Pankratz Suderman: In the days before chickens had been bred to lay eggs in the wintertime, it was customary to preserve eggs in waterglass. The Pankratz chicken barn did not hold a big flock, but, before the weather got very cold, there were more eggs than needed, so we laid them in stone jars and covered them with the solution called waterglass. This liquid looked for all the world like pure water, but it felt very cold when one's hand was plunged into it to retrieve the eggs.[2]

Mariam Penner Schmidt: In fall, just before the last frost, Grandmother pulled the tomato vines and hung them in the granary. Sometimes we had tomatoes until Thanksgiving.

Minnie Jost Krause: Carrots weren't canned. A hole was dug in the ground below the frost level to store vegetables such as carrots, beets and turnips. Cabbage was wrapped in paper to keep it clean and also stored in a hole or trench. It remained crisp until as late as March.

Frieda Pankratz Suderman: Sometimes Papa buried apples and potatoes in a pit southeast of the house. He would dig a circular hole about two feet deep and line it with straw. The things to be buried were carefully arranged in the center of this pit and covered with another layer of straw. Papa covered the whole thing with earth, making sure the outside edges were protected. After Christmas when the pit was emptied, the apples were still crackly firm but they had a faint taste of straw. The Regier farm had an apple cellar in which the winter apples were kept. Most of the apples were packed in wooden boxes and stacked almost to the ceiling. Culls were kept in bins near the bottom of the rock steps. That was where we were allowed to help ourselves to eating apples.[3]

Drying Fruit in West Prussia

Before the days of canning, when the Mennonites lived in the Vistula Delta, drying fruit was the main method of preservation. Every old farmstead had its own bakehouse with a *Pflaumendarre,* or plum drying kiln. For proper drying it was necessary to have a good fire for this operation. At the same time, the heat needed to be steady and even to dry nine containers of fruit simultaneously. If the fire was too hot, the plums popped open. Plum drying, like preparation for *jedräjde Aupelstekja* (dried apple slices), became a neighborhood project in which old and young joined. According to Siegfried Rosenberg, the young, especially, used those days as a time for singing and storytelling along with the work.

Drying Fruit In Russia

Agatha Epp: We had a big garden with large old trees hanging full of apples and pears. We sold and we gave them away. All the poor of the village came with their *Kinderwagen* to get fruit. We dried it. Our David liked to fill his pockets with dried apricots to eat at school.[4]

Mary Dirks Janzen: All summer there would be drying racks, covered with muslin, where sliced fruits would dry for winter's use. On the racks you found apricots, cherries, apples and pears. To make prunes we had an oven where the plums slowly steamed, all covered to keep their moisture in. Our parents, like all others in our village of Gnadenfeld, were thrifty. They carefully gathered all dropped-off fruits and used them for drying.

Apple Drying Time in the United States

Helen Peters Epp: My Grandmother Hiebert and the aunts would dry apples and store them in wooden barrels in the attic of the old sod house. One barrel had sugared-down apples. This was our candy. Often women from neighboring villages walked over to help Grandmother during "*schnitzing* time" [cutting time].[5] It took a bushel of apples to make one and a half gallons of dried apples. Through the years she probably dried wagonloads of apples.

I loved Grandmother's apple pie. She cooked the apples until done, added sugar and shoved them to the back of the stove. There they gently stewed until dark brown. Her pie was delicious hot or cold.

Frieda Pankratz Suderman: Apple varieties that were not "keepers" were used for drying. To process the apples for drying, Mrs. Janzen, the lady who often helped with time consuming extra work, came for the day and other women sat in the dining room with pans of apples in their laps. They peeled and snipped as they talked. Apple peeling days were fun because the conversation was interesting and the apple slices we snitched from the stone crocks placed conveniently on nearby chairs were the most delicious in the world.

When crocks were filled, they were taken up the stairs and spread on the tin roof of the kitchen, which could be reached through the south bedroom window. The tin roof was so hot that the flies were not interested, but to make sure they would not have a chance, window screens were used to cover the apple slices. By evening they were limp and juiceless. Then they were rolled up in the muslin on which they had been spread and taken in for the night. Next morning they were spread out again. After a few days the drying process was finished, and apples were stored in gallon syrup buckets with tight lids or in flour sacks. Dried apples make delicious pies, and, when stewed with raisins, they are superior to apple sauce.[6]

Over the Canning Kettle

Canning revolutionized food preservation. Until the late 1700s the main method of preservation was drying. Around that time Napoleon actually offered a prize to any person who could develop a successful method for preserving foods. A French candy maker, after experimenting for ten years, discovered that if food could be kept away from air, it would remain edible for a long time.

Canning became widespread and common, but nobody understood why it worked or even why some food kept and some spoiled. Louis Pasteur's discovery of bacteria in the mid 1800s led to better methods of canning.

In 1858 John L. Mason invented the Mason jar which permitted a metal cap to be screwed onto a glass jar. In 1902 Alexander Kerr perfected a lid with a sealing gasket of rubber attached to the lid. The two-piece lid we know today was invented in 1914.

Mennonite women who came to America in the 1870s benefited from these improvements and new techniques, while those who stayed in Russia continued to use the older methods.

Canning in Russia

Anna von Kampen Funk: In Russia canning was done in several ways. Really it was preserving. Cherries, gooseberries and red currants were placed in narrow-necked bottles. The fruit was dropped into the jars, one by one. The bottles were sealed with a cork, which in poorer times was made of dry corn husks and sealed with tallow.

Beans were salted down in crocks, as was sauerkraut. A piece of cloth with a wooden lid or plate was placed on top and weighted down with a stone. The mold which formed was cleaned off each week and the cloth, stone and lid were washed.

Betty Schmidt Epp: Fruit was canned in narrow-necked bottles. When taking out the fruit, we used a long hook. Vegetables were never canned.

Filling the Fruit Cellar in the United States

Minnie Jost Krause: One year we put up seven hundred quarts of food from the garden and orchard. We had ten or twelve gallons of sauerkraut in big crocks.

Bertha Nickel: All Mennonites had orchards. We canned all summer, often as many as three hundred quarts of fruits and vegetables.

Marie Harms Berg: I remember canning forty-eight quarts of beets one day. We pulled and capped them, scrubbed them and put them into the large iron kettle to boil till soft. Next we slipped the skins off and packed them into well-cleaned glass jars. Meanwhile Mamma prepared a juice with vinegar, water, sugar and spices. We filled the jars with juice and processed them for an hour or so in the kettle. After the beet jars were lifted out, we closed them tightly. Then they were set to cool. Next day we carried all forty-eight quarts of beets into the cellar. This constituted the supply for the winter. They were so good as a side dish with fried potatoes.

Frieda Pankratz Suderman: The method used to preserve corn must have destroyed every vitamin that was in it, but since no one knew about vitamins it did not matter. Field corn was cleaned and cut from the cob. Then it was cooked until almost done using a cup each of salt, sugar and water for each twelve cups of corn. It was sealed in glass jars until needed, but with all that salt it was not edible as it came from the jar. It had to be rinsed, soaked in clear water for hours, drained and finally cooked again before it could be served.[7]

Tina Friesen Klassen: We canned grapes, cold packed in half-gallon jars. In fact, all our fruit was canned in half-gallon jars. We had a cherry orchard of around twenty trees. Our orchard produced lots of apples, pears, apricots and peaches.

ſTINKY CHEESE

Take real dry cottage cheese. [Anna takes the top off homemade buttermilk.] Put into a crock and let stand in a warm place 4 – 5 days, stirring now and then. Cover with a damp cloth. Add salt and caraway seed. Roll into balls. Let dry until ripe, 5 – 7 days.

—Anna Epp Entz (Mrs. J.E.)
— Helen Peters Epp

OLD-FASHIONED SPICY DILLS

Anna Rosenfeld learned the art of making good dill pickles from her mother. These old-fashioned cucumber dills have a slightly piquant flavor — perhaps reminiscent of cucumber pickles in the Ukraine.

Mrs. Rosenfeld helped edit the enduring *Mennonite Treasury of Recipes*. She has been active at the Mennonite Village Museum in Steinbach, where she lends historical information as well as cooking and quilting skills. This recipe appears in the Steinbach cookbook.

100 medium-sized cucumbers
½ cup pickling salt to each 4 quarts water
Fresh dill stalks
Cherry or grape leaves
Small, hot red peppers
Alum

Fresh garlic
10 quarts water
1 quart vinegar
2 cups pickling salt
1 cup mustard seed (optional)
1 cup horseradish, shredded (optional)

Make a brine out of ½ cup salt to each 4 quarts of water. Soak the cucumbers in this overnight. The next morning drain and wipe dry. Now pack cucumbers in layers in crocks or jars and between each layer of cucumbers, place a thin layer of dill. (You may use leaves, stalks or seeds.) Add a cherry or grape leaf every two or three layers. Add a small, hot red pepper, a piece of alum the size of a bean and a clove of garlic to each quart of pickles.

Boil 10 quarts water, vinegar and salt for 5 minutes. If using mustard seed and horseradish, add at this time. Let the brine stand overnight and then pour over the pickles. Fill jars or crocks with cold brine. Cover, but do not seal tightly until they have finished fermenting, which will take about 3–4 weeks.

Should the brine become cloudy and sour, drain and replace with fresh brine. Heat, cover and seal, or pour a layer of paraffin over the top of each jar. These dills will keep all winter in a cool place.

—*Anna Derksen Rosenfeld*

*W*HOLE BRINED WATERMELON IN A BARREL
(*Süare Arbusen*)

Helen Peters Epp: This is a very old recipe, brought directly from Russia in 1874. These pickles are very good served with fried potatoes. This is the original recipe, reprinted exactly as it was written.

50 gallon barrel or 10 gallon crocks
Small 2–3½ lb. watermelons
Pulp of several melons

10 lbs. meat salt
2 lbs. salt
Dill and cherry or grape leaves

Place melons in barrel. Fill remainder of space with clear water. Lots of dill, grape leaves. Leave until the pulp becomes transparent. You may add green tomatoes. Weight pulp down with a board. Put smaller crock on top of water on top. Cover with tea towel. Let stand 5–6 weeks.

—*Helen Peters Epp*

ℬERRY JELLY

Pick whatever kind of berries are available. Wash and place in a pan with a small amount of water — only enough to keep from scorching. As the berries cook, they produce their own juice. Berries should be soft. Cool.

Strain the juice through a double layer of cheesecloth. (Women used to use cloth flour and sugar sacks). Squeeze out all the juice. Measure juice and place in a jelly kettle. Add one cup of sugar for every cup of juice. Bring to a slow boil, stirring often. Keep boiling until it makes jelly. (Pectin content is higher in some berries, so less sugar is required.)

ℬERRY JAMS

9 cups crushed berries
6 cups sugar

Pick whatever kind of berries are available. Wash. Combine berries and sugar. Bring slowly to boil, stirring occasionally until sugar dissolves. (As they cook, they produce their own juice.) Cook rapidly to, or almost to, jelling point, depending upon whether a firm or soft jam is desired. As mixture thickens, stir frequently to prevent sticking. Pour into sterilized jars. Seal with paraffin or sealer lids.

Mie Hungat (I'm Hungry)

Mie hun-gat, mie pun-gat, mie schlac-kat de Buck, Bie
Grooss-ma em Kjal-la, doa ess ee-ne Kruck/Wruck. Wäa
dee, dee wel ha-be, dee kjemt en sajcht, Bie
Grooss-ma em Kjal-la, doa ess ee-ne Kruck/Wruck.

Translation

I'm hungry, I'm hungry, my stomach is flapping around,
At grandmother's, in the basement, here is a crock/turnip,
Whoever, whoever wants it, simply comes and says so,
At grandmother's, in the basement, there is a crock/turnip.

From the Larder

The cellar and attic, the vegetable pit and the granary were Grandmother Jost's own personal grocery store, stocked with everything she needed to feed her large brood. It was from this larder that she was able to accommodate many unexpected guests and produce a complete meal without making a trip to the store or running to the neighbors. Her son Bill remembers her as "always having room for one more."

Few were the items not raised on the farm — coffee, spices, sugar. Trips to the store in town to lay in those extras were infrequent and often made by the men, as the following story indicates.

Ann Eck Sykes: My father would pick the coldest, snowiest time of winter to go to town for supplies. He would bring back a hundred pounds of flour, rice, corn meal, a little sugar, herring in a keg, salt and coal. He would arrive home late at night with the wagon, icicles dripping from his beard and mustache, and call for one of us children to hold the lantern while he unhitched the horses and unloaded the wagon. Sometimes we girls stood out in the snow in our nightgowns holding the lantern.

Keeping Foods Cool

Mariam Penner Schmidt: We had no refrigeration. Grandmother Penner kept food cool by putting it into the basement in the coolest, darkest place.

Helen Peters Epp: Cooling was done in the well. After dinner a trip was made outside to return the butter and milk to the well. They were placed in a box and let down on a rope. In winter there was the cold back porch for storing cookie dough and special foods. In winter the pantry also proved to be a fairly cool spot for food.

Harvesting Ice from Lake and Pond

Dan G. Jost: There was an ice plant in Hillsboro, but when we lived on the home place we made ice from the pond. The ice cutter would stand and push a saw blade up and down. He would cut slabs maybe about sixty pounds apiece, and we would haul them to town to store them in one of the buildings Dad bought. We packed sawdust around the chunks of ice. Ice was always available.

The Early Icebox

What we call a refrigerator was originally called an icebox and was advertised as early as 1897 in the *Sears & Roebuck* catalog. The interior was a zinc-lined insulated cabinet. The iceman delivered ice by cart or truck. Ice blocks, covered with large dark blankets, came in chunks weighing 25, 50 or 100 lbs. Every household bought as much ice as the icebox would hold.

On the day of ice delivery, the housewife put out an ice card in her window, indicating how much ice she wanted. The iceman picked up the chunk with tongs and swung the block over his shoulder, bringing it inside. He left a dripping trail on his way through the house to the icebox. Sometimes he felt generous and gave us small pieces of ice to hold in our hands and suck like a lollipop.

Food was stored in the lower part of the box. Ice chilled the food and retarded spoilage. It was not cold enough to store ice cream. In fact, foods from the icebox were never really cold.

"Refrigerators," as the *Sears & Roebuck* catalog called them, were available in a number of styles from a spartan model for $5.60 to a fancy model with a sideboard at $22.93.

Marie Loewen Franz: We had one of those wooden "ice chests" that resembled a storage cabinet, made of oak, with two small doors in front. The inside was lined with a rustproof metal. It had a special compartment for about a forty-pound block of ice, which the iceman brought in every three or four days, dripping water all the way through the house. It was wonderful to drink iced tea or cold lemonade or even chomp on a piece of ice. Butter wasn't runny anymore, milk did not sour and potatoes did not turn moldy. We loved the luxury of our ice chest, even though there was only a very small space for food, probably no more than two square feet. It's hard to imagine how mothers with large families got along without refrigerators or freezers at all. How well they must have planned the meals, so as not to have any leftovers.[8]

Russian
Mennonite Menus

De Kjäakjsche onn de Kaut senn emma saut.

The cook and the cat are never hungry.
— *Low German Maxim*

Waut dee Büa nijch kjant, frat hee nijch.

What the farmer doesn't recognize,
he won't eat.
— *Werder Plattdeutsch Saying*

Typical Menus from the Russian Mennonite Kitchen

Wää lang läwe well mot Tsemorjest äte
aus en Kjeisa, opp Meddach aus en Kjeenijch,
on Tseowent aus en Pracha.
He who would live long must eat like an
emperor in the morning, at noon like a king,
and in the evening like a beggar.
— *Low German Maxim*

When young Kaethe called out to her mother, "What's for dinner?" and her mother replied, "*Borscht,*" Kaethe could be sure it was Thursday. In the Kasdorf family home in Osterwick (Chortitiza Colony), they always served *Borscht* on Thursday.

In Russia, and earlier in West Prussia, it was customary in Mennonite homes to follow a weekly routine or a rotating menu. In every family there was a meat day or a *Kjielkje* day. On Fridays at the Kasdorfs it was customary to have ham or fish from the market. Almost every family had pancakes at least once a week. In the village of Lupushorst (Vistula Delta) where some of my Golbeck ancestors lived, there was this saying:

Weetst doch daut fonndoag Dinjsdach es   Don't you know that today is Tuesday
onn Muttakje bruckt de Paun.   and Mother needs the pan.
Daut jeft doch fonndoag Flinse.[1]   Today is the day for pancakes.

Anna Lohrenz: In our home on Tuesdays we always had chicken soup or chicken of some kind.

Helen Pankratz Siemens: Once a week we had *Varenikje.* We also had *Kjielkje* once a week.

Anna Derksen Rosenfeld: One day a week there were jacket potatoes on the menu. Another day: pancakes or waffles.

A routine menu simplified mealtime planning and preparation for the cook, and it satisfied hungry eaters as well. Mary Dirks Janzen adds, "The rich people ate the same menus as the rest of us, except perhaps on holidays."

Despite the best efforts of the cook, food at times must have been very monotonous. The cook was entirely dependent on food raised in the garden and what could be preserved from that. For meat she relied almost entirely on the butchering of hogs. Food was solid, satisfying and, by our standards, often rich and fatty.[2] However, the Mennonite immigrants were usually engaged in hard work — clearing the swamps, digging canals by hand, building dikes and dams — so the fat poured over noodles or potatoes was quickly burned up. Fatty dishes, even in small amounts,

Members of a large Russian Mennonite family gather in front of their parents' village home.

Rooftops of the village of Rosenthal, Chortitza Colony.

satisfied the appetite, without burdening the stomach. The Mennonite farmer of the Grosses Werder and the Chortitza and Molotschna colonies was a hearty eater, satisfied with a steady diet of meat, potatoes and *Kjielkje*.

Weddings, holidays and birthdays provided exceptions to the routine simplicity. To celebrate such events the hostess prepared more elaborate foods and baked special breads and *Kuchen*. In the Grosses Werder Mennonites were known for their fine hospitality and good food at weddings.[3]

The Russian Mennonite cuisine of the past is basically Prussian/Russian with remnants of food brought from Holland in the sixteenth century. The greatest changes in our food have come since living in North America. Today our Mennonite food is basically North American with remnants of the Prussian/Russian days, served on special occasions and at special events.

Some Typical Mennonite Foods of the Vistula Delta (ca. 1600–1800)

Meats: Pork, bacon, ribs, fried meat balls (*Klopps*), boiled ham, pork sausage, head cheese, *Bratwurst*, pickled pork, roast goose, fish, eel.

Vegetables: Potatoes, cabbage, sauerkraut, carrots, parsnips, cauliflower, peas, turnips, beets.

Cereals and Grains: Oatmeal, barley, wheat, rice.

Soups: Water base soups with flour, milk base soups with flour or quick dumplings (*Kjlieta*); milk soups with cereal, beer, vegetable, fish, fruit (*Mooss*), potato, butter, bean, barley-buttermilk, pea (porridge or gruel).

Pasta-Style: *Kjlieta, Kjielkje,* noodles, steamed dumplings.

Breads: Rye, *Semmel* (hard rolls), wheat bread, *Plautsje,* pancakes, waffles.

Festive Breads: *Stretsel* (white bread), raisin *Stretsel, Kuchen, Plauts,* poppyseed rolls, *Schnetje, Portselkje,* crullers.

Cookies: Honey cookies, *Pfefferkuchen, Päpanät, Kjrinjel.*[4]

A Weekly Family Menu in Russia

The following is a weekly menu shared by Kaethe Kasdorf Warkentin from her home in Osterwick, Chortitza Colony. "Every day we had potatoes in some form. In winter it was jacket potatoes with gravy. We never had vegetables."

A typical family sat together for meals often arranged around the table according to age. No one ate until everyone was there and the father had said the blessing. Children remained at the table until granted permission to leave.

Monday	*Kjielkje,* sausage, fried onions.
Tuesday	Potatoes in some form (mashed, cooked and salted), sauerkraut, watermelon and dill pickles.
Wednesday	Pancakes, *Rundeküake* (fritters), etc. In winter we ate them with jam and watermelon syrup. In summer mother made pancakes to go with watermelon.

257

Thursday	*Borscht, Salankje* or beef soup. Sometimes sauerkraut was made into soup with salt pork.
Friday	In summer we always had ham. Or we would have fish from the market at the Dnieper. We also had *Schnetje* and *Bobbat.*
Saturday	Beans with onion and pork, sausage or liver sausage.
Sunday	Roast beef, veal, lamb, chicken or goose.

Table Manners and Eating Patterns

Wilma Toews: Honesty and morals were probably more important than table manners. We were usually admonished not to "cut up" at the table.

Nellie Lehn: In our home we were often quiet at the table. Children were to be seen and not heard.

Mariam Penner Schmidt: Grandpa always insisted on promptness at the table. "When you are called, you must come, no dilly-dallying, because you must be there when we bow our heads and say, *"Komm Herr Jesu, sei Du unser Gast, und segne was Du uns bescheret hast. Amen."* [Come Lord, Jesus, be our guest and let this Thy food to us be blest.] And no one — NO ONE! left the table until he said, *"Danket dem Herrn, denn er ist freundlich und seine Güte währet ewiglich. Amen.* [Thank the Lord, for He is gracious and His goodness endures forever.]

Anna Epp Entz: My family was Russian Mennonite. They were more informal than the Prussians. When my husband's family [Prussian] came to visit, they stayed in the living room. When my people [Russian Mennonite] visited, they came right into the kitchen.

Menus for All Seasons from Russia

The seasonal menus in the following section were recorded by D.H. Peters, formerly of Blumengart, Chortitza Colony in the Ukraine. Peters was the *Schultze* (Low German, *Schult)* or mayor in his village from 1930–1940. In 1948, at the age of seventy, he immigrated to Hillsboro, Kansas, where he became a United States citizen and also a member of the Ebenfeld Mennonite Brethern Church. He left a very complete record of typical Mennonite village food after the turn of the century (1900s).[5]

Spring Menus

Spring menus in the Russian Mennonite home reflected several new seasonal additions. Cattle, penned up through the winter, were back grazing on new, lush pasture grass, so the family had milk at mealtime. They also had "white coffee" or coffee with cream and there was cream for the *Mooss.* A typical spring supper included clabbered milk with hard-cooked eggs and perhaps fresh garden lettuce — a kind of "soup-salad." Rhubarb, thick, red and tender from the garden, provided inspiration for a wonderful *Plauts* on Saturday night. Rhubarb also appeared in the sauce over waffles on Friday. The hens, too, were laying again so there were fresh eggs for breakfast.

Spring
April, May, June
Menus for one Week

SUNDAY

Breakfast	Noon	Faspa	Supper
Scambled Eggs*	Boiled Potatoes*	Zwieback	Fried Potatoes
Rye Bread	Cream Gravy*	Jam	Rye Bread
Zwieback	Rye Bread	Coffee/Cream*	Menjselmooss*
Jam	1 Glass Milk*		Sweet Milk*

MONDAY

Fried Potatoes w/Eggs	Kjielkje w/Onion Gravy	Bulkje	Boiled Potatoes & Fresh Cream
Bulkje	Rye Bread	Watermelon Syrup	Gravy*
Watermelon Syrup	1 Glass Milk*	Coffee/Cream*	1 Glass Milk*
Coffee/Cream*			

TUESDAY

Scrambled Eggs*	Rollküake	Bulkje	Schmauntsupp*
Rye Bread	(crullers)	Watermelon Syrup	(Clabbered Milk
Bulkje	Jam	Coffee/Cream*	w/Boiled Eggs)
Watermelon Syrup	1 Glass Milk*		Vinegar
Coffee/Cream*			Boiled Potatoes

WEDNESDAY

Fried Potatoes w/ Eggs*	Cottage Cheese	Clabbered Milk	Fried Potatoes w/Eggs
Rye Bread	Varenikje w/Sour Cream	Rye Bread	1 Glass Milk*
Bulkje	Gravy	Butter*	
Watermelon Syrup			
Coffee/Cream*			

THURSDAY

Fried Onions	Fried Ham	*Bulkje*	Egg Salad*
Rye Bread	Boiled Potatoes	Watermelon Syrup	Summer Dill
Bulkje	Sour Cream	Coffee/Cream*	Pickles*
Watermelon Syrup	Rye Bread		Clabbered Milk
Coffee/Cream*	1 Glass Milk*		

FRIDAY

Fried Potatoes	Waffles	*Bulkje*	*Joaschtnejrett**
w/Eggs*	Rhubarb Sauce*	Watermelon Syrup	(Cold Barley
Rye Bread	Clabbered Milk	Coffee/Cream	Soup)
Watermelon Syrup			Rye Bread
Coffee/Cream*			Butter*

SATURDAY

Scrambled Eggs*	Cooked Beans &	*Bulkje*	Large Rhubarb
w/Potatoes	Onion Gravy	Watermelon Syrup	Plauts*
Rye Bread	Rye Bread	Coffee/Cream*	Fruit Juice*
	Clabbered Milk		Tea

*Spring seasonal items.

Summer Menus

During the summer the garden and melon patches were at their peak. Fruits and vegetables were produced abundantly. Fruit *Plauts* was baked and served for breakfast. Sunday's dinner included lamb. There were fresh cherries for *Mooss* and *Perieschkje*. The first watermelon and cantaloupe were ready and appeared frequently at the *Faspa* table along with thick slices of white bread and butter. At other seasons of the year butter was not served for *Faspa*.

Helen Pankratz Siemens remembers summer *Faspa* time: "During the time of hard work, Mother often served *Faspa* outside under the trees where it was cool and restful. We often had bread, butter, jam and fresh cucumber pickles."

This was the time women made large crocks of summer dills which, in a few days, were crisp and slightly sour, delicious to the taste. New potatoes and fresh green beans appeared on the menu along with new boiled potatoes and sour cream gravy. The *Schnetje* for Wednesday's breakfast were made with home-rendered lard and fresh butter.

Summer
July, August, September
Menus for a Week

SUNDAY

Breakfast
Fruit *Plauts**
Coffee/Cream*

Noon
Roast Lamb*
Potatoes
Rye Bread
Fresh Fruit*
Fruit Juice*

Faspa
Rhubarb *Plauts**
Fruit Juice*
Tea

Supper
Potato Soup
  (*Bottasupp*)
Rye Bread
Butter*

MONDAY

Scrambled Eggs*
Fruit *Plauts**
Coffee/Cream

Fried Ham
Kjielkje
Rye Bread
Bulkje
Fresh Watermelon*

Bulkje
Jam
Coffee/Cream

Fish Soup
Rye Bread
Butter
Glass of Milk*

TUESDAY

Scrambled Eggs*
Bulkje
Watermelon Syrup
Coffee/Cream

Fresh Green Bean
  Soup*

Bulkje
Butter
Watermelon*
Cantaloupe*

Buttermilk Soup
Fried Potatoes
Rye Bread

WEDNESDAY

Fried Potatoes
Rye Bread
Schnetje

Rhubarb *Mooss*
Fried Ham
Rye Bread

Bulkje
Butter
Watermelon*
Cantaloupe*

Cherry *Mooss**
Fried Potatoes
Rye Bread

THURSDAY

Scrambled Eggs*
Bulkje
Watermelon Syrup
Coffee/Cream

Rhubarb *Plauts*
Clabbered Milk*

Bulkje
Jam
Coffee/Cream

Boiled Potatoes &
  Sour Cream
  Gravy*
Rye Bread
Glass Milk*

FRIDAY

Fried Potatoes	Rhubarb	*Bulkje*	*Glommsküake*
Rye Bread	*Perieschkje*	Butter	(Cottage Cheese
Bulkje	Clabbered Milk	Watermelon*	Cakes)
Watermelon Syrup		Cantaloupe*	Boiled Milk
Coffee/Cream			White Bread

SATURDAY

Scrambled Eggs*	Cooked Beans*	*Bulkje*	French Toast
Rye Bread	w/Fried Onions	Butter	(*Arme Ritter*)
Bulkje	Rye Bread	Watermelon Syrup	Sweet Milk*
Coffee/Cream	Clabbered Milk	Coffee/Cream	*Bulkje*

* Summer seasonal items

Autumn Menus

Plums of all kinds were considered a delicacy and damson plums (*Kjräkjle*) were the best loved of all. They made lovely *Plauts,* and making damson plum preserves was a common fall activity. Damsons' tangy flavor made the Christmas *Perieschkje* especially appealing. Melons, so abundant in summer, were packed into straw and lasted until Christmas. You will note they are still on the menu for almost every meal. Early December was the time of hog butchering, another of the special events of the year. It was almost like a celebration, some said. The Sunday dinner of chicken and *Bobbat* reflected the coming of cooler weather.

Autumn
October, November, December
Menus for a Week

SUNDAY

Breakfast	Noon	*Faspa*	Supper
Plum *Plauts**	Roast Chicken	Plum *Plauts*	Boiled Potatoes
Zwieback	*Bobbat* Filling	Apricot Jam	w/Cream Gravy
Tea or Coffee/	Potatoes & Gravy	Coffee/Cream	*Safflo* Oil
Cream	Watermelon		Pickled
	Cantaloupe		Watermelon

MONDAY

Fruit *Plauts*	Fried Ham	Fruit *Plauts*	Fried Noodles
Bulkje	*Kjielkje*	Watermelon	Rye Bread
Jam	Fresh Fruit		Watermelon
Coffee/Cream	Watermelon		Cantaloupe
	Cantaloupe		

TUESDAY

Fried Potatoes	Fruit *Varenikje*	*Bulkje*	*Holubtsi*
Bulkje	w/Sugar	Butter	(Cabbage Rolls)
Rye Bread	Watermelon	Watermelon	Watermelon
Jam	Cantaloupe	Cantaloupe	
Coffee/Cream			

WEDNESDAY

Fried Potatoes w/	Fresh Plum *Plauts**	*Bulkje*	Fresh Plum *Plauts**
Eggs	Watermelon	Butter	Watermelon
Bulkje	Cantaloupe	Watermelon	Cantaloupe
Jam		Cantaloupe	
Coffee/Cream			

THURSDAY

Fried Potatoes	Chicken *Borscht**	*Bulkje*	Cabbage *Borscht*
Rye Bread	Watermelon	Butter	*Bulkje*
Bulkje	Cantaloupe	Watermelon	Watermelon
Jam		Cantaloupe	Cantaloupe
Coffee/Cream			

FRIDAY

Scrambled Eggs	Fried Ham	*Bulkje*	Fried Ham
Rye Bread	*Plümemooss*	Butter	Boiled Potatoes
Bulkje	*Rye Bread*	Watermelon	Rye Bread
Jam	*Bulkje*	Cantaloupe	Watermelon
Coffee/Cream	Watermelon		Cantaloupe
	Cantaloupe		

SATURDAY

Clabbered Milk	Fried Ham	*Bulkje*	*Süaramalkjsche-*
w/Eggs &	Bean Soup	Butter	*mooss* with
Onion	Rye Bread	Watermelon	*Kjlieta* (Hot
Potatoes	*Bulkje*	Cantaloupe	sour milk soup
Dill Pickles	Watermelon		with tiny
Bulkje	Cantaloupe		noodles)
Coffee/Cream			Fresh Plum *Plauts**

* Autumn seasonal items

Winter Menus

This was the season which offered the least variety in the menu. Fresh fruits and vegetables were no longer available. Pickled tomatoes and watermelon became the "salad substitutes." Fresh pork from butchering added variety—cracklings for breakfast, sausage in the sauerkraut *Borscht* and pork jowls with noodles (*Kjielkje*). There was an ample supply of watermelon syrup served every afternoon for *Faspa* (along with white bread) and also for breakfast. Fruit-filled fritters were on the menu on Tuesday—perhaps this was New Year's Day. The fritters may have been the traditional *Portselkje* especially made for that day. Coffee was served without milk or cream. Bread was spread with watermelon syrup and occasionally jam.

Winter
January, February, March
Menus for a Week

SUNDAY

Breakfast	Noon	*Faspa*	Supper
Fried Cracklings*	Preserved Quail	White Bread	Fried Sausage*
Brown Bread	Apple *Mooss*	Jam	Baked Potatoes
Buns/*Zwieback*		Coffee	Pickled Tomatoes
Coffee			Brown Bread

MONDAY

Fried Potatoes	*Kjielkje*	*Bulkje*	Boiled Potatoes
Brown Bread	Fried Onions	Watermelon Syrup	w/Crackling
Bulkje	Fried Pork Jowl	Coffee	Fat*
Watermelon Syrup	Pickled		Pickled Tomatoes
Coffee	Watermelon		

TUESDAY

Fried Potatoes	Fruit-Filled Fritters	*Bulkje*	Butter Soup
Rye Bread	Watermelon Syrup	Watermelon Syrup	Fried Jowl*
Watermelon Syrup	Pickled	Coffee	Pickled Tomatoes
Coffee	Watermelon		

WEDNESDAY

Fried Cracklings	Smoked Sausage*	*Bulkje*	Cabbage
Rye Bread	Sauerkraut	Watermelon Syrup	*Perieschkje*
Bulkje	*Borscht**	Coffee	w/Raisins*
Watermelon Syrup	Rye Bread		Pickled Tomatoes
	Watermelon		
	Pickles		

THURSDAY

Fried Potatoes	Boiled Potatoes	*Bulkje*	*Schnetje*
Bulkje	Cracklings*	Watermelon Syrup	Watermelon Syrup
Watermelon Syrup	Watermelon	Coffee	Watermelon
Coffee	Pickles		Pickles

FRIDAY

Fried Potatoes	Cherry *Varenikje*	*Bulkje*	Fried *Varenikje*
Bulkje	Vanilla Sauce	Watermelon Syrup	Pickled Tomatoes
Coffee	Sugar	Coffee	
	Gooseberry *Mooss*		

* Winter seasonal items

Christmas Dinner (USA)

Baked Homemade Sausage
Fried Potatoes
Horseradish & Mustard
Pickles
Rye Bread
Zwieback
Plümemooss
Assorted Peppernuts & Christmas Cookies
Coffee

New Year's Day Lunch

Large platter of *Portselkje*
Coffee
Milk

Easter Dinner

Boiled Ham
Fried Potatoes
Bread & Butter
Homemade Mustard
Plümemooss
Colored Hard-Cooked Eggs

Easter *Faspa*

Paska & Cheese Spread
Canned Fruit
Coffee & Sugar Cubes
Colored Hard-Cooked Eggs

Pentecost Sunday Dinner
(Molotschna Colony)

On Pentecost Sunday the trees were in new bloom. Many branches were brought into the house and walls were decorated with foliage. Flowers were in bloom, and they, too, were brought in to decorate the tables.

Breakfast
(Early 1900s, Kansas)

Scrambled Eggs
White & Dark Rye Bread
Homemade Butter
Molasses
Canned Fruit
Coffee

Noon Meal
(Molotschna Colony)

Butchering Day Celebration

"Butchering Day was an incredibly joyous event."
—*Dan G. Jost*

It was customary for the families to arrive before dawn on the appointed day, gathering at the host's house for a hearty breakfast. When the first rays of the sun appeared and the stars faded away, it was time to go outdoors for the shooting. A glass of wine, on occasion, preceded this event.

Breakfast
(Early 1900s, Kansas)

Scrambled Eggs
White & Dark Rye Bread
Homemade Butter
Molasses
Canned Fruit
Coffee

Noon Meal
(Molotschna Colony)

Roast Duck
Fruit *Bobbat* Stuffing
Cream of Wheat Pudding
Cherry or *Plümemooss*

Usually a group of school children poured into the house for the noon meal. Sometimes they brought the teacher with them.

Faspa
Zwieback
Zuckerkuchen
Raisin *Stretsel*
Coffee & Sugar Cubes

Supper
(Canada, 1890s)

Fresh Spareribs
Fresh Liverwurst
Tangy Homemade Mustard
Raw Fried Potatoes
Rye Bread
Molasses
Plümemooss
Coffee

After supper the guests were invited into the living room to relax. The children usually played games outside in the dark. Everyone was presented with a bag of cookies and freshly cooked liverwurst.

Wheat Harvest (USA)
(1920s)

Mid-Morning Lunch
(served in the field)

Doughnuts
Sugar Cookies
Molasses Cookies
Lemonade
Coffee

Grandmother Jost's Threshers' Dinner

Fried Spring Chicken
Baked or Boiled Ham
Country Fried Sausage
New Potatoes & Peas in Cream
Buttered Green Beans
Cabbage Slaw
Cucumbers & Onions in Sour Cream
Watermelon Pickles
Dill Pickles
Rye & White Bread
Wild Sand Plum Jam
Peach Jelly
Apple, Coconut & Chocolate Pies
Lemonade, Milk & Coffee

Afternoon Faspa
(served in the field)

Bologna Sandwiches
Cheese
Cinnamon Rolls
Coffee

Preparations for the harvest meals began several days in advance. The menus were banquets; feasts prepared under difficult conditions with limited equipment. Young girls served lunch in the field. Praise and compliments were the women's rewards.

Farm Breakfast for Company
Old Colony Mennonite Home in Mexico

Since the days in West Prussia, Mennonite homes have been known for their hospitality, often extended without prior notice. Following is a description of the warm, friendly *Gast-*

freundlichkeit (hospitality) in an Old Colony Mennonite home in Mexico.

Walter Schmiedhaus: We took our places at the breakfast table in the kitchen and were served. God knows, that was not bad! Fried eggs with ham lay in the frying pan. Smoked pork came to the table along with a pan of *Bratwurst.* In addition there were waffles with *Plümemooss,* and the wonderful home-baked bread, both white and dark, with the best butter and fresh cheese. We had as many cups of coffee as we wished."[6]

Hard Times Menus in Paraguay

Frieda Siemens Kaethler: I was a five-year-old when our family pioneered in Paraguay. I remember one time our family was sitting at the crude table with the buggy old beans (beans with bugs) in front of us.

We children were murmuring. We were hungry for meat, fruits and vegetables. But then Father admonished us. He said, "Children, we must not be ungrateful. Our relatives in Russia would be glad to have beans. And we also have freedom and can sleep in peace without fear of the police." Ashamed and quiet, we ate our beans.

The pioneer woman was a resourceful cook. How do you make scrambled eggs without eggs or milk? Well, she took flour, baking soda and water and made scrambled eggs without eggs.

When we were hungry for meatballs and there was no meat, she took boiled rice, formed balls and fried them in tallow.

How do you make *Plümemoos* without fruit? She took water, vinegar, sugar and flour and made *Blinjemooss.* Later we learned to know the nonpoisonous berries in the bush which were used for pies and *Mooss.*

Famine Menu

In the midst of our plenty, we must not forget the times of great tragedy in the history of our people in Russia. As the famine in the Ukraine intensified late in 1921, anything edible was included in the menu. "At first the famine struck unevenly. In some areas it reached crisis proportions as early as August, 1921, while others managed to stave off starvation until 1922."[7]

Dried pumpkins
Dried beets
Chaff
Dried weeds
Ground-up corncobs

Dogs
Cats
Gophers
Remains of processed linseed

BEGGAR'S SOUP—POTATO SOUP WITH *KJIELKJE*
(*Prachasupp* or *Kjielkjesupp*)

No meat. No butter. No cream. So say the "old-timers." This soup was plain and inexpensive, but filling. The potatoes are enhanced by adding an equal amount of *Kjielkje*. Its good taste shouldn't be reserved for beggars.

Sylvia Unruh Abrahams: Prachasupp really needs homemade bread with it. This is a simple soup but very tasty. We tried it with and without butter — the butter really adds to the flavor. The dumplings add thickening, which we liked. It is not too watery.

Elizabeth Baerwald: This soup was usually served with smoked, raw sausage and thinly sliced Spanish onions. It may also be accompanied by rye bread and butter.

2 potatoes, diced	½ medium onion, chopped
4 cups water	*Kjielkje*
1 bay leaf	1 Tbsp. butter (optional)
½ tsp. salt	1 sprig fresh parsley, chopped
⅛ tsp. pepper	

Peel and cut potatoes into boiling water. Add seasonings and onion and cook until potatoes are almost soft.

Make a *Kjielkje* dough with egg and water beaten together. Add enough flour to make a medium-thick dough. (*Kjielkje* cannot be made in a hurry.)

With kitchen shears snip off pieces of dough the size of peas and drop into the boiling potatoes and cook for several minutes. Before serving, add butter and parsley.

KJIELKJE FOR *PRACHASUPP*

1 egg	⅔ – 1 cup all-purpose flour
2 Tbsp. water	¼ – ½ tsp. salt

Beat egg and water together. Add salt and enough flour to make a medium-thick dough. Here are two methods of working with this dough to get it like our grandmothers made it.

1) Take a small amount of the dough and roll it in flour. Then roll in your hand and make a thin rope. Snip pieces into a small amount of flour, so they do not stick together. Place in a

strainer and shake flour from dough before adding them to the soup.

2) With a scissors cut the *Kjielkje* directly into the hot soup. Occasionally, dip the shears in the hot soup to keep dough from sticking.

*D*ROP *KJIELKJE*

In her book, *Oma's Schattelbank,* Elizabeth Baerwald suggests making a softer batter which can be dropped by teaspoonsful into the soup. Use a regular *Kjielkje* recipe, but reduce the flour so the dough has spoon-drop consistency. Drop into boiling soup. Cover and simmer until all the *Kjielkje* rise to the top. Baerwald flavors her soup with buttermilk and cream.

Handwritten
Cookbooks

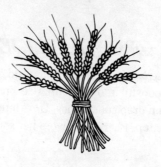

Handwritten Cookbooks —Treasures from Our Past

Among the Mennonite women of the Vistula Delta and the early villages in Russia, commercially printed cookbooks were practically unheard of. Few if any such cookbooks found their way to North America. Those of our grandmothers and great-grandmothers who came here brought most of their recipes "in their heads." Their cooking was basic and simple. Most times the ingredients were easy to remember. Cooking was learned by experience, not by reading a book.

The first "receipt books" among Mennonites in Russia were handwritten. Some of those handwritten cookbooks were carried to North America and are found primarily among Mennonite families now living in Canada. The compilers of these books started collecting recipes as young girls in their mothers' homes. The writing was usually in old High German script, learned in the village school and now only deciphered by older folks. Occasional recipes were written in Russian. Long after these women learned to speak English, they continued to write in German.

Handwritten cookbooks were mainly used as a memory aid and as a place to write down recipes one had enjoyed in someone else's home. As recipes became more sophisticated and as greater varieties were desired, women began recording those which were more difficult to remember or those which were used only during certain seasons such as peppernuts or *Portselkje*.

Routine, familiar recipes — bread or *Zwieback*—were never written down. The dough was simple and the instructions were automatic. The same was true of most soup recipes. Grandmother Jost gave me her *Borscht* recipe at my wedding shower. Written in pencil in German on a uniform recipe card which I gave her, it lists only ingredients. No measurements or instructions are included.

*   *   *

In the old handwritten books one finds numerous unusual measurements:

1. 1 *Glas* (Russian) is slightly less than 1 U.S. liquid cup
2. 1 spoonful of salt
3. 1 big spoonful of flour
4. 3 kopeks worth ammonia
5. 1 15-cent bottle oil of anise
6. 1 *Stoff* or *shtof* (Russian) equals 1.23 liters or 1.3 U.S. quarts
7. 1 *lot* (Russian) equals about ½ ounce or about 1 U.S. tablespoon
8. A little vinegar
9. A few sprigs *Päpakrüt* (summer savory)

Flour quantities were rarely specified even though flour measurement is often crucial to texture. All women, of necessity, were veteran bakers and knew by experience and touch how much flour to add. None of the *old* peppernut recipes which I found in the research for both volumes of this book gave specific flour measurements. Words such as "flour to make a stiff dough" can be quite puzzling to contemporary bakers.

Russian Mennonite women were the persons responsible for all the cooking in the homes and communities. Mothers wrote down recipes for their daughters. Daughters laboriously copied their mothers' "receipt books" and used them for their own households. These were passed on from one generation to another. On rare occasions men recorded information about food. Margaret Klassen Sawatsky's father kept a journal in Russia which included several family recipes—one for *Schneeballen* (snowballs, a custard dessert with meringue) and one for *Paska*. Sometimes the men were more educated and could write more easily.

My own mother, Helen Taeves Jost, began a recipe collection as a young woman when she went to work for a Swedish family in McPherson, Kansas. Her early recipes reflect the "new ways" and are primarily for desserts, pastries and salads, most of which were unknown in Mennonite homes. The pages in her book from this era are yellowed and crumbling.

Other recipes in her collection were jotted on scraps of paper or on the backs of handy envelopes and were filed in a fancy old tin chocolate box. Many of these give only partial information. The recipes for the foods of our childhood—the dishes we really loved such as *Varenikje, Kjielkje* and Russian pancakes—had to be coaxed from her and became long, rambling narratives. She cooked by feel, touch and taste, not by precise measurements. It would have been superfluous for her to record those recipes. Mother had few commercially printed cookbooks. Those she did have were "giveaways" from various businesses.

Old handwritten cookbooks are true family treasures—for collectors and cooks alike. They reveal much about our past: what was cooked in the home, our eating culture, something of the social class of the family and the dishes which were popular at the time the book was recorded. While doing research for this book, I had the rare privilege of holding in my hands three of these treasures from our past. The following pages include short descriptions of these wonderful books.

Agnes Rempel Braun Cookbook

Agnes Rempel Braun grew up in the village of Tiegenhagen, Molotschna, Ukraine. Cooking for a family of fifteen and five hired workers took much of her mother's and older sisters' days. Younger ones, like Agnes, had the task of gathering fuel and keeping the large brick oven fired for baking and cooking. Among her fond memories of childhood in Russia are summer weekends playing circle games with friends.

In 1927, two years after arriving in Manitoba, Agnes married George Braun, a former neighbor from Russia. As a young bride she polished her own cooking skills, continued her mother's Russian Mennonite-style of cooking, had a large garden and regularly raised a flock of sixty geese. Sundays she frequently served chicken baked with fresh tomatoes or roast goose with *Bobbat* stuffing. A favorite food memory from childhood is her mother's large roaster filled to the corners with baked young doves, one or two for each person.

Agnes Braun recorded her recipes in a blue account ledger. Reflecting the changes in her life, many of the German handwritten receipts include sprinklings of English words.

Agnes Braun now lives in a Winnipeg retirement center where she still bakes and offers guests a variety of sweets and baked delicacies.

Anna Reimer Dyck Cookbook

The early pages of Anna Reimer's handwritten cookbook were started when she was a young girl in her parents' home. The Reimer family lived on a large estate in the Kuban where she enjoyed an idyllic childhood and also attended school. Anna's mother, Emilie Zeh Reimer, was Swabian in background and "the Swabians are noted for their good cuisine." Her recipes were a blend of the best of two styles of cooking — Mennonite and South German. Emilie was also noted for her pastries and Christmas baking.

Years of turmoil, war and famine ended the happy, beautiful years in the Kuban. In 1924 Anna left her family to join her fiance, Willy Dyck, who had already gone to Canada. Among her belongings she carried a black, hardcover notebook with her mother's cherished recipes. During her busy life, she added many of her own recipes to the collection. Anna Reimer Dyck was a mother, a pastor's wife and for a time she also ran her own private kindergarten. Her home was in Niverville, Manitoba. Her life story is told in the book, *Anna, From the Caucasus to Canada.*

Maria Martens Schapansky Cookbook

Lena Schapansky: My mother-in-law loved to cook. She had a reputation for brewing the best coffee in the French district of Manitoba where she and her husband first farmed. Also the French neighbors tell of her delicious buns and *Plümemooss.* Her best cooking was always done when there was a large crowd. This was during threshing, butchering bees and family gatherings. She made her own raspberry or chokecherry wine and used it as punch to serve with meals. My husband said she didn't cook as well in later years. "It doesn't pay to cook for just three people," was her reply.

Jacob and Maria Schapansky both grew up in the village of Steinfeld in the Molotschna Colony. They were married in 1923. When times became hard in Russia, they immigrated to Canada and settled near Kleefeld, Manitoba, where they were farmers.

Her recipes are neatly written in old High German script which she learned in a Russian village school. Some of them are Russian in origin and use Russian measurements. One of the recipes most treasured by the Schapansky family today is called *Pomashka.* It is translated into English on page 85 of this book.

Notes

The Mennonite House

[1] *Mennonite Encyclopedia*, vol. 1 (Scottdale, Pa.: Mennonite Publishing House, 1955), p. 150.

[2] *Mennonite Encyclopedia*, vol. 2 (Scottdale, Pa.: Mennonite Publishing House, 1956), p. 312.

[3] *Mennonite Encyclopedia*, vol. 4 (Scottdale, Pa.: Mennonite Publishing House, 1959), pp. 922–923.

[4] *Mennonite Encyclopedia*, vol. 4, p. 386.

[5] Delbert F. Plett, *History and Events of Earlier Times* (Steinbach, Man.: D.F. Plett Farms, Ltd., 1982), p. 102.

[6] Julius G. Toews and Lawrence Klippenstein, eds., *Manitoba Mennonite Memories* (Altona and Steinbach, Man.: Manitoba Centennial Committee, 1974), p. 313.

[7] Siegfried Rosenberg, *Geschichte des Kreises Grosses Werder* (Schwentine, Poland: Danziger Verlagsgesellschaft Paul Rosenberg, 1940), p. 79.

[8] Helmut T. Huebert *Hierschau, an Example of Russian Mennonite Life* (Winnipeg: Springfield Publishers, 1986), p. 338.

The Russian Mennonite Oven

[1] Arnold Dyck, *Lost in the Steppe* (Steinbach, Man.: Derksen Printers, 1977), p. 34.

Plautdietsch — Our Low German Language

[1] Jacob H. Janzen (1878–1950) was born in Steinbach, Molotschna Colony. He was a teacher and after World War I continued his education in Germany, returning to Russia to teach in Tiege. In 1924 he immigrated to Canada. Janzen wrote more than a dozen books in German as well as several plays in *Plautdietsch*, including the very first play in the Low German of the Mennonites, *Dee Bildung* (1912).

[2] Henry Dietrich Dyck, "Language Differences in Two Low German Groups in Canada" (Ph.D. diss., University of Michigan, 1964), p. 5.

[3] Henry Dietrich Dyck, p. 6.

[4] Reuben Epp, "*Plautdietsch*: Origins, Development and State of the Mennonite Low German Language," *Journal of Mennonite Studies*, 1987, pp. 62–67.

When a Low German speaking person is confronted with English words which he or she finds hard to grasp, he or she may well say, "*Kannst mie dat nich Platt seggen?*"

[5] Epp, p. 67.

[6] Epp, p. 62.

[7] Epp, p. 63.

[8] Epp, p. 63.

[9] Epp, p. 63.

[10] Rosenberg, p. 207.

[11] Epp, p. 65.

[12] Henry Dietrich Dyck, p. 7.

[13] Rosenberg, p. 207.

[14] Epp, p. 67.

There were many variations of East and West Prussian *Plattdeutsch* in this area which was less than half the size of Florida and only one-tenth the size of Manitoba. *Plautdietsch* was only one of more than nine different dialects.

[15] Henry Dietrich Dyck, p. 9.

[16] Victor Carl Friesen, *The Windmill Turning* (Edmonton, Alta.: University of Alberta Press, 1988), p. 21.

[17] Al Reimer, Ann Reimer and Jack Thiessen, *A Sackful of Plautdietsch; A Collection of Mennonite Low German Stories and Poems* (Winnipeg: Hyperion Press, Ltd., 1983), p. 3.

[18] Reuben Epp, "Low German, Where It Came From and Where It Is Going," *Mennonite Mirror* (Jan. 1989), p. 6.

[19] Henry Dietrich Dyck, p. 9.

[20] There are Low German speaking Mennonites living in Canada, Germany, the United States, the Union of Soviet Socialist Republics, Mexico, Paraguay, Uruguay, Brazil, Bolivia, Belize and Argentina.

Early Russian Mennonite Education

[1] N.J. Kroeker, *First Mennonite Villages in Russia* (Cloverdale, B.C.: D.W. Friesen, 1981), p. 146.

[2] *Mennonite Encyclopedia,* vol. 2, pp. 156–157.

[3] N.J. Kroeker, p. 147.

[4] Mary Dirks Janzen, unpublished autobiography, Mennonite Library and Archives, North Newton, Kan.

[5] Janzen autobiography.

[6] Anna Reimer Dyck, *Anna: From the Caucasus to Canada* (Hillsboro, Kan.: Mennonite Brethren Publishing House, 1979), p. 40.

[7] N.J. Kroeker, p. 154.

[8] O.L. Davis, Jr., *Schools of the Past* (Bloomington, Ind.: Phi Delta Kappa Foundation, 1976), p. 10.

[9] Raymond F. Wiebe, *Hillsboro, Kansas, The City on the Prairie* (Hillsboro, Kan.: Multi-Business Press, 1985), p. 61.

[10] Mennonite Heritage Village brochure, Steinbach, Manitoba.

[11] Plett, p. 123.

[12] Peter D. Zacharias, *Reinland, An Experience in Community* (Altona, Man.: D.W. Friesen & Sons, 1976).

[13] John H. Enns journal, "The Settlement of Reesor, Ontario," Mennonite Heritage Center Archives, Winnipeg.

[14] Marie Loewen Franz, *Word Pictures of Yesteryear* (Montezuma, Kan.: Montezuma Press, 1985), p. 8.

[15] Frieda Pankratz Suderman, *You Just Can't Do That Anymore* (Hillsboro, Kan.: Mennonite Brethren Publishing House, 1977), p. 189.

[16] *Harvest Anthology of Mennonite Writing in Canada, 1874–1974* (Altona and Steinbach, Man.: Manitoba Centennial Commitee, 1974), p. 17.

[17] One of the more unique families to settle in the Gnadenau area during the early 1870s was the Charles Flippin family. Flippin, a black physician, operated a molasses press in the Gnadenau district and later opened a medical practice in Peabody, Kansas.

The Mennonite Church

[1] C. Henry Smith, *Smith's Story of the Mennonites* (Newton, Kan.: Faith and Life Press, 1981), p. 167.

[2] *Mennonite Encyclopedia,* vol. 2, p. 176.

[3] *Mennonite Encyclopedia,* vol. 1, p. 150.

[4] Anna Rempel Dyck, unpublished autobiography, Mennonite Library and Archives, North Newton, Kan.

[5] *Mennonite Encyclopedia,* vol. 3 (Scottdale, Pa.: Mennonite Publishing House, 1957), p. 794.

[6] Anna Rempel Dyck autobiography.

[7] Smith, pp. 278–279.

Mennonite Encyclopedia, vol. 2, pp. 658–659.

The Festive Sabbath
[1] Franz, p. 7.
[2] Franz, p. 24.
[3] Franz, p. 54.
[4] Franz, p. 54.
[5] Franz, p. 13.
[6] *Mennonite Life,* Centennial Issue, 1974.
[7] Suderman, p. 92.
[8] John H. Enns journal.
[9] Franz, p. 18.
[10] Peter Epp, ***Eine Mutter*** (Bluffton, Oh.: Libertas Verlag, 1932), p. 24.
[11] Ray Plett, "*Faspa*" (Winnipeg: Locusts and Wild Honey), original lyrics for song.

Celebrations among Russian Mennonites
[1] Arnold Dyck, *Lost in the Steppe* (Steinbach, Man.: Derksen Printers, 1974), pp. 156, 161.
[2] Anna Reimer Dyck, pp. 33–35.
[3] Mary M. Enns, *Mia, The Story of a Remarkable Woman* (Winnipeg: A.A. DeFehr Trust), p. 45.
[4] Debbie Kilpatrick, unpublished biography of Suse Rempel, Mennonite Heritage Center Archives, Winnipeg.
[5] H.B. Friesen, unpublished autobiography, Mennonite Library and Archives, North Newton, Kan.
[6] Suderman, pp. 142–143.
[7] Rosenberg, p. 215.
[8] Anna Rempel Dyck autobiography.
[9] Mary M. Enns, p. 39.
[10] Arnold Dyck, p. 177.
[11] Delbert F. Plett, p. 96.
[12] Anna Reimer Dyck, p. 35.
[13] Rosenberg, p. 214.
[14] Anna Reimer Dyck, pp. 104–105.
[15] Anna Reimer Dyck, p. 37.
[16] A very old belief, once found in most parts of Great Britain and Ireland, held that the sun danced for joy that the Lord Jesus had risen at its rising each Easter morning. A similar belief, less widespread than the dancing tradition but very firmly held in some districts, maintained that the Lamb of God carrying a red cross banner appeared in the center of the sun's disk each Easter morning. It was visible for only the first few moments after the sun had broken the horizon and people eagerly watched the sunrise in order to see the Lamb and Flag image.
Christina Hole, *Easter and Its Customs* (New York: M. Barrows, 1961), pp. 57–58.
[17] Toews and Klippenstein, p. 99.
[18] Henry B. Tiessen, *The Molotschna Colony* (Kitchener, Ont.: Henry B. Tiessen, 1981) p. 18.
[19] Tiessen, p. 92.
[20] Anna Reimer Dyck, pp. 32, 40.
[21] Mary M. Enns, p. 38.

Russian Mennonite Wedding Customs
[1] *Mennonite Encyclopedia,* vol. 4, p. 772.
[2] *Mennonite Encyclopedia,* vol. 3, p. 505.

³ *Mennonite Encyclopedia,* vol. 3, p. 505.

⁴ Rosenberg, p. 219.

⁵ *Mennonite Encyclopedia,* vol. 2, p. 732.

⁶ Anna Rempel Dyck autobiography.

⁷ Rosenberg, p. 219.

⁸ Dennis Stoesz, unpublished biography of David Stoesz, Mennonite Heritage Center Archives, Winnipeg.

⁹ The colonies supported various higher schools which were located in different villages.

¹⁰ Anna Rempel Dyck autobiography.

¹¹ Katherine Woelk van den Haak, unpublished research paper, Mennonite Library and Archives, North Newton, Kan.

¹² Johann J. Neudorf, Heinrich J. Neudorf and David D. Rempel, comps., *Osterwick, 1812–1942* (Clearbrook, B.C.: A. Olfert & Sons, 1973), p. 81.

¹³ Cornelius Goosen, unpublished autobiographical paper, Mennonite Heritage Center Archives, Winnipeg.

¹⁴ Anna Reimer Dyck, conversation with the author, Fresno, Ca., July 1987.

¹⁵ Mary Francis manuscript, "Autobiographical Sketches of Childhood in Russia," Mennonite Heritage Center Archives, Winnipeg.

¹⁶ Rosenberg, p. 221.

¹⁷ Anna Rempel Dyck autobiography.

¹⁸ Cornelius and Agnes Wall, *As We Remember* (Hillsboro, Kan.: Mennonite Brethren Publishing House, 1979), pp. 21–22.

¹⁹ Maria Penner Weise, conversation with the author, Winnipeg, September 1984.

²⁰ Zacharias, p. 292.

²¹ Marie Berg's grandparents were Rev. Peter A. and Sarah Voth Wiebe. Rev. Wiebe was an elder in the Springfield Krimmer Mennonite Brethren Church near rural Lehigh, Kansas.

²² John H. Enns journal.

²³ Barbara Funk, unpublished paper, Mennonite Library and Archives, North Newton, Kan.

²⁴ Franz, p. 64.

²⁵ Mary M. Enns, p. 127.

The Seasons

¹ Arnold Dyck, p. 178.

² N.J. Kroeker, p. 200.

³ N.J. Kroeker, p. 215.

⁴ Franz, pp. 24–25.

⁵ Arnold Dyck, p. 35.

⁶ N.J. Kroeker, p. 180.

⁷ Suderman, p. 25.

⁸ Mary M. Enns, p. 34.

⁹ N.J. Kroeker, p. 215.

¹⁰ Suderman, p. 28.

¹¹ Franz, p. 11.

¹² Suderman, p. 18.

¹³ David V. Wiebe, *Grace Meadow* (Hillsboro, Kan.: Mennonite Brethren Publishing House, 1967), p. 33.

¹⁴ *Harvest Anthology,* p. 17.

Wheat Harvest from the Steppes to the Plains

[1] Cornelius Krahn, *From the Steppes to the Prairies* (Newton, Kan.: Mennonite Publication Offices, 1949), pp. 3–4.

[2] Katherine Nickel, *Seed from the Ukraine* (New York: Pageant Press, 1952), pp. 42–43.

[3] N.J. Kroeker, p. 71.

[4] Tiessen, p. 38.

[5] Tiessen, p. 39.

[6] Rosenberg, p. 219.

[7] Raymond F. Wiebe, pp. 17–18.

[8] Accompanying the Fasts were a son-in-law and daughter, Heinrich A. and Helena Fast Flaming, and their children. One of these children was my husband's grandmother who was seven years old at the time.

[9] Smith, p. 431.

[10] David V. Wiebe, *They Seek a Country* (Freeman, S.D.: Pine Hill Press, 1974), p. 55.

[11] Clarence Hiebert, *Brothers in Deed to Brothers in Need* (Newton, Kan.: Faith and Life Press, 1974), p. 451.

One evening near the end of Schmidt's trip to the Ukraine, he was driving from Mariawohl to Ruckenau when a man on horseback suddenly galloped up beside his carriage. He had been sent with a message that three mounted *gens d'armes* were at Schmidt's heels and would probably catch up to him by nightfall. His alarmed driver dropped Schmidt off at a blacksmith shop and ordered him to wait until the way was clear. Later that night, escorted by two young Mennonites, Schmidt set out for the railway station in Melitopol which was about 70 miles away. He reached Melitopol safely and left Russia for Austria.

[12] Smith, p. 441.

The Mennonite immigrants settling in Canada in 1874 also brought wheat seeds from the Ukraine. However, the hard winter wheat for which they became famous in Kansas did not do well in Manitoba. In Manitoba spring wheat, oats and barley became the staple crops.

[13] Raymond F. Wiebe, p. 140.

[14] Raymond F. Wiebe, p. 140.

[15] Raymond F. Wiebe, p. 140.

[16] Raymond F. Wiebe, p. 27.

[17] Raymond F. Wiebe, p. 38.

[18] David V. Wiebe, *Grace Meadow*, p. 89.

[19] David V. Wiebe, *They Seek a Country*, p. 92.

[20] Raymond F. Wiebe, pp. 27, 31, 140.

[21] David V. Wiebe, *They Seek a Country*, p. 55.

[22] Hiebert, p. 253.

[23] David V. Wiebe, *Grace Meadow*, p. 47.

[24] David V. Wiebe, *They Seek a Country*, p. 95.

The Celebration of Butchering

[1] Zacharias, p. 28.

[2] *Harvest Anthology*, p. 18.

[3] *Harvest Anthology*, p. 18.

[4] Mary M. Enns, p. 33.

[5] Suderman, p. 102.

[6] Stella and Orpha Schrag, *Mennonite Life*, Centennial Issue, 1974.

[7] Zacharias, p. 28.

[8] Arnold Dyck, p. 217.

[9] Tiessen, p. 48.

[10] Tiessen, p. 48.
[11] John H. Enns journal.

Busy Days

[1] Suderman, p. 116.
[2] Arnold Dyck, p. 110.
[3] Franz, p. 25.
[4] Suderman, p. 25.
[5] Franz, p. 24.
[6] Franz, p. 7.
[7] Suderman, pp. 12–13.

Orchards and Gardens

[1] *Mennonite Encyclopedia,* vol. 1, p. 312.
[2] *Mennonite Encyclopedia,* vol. 1, pp. 716–717.
[3] Nickel, p. 31.
[4] Anne Volokh, *The Art of Russian Cuisine* (New York: Macmillan Publishing Company, 1983), p. 448.
[5] Mary M. Enns, p. 32.
[6] N.J. Kroeker, pp. 214–215.
[7] Toews and Klippenstein, p. 296.
[8] Franz, pp. 12–13.
[9] Raymond F. Wiebe, pp. 28–29.

Food Preservation

[1] Arnold Dyck, pp. 152, 155.
[2] Suderman, p. 104.
[3] Suderman, p. 100.
[4] Peter Epp, p. 118.
[5] *Schnitz* is not a Low German word. It was probably borrowed from the Pennsylvania Dutch language.
[6] Suderman, pp. 100–101.
[7] Suderman, p. 100.
[8] Franz, p. 29.

Russian Mennonite Menus

[1] Ulrich Tolksdorf, *Essen und Trinken in Ost- und West-Preussen* (Marburg: E.G. Elwert Verlag, 1975), p. 231.
[2] Soldiers from Napoleon's army who spent some time quartered in various homes throughout the Vistula Delta went back to France with the report that the area was a *Schmalzgrube* (lard pit) or *Schmalzinsel* (lard island).
[3] Rosenberg, p. 206.
[4] Rosenberg, p. 206.
[5] N.J. Kroeker, pp. 80–82.
[6] Walter Schmiedhaus, *Die Altkolonier Mennoniten in Mexico* (Winnipeg: Canadian Mennonite Bible College Publications, 1982), p. 161.
[7] John B. Toews, *Czars, Soviets and Mennonites* (Newton, Kan.: Faith and Life Press, 1982), p. 112.

Readings and Sources

Bethel College Women's Association. *Melting Pot of Mennonite Cookery*. North Newton, Kansas: Mennonite Press, 1974.

Dyck, Anna Reimer. *Anna: From the Caucasus to Canada*. Hillsboro, Kansas: Mennonite Brethren Publishing House, 1979.

Dyck, Anna Rempel. Unpublished autobiography. Mennonite Library and Archives, North Newton, Kansas.

Dyck, Arnold. *Lost in the Steppe*. Steinbach, Manitoba: Derksen Printers, 1974.

Dyck, Henry Dietrich. "Language Differences in Two Low German Groups in Canada." Ph.D. diss., University of Michigan, 1964.

Enns, Mary M. *Mia, The Story of a Remarkable Woman*. Winnipeg: A.A. DeFehr Trust.

Epp, Reuben. "*Plautdietsch:* Origins, Development and State of the Mennonite Low German Language." *Journal of Mennonite Studies* (1987): 62–67.

Fast, Johannes and Elisabeth Isaac. Letters, 1873–1874. Mennonite Library and Archives, North Newton, Kansas.

Franz, Marie Loewen. *Word Pictures of Yesteryear*. Montezuma, Kansas: Montezuma Press, 1985.

Friesen, Victor Carl. *The Windmill Turning: Nursery Rhymes, Maxims, and Other Expressions of Western Canadian Mennonites*. Edmonton, Alberta: University of Alberta Press, 1988.

Harvest Anthology of Mennonite Writing in Canada, 1874–1974. Altona and Steinbach, Manitoba: Manitoba Centennial Committee, 1974.

Hiebert, Clarence, editor. *Brothers in Deed to Brothers in Need: A Scrapbook about Mennonite Immigrants from Russia 1870–1875*. Newton, Kansas: Faith and Life Press, 1974.

Huebert, Helmut T. *Hierschau, An Example of Russian Mennonite Life*. Winnipeg: Springfield Publishers, 1986.

Janzen, Mary Dirks. Unpublished autobiography. Mennonite Library and Archives, North Newton, Kansas.

Klassen, Doreen Helen. *Singing Mennonite: Low German Songs Among the Mennonites*. Winnipeg: University of Manitoba Press, 1988.

Klassen, Peter J. *A Homeland for Strangers, An Introduction to Mennonites in Poland and Prussia*. Fresno, California: Center for Mennonite Brethren Studies, 1989.

Krahn, Cornelius. *From the Steppes to the Prairies (1874–1949)*. Newton, Kansas: Mennonite Publication Offices, 1949.

Kroeker, N.J. *First Mennonite Villages in Russia*. Cloverdale, British Columbia: D.W. Friesen & Sons, 1981.

Mennonite Encyclopedia, The. Volumes 1–4. Scottdale, Pennsylvania: Mennonite Publishing House, 1955–1959.

Nickel, Katherine. *Seed from the Ukraine*. New York: Pageant Press, 1952.

Plett, Delbert F. *History and Events of Earlier Times*. Steinbach, Manitoba: D.F. Plett Farms, Ltd., 1982.

Reimer, Al, Anne Reimer and Jack Thiessen. *A Sackful of Plautdietsch; A Collection of Mennonite Low German Stories and Poems*. Winnipeg: Hyperion Press, 1983.

Rempel, Herman. *Kienn Jie Noch Plautdietsch? A Mennonite Low German Dictionary*. Winnipeg: Mennonite Literary Society, 1984.

Rosenberg, Siegfried. *Geschichte des Kreises Grosses Werder*. Schwentine, Poland: Danziger Verlagsgesellschaft Paul Rosenberg, 1940.

Rosenfeld, Mrs. Peter, Mrs. Jacob H. Peters and Mrs. D.D. Warkentin, editors. *A Mennonite Treasury of Recipes*. Steinbach, Manitoba, 1962.

Smith, C. Henry. *Smith's Story of the Mennonites*. 5th ed. Revised and enlarged by Cornelius Krahn. Newton, Kansas: Faith and Life Press, 1981.

Suderman, Frieda Pankratz. *You Just Can't Do That Anymore*. Hillsboro, Kansas: Mennonite Brethren Publishing House, 1977

Tiessen, Henry B. *The Molotschna Colony:* Kitchener, Ontario: Henry B. Tiessen, 1981.

Toews, John B. *Czars, Soviets, and Mennonites*. Newton, Kansas: Faith and Life Press, 1982.

Toews, Julius G. and Lawrence Klippenstein, editors. *Manitoba Mennonite Memories*. Altona and Steinbach, Manitoba: Manitoba Centennial Committee, 1974.

Tolksdorf, Ulrich. *Essen und Trinken in Ost- und West-Preussen*. Marburg, Germany: E.G. Elwert Verlag, 1975.

Wall, Cornelius and Agnes. *As We Remember*. Hillsboro, Kansas: Mennonite Brethren Publishing House, 1979.

Wiebe, David V. *They Seek a Country: A Survey of Mennonite Migrations*. Freeman, South Dakota: Pine Hill Press, 1974.

Wiebe, David V. *Grace Meadow*. Hillsboro, Kansas: Mennonite Brethren Publishing House, 1967.

Wiebe, Raymond F. *Hillsboro, Kansas, The City on the Prairie*. Hillsboro, Kansas: Multi-Business Press, 1985.

Zacharias, Peter D. *Reinland, An Experience in Community*. Altona, Manitoba: D.W. Friesen & Sons, 1976.

Recipe Index

Anise
   chicken,7
   peppernuts, 99-100
   syrup cookies, 133-134
Ammonia
   cookies (*Gruznikje*), 94
   cookies, yellow (*Gruznikje*),
      93
   Sockanat/Zuchernüsse, 96-97
Apricot filling for cookies, 93

Barley-buttermilk *Mooss*, 172
Beef
   broth with noodles, 165
   meat balls (*Klopps*), 168
Beet *Borscht*, 166
Berry jam, 251
Berry jelly, 251
Bierocks
   easy II, 218
   regular, 217
Biscuits, yeast, 163
Bobbat dressing for chicken,
   71
Borscht
   beet, 166
   lamb, 216
   sauerkraut, 164
   sorrel, 173
Breads, sweet yeast
   double quick dough for,
      221
   Korintestretsel, 150, 151
   Paska, 121
   Porselkje, 106
      Schmeck Haus #2,
      106-107
   Peppernuts, Russian, 103
      syrup, 84
      yeast, 83
Breads, yeast
   Bulkje, 28
   Franzoli, about, 32
   Hollandisches, about, 31
   Kringel/Kjrinjel (bubliki), 30-
      31
   Langfuhr, about, 32
   oatmeal-cracked wheat, 27

raisin, 29
raisin/potato, 210
Roggebroot, bazaar, 25-26
   store, about, 221
   wheat, whole, 26
Brown sugar peppernuts, 100
Bulkje (white bread), 28
Buns, *Zwieback*, 151-152

Cabbage, stewed, 168-169
Cake, syrup, 131
Canadian peppermint
   cookies, 94
Candy, *Pomashka*, 85
Cheese, *Paska*, 124
Cheese, stinky, 249
Cherry-plum *Mooss*, 70
Chicken
   anise, 70
   dressing for, 71
   fried, tips for, 197
   roast with *Bobbat*, 210
Christmas, see cookies,
   peppernuts, candy
Clabbered milk
   dessert, 178
   Dikje Malkj, 172
   with noddles
      (*Kjielkjesalaut*), 178
Cookies
   anise syrup, 133
   dark molasses, 193
   soft molasses, 132
   sour cream, 133

Eggs, scrambled (*Rearei*), 179

Franzoli Brot, about, 32
French toast, 163-164
French steak, 243
Fruit
   Mooss or soup
      cherry-plum, 70
      dried fruit, 69
      fruit, 195
   gooseberry, canned, 211
   Plauts, summer, 75-76
   Varenikje, summer, 242

Gooseberry *Mooss*, canned,
   211
Grandma Funk's bushel
   cookies, 193-194
Grandma's dark molasses
   drops, 193
Gruznikje, 93, 94

Ham, boiled, 209
Hollandisches Brot, about, 32
Honey cookies, Mother's, 95

Jam, berry, 251
Jelly, berry, 251

Kholodnyk, Ukrainian, 172
Kjielkje, 218
   drop, 271
   for soup, 270
Klopps, 168
Knick Knack cookies, 92
Korintestretsel, 150-151
Kringel/Kjrinjel
   about, 30
   buns, 30-31
Kruidnootjes, Dutch, 102

Lamb, 216
Lamb, roast leg of, 122
Langfuhr Brot, about, 32
Lebkuchen, 95

Main dishes
   Bierocks, 217
      easy, II, 218
   Bobbat, fruit, 71
   Kjielkje, 218
   pancakes, potato, 219
   Perieschkje, meat-filled,
      167-168
   Rearei, 179
   Varenikje
      cottage cheese for,
      167
      dough for, 121-122
      filling for, 242
Meat
   chicken, fried, 197

chicken, roast with *Bobbat*, 210
duck, roast with *Bobbat*, 210
ham, boiled, 209
Klopps, 168
lamb, roast leg of 122
Perieschkje, meat filled, 167-168
    pork loin roast and gravy, 209
    steak French, 243
Milk, clabbered, 178
Milk soups, see Soup
Molasses cookies
    Grandma's dark drop, 193
    soft drop, 132
Mooss
    barley-buttermilk, 172
    cherry-plum, 70
    fruit, 195
    fruit, dried, 69
    gooseberry, canned, 211
Mother's honey cookies, 95
Mustard, hot, 121-122

Noodles, homemade, 165

Oatmeal-cracked wheat
    bread, 27
Oklahoma frontier biscuits, 163

Pancakes
    cottage cheese, 220
    plain, 219
    potato, 219
Paska, Easter bread, 121
    cheese spread for, 124
    traditional, 124

Peppernut cookies, see
    Ammonia cookies
Peppernuts
    anise, 99-100
    brown sugar, crunchy, 100
    Danish *pebernodder*, 103
    Dutch *Kruidnootjes*, 102
    Dutch *pepernoten* II, 101
    easy, 98-99
    raisin-nut, 101
    Siaroppspapanat, 98
    Sockanat/Zuckernüsse, 96

    with ammonia, 96-97
    syrup, 97, 98
Peppernuts, yeast
    Russian, 103
    syrup, 84
    yeast, *83*
Perieschkje
    meat-filled, 167-168
    quick and easy, 197
Pickles
    dill, spicy, 249-250
    watermelon, brined, 250
Plauts
    summer fruit, 75-76
    Village Museum, 196
Pomashka, 85
Pork loin roast and gravy, 209
Portselkje, 106
    Schmeck Haus #2, 106-107
Potato
    panckaes, 219
    soup with *Kjielkje*, 270

Raisin
    bread, 29
    nut peppernuts, 101
    potato bread, 210
Rearei, 179
Roggebroot, 25-26
Rollkuchen, 177-178
Russian
    jam-filled cookies, 92
    peppernuts, yeast, 83, 103
    wafer cookies, 92

Sauerkraut *Borscht*, 164
Schmeck Haus Portselkje II, 106-107
Siaroppspapanat, 98
Soap, laundry, 225
Sockanat/Zuckernüsse, 96
    with ammonia, 96-97
Sorrel *Borscht*, mock, 173
Soup(s), main dish
    beef broth with noodles, 165
    Borscht
        beet, 166
        sauerkraut, 164
        sorrel, 173
    Kjielkje , 270

    drop, 271
    noodles for, 165
    pick and choose, 165
    potato with *Kjielkje*, 270
Soup, milk
    barley, buttermilk, 172
    clabbered milk, 172
    Kholodnyk, Ukrainian, 172
    Schmauntsupp, 172
Sour cream drop cakes, 133
Steak, French, 243
Store bread, about 221-222
Stretsel, Korinte, 150-151
Sweet bread dough, 221
Syrup
    cake, 131
    cookies, anise, 133-134
    cookies, Rempel family, 194-195
    peppernuts, 97, 98
    peppernuts, yeast, 83, 84, 103

Topping for *Plauts*, 76

Ukrainian
    bubliki/Kringel, 30-31
    Paska, 121
        cheese for, 124
    Pomashka, 85
    Varenikje, see below

Varenikje
    cream gravy for, 242
    dough for, 121-122
    cottage cheese, 167
    fruit, 242

Waffles, basic, 220
Watermelon, brined, 250
Wheat, whole, bread, 26

Yeast
    biscuits, 163
    bread, see breads
    peppernuts, 83, 84, 103

Zuckernüsse/Sockanat, 96-97
Zwieback, 151-152
    contemporary version, 75
    summer fruit *Plauts*, from, 75-76

Index

Agricultural Association, Mennonite
  (*Mennobschevtso*), Russia, 117, 181
Alcoholic beverages and butchering,
  204, 207
Alexanderkrone (village), 120
Alliance School, Gnadenfeld (village),
  43, 44
Annenfeld (village), Crimea, 67, 185,
  186, 187
Ant hill ovens, Paraguay, 21
Architecture, early Mennonite
  churches, Holland, Vistula Delta,
  Russia, North America, 57
Architecture, early Mennonite houses
  in Friesland, Vistula Delta, Russia,
  North America, 8 12-13, 14;
  remaining today, 14
Attic (*Bowaban*) in Mennonite house,
  11, 182, 245, 252

Bake house,Vistula Delta, 17
Barn (*Staul*) and Mennonite house, 11
Barn annex (*Schien*) and Mennonite
  house, 11, 145, 155
Baschtan, 235
Bells, Russian church, 115
Bernay, C.L., on Mennonite farming,
  189
Berry picking, 236, 239, 240
Birthday celebrations, Russia, 131
Black bow ceremony (wedding), 148
Blumengart (village), menus from,
  259-265
Brick ovens (Russian *pietsch*), 17-18
Brick ovens, how to build, 19-20
Brommtopp song, Vistula Delta, 110
Brommtoppspala, Russia, 109, 112;
  Canada, 112
Busy days for women, 213-215
Butchering, hog, 202-208

Cake walks and basket socials, rural
  schools, North America, 54
Canning, 173, 179, 245, 246, 248, 249
Canadian government offers to
  immigrants, 1874, 186
Catechism in Mennonite schools, 39,
  42-43
Catherine the Great, 184, 186
Cauldron, copper, see *Miagrope*
Celebrations, village schools, Russia,
  44-45
Chaco jungle, 15
Chortitza colony, 11, 36, 39, 42-43, 46,
  107, 113, 161, 175
Chortitza Low German dialect, 36
Chortitza village school, 42, 43
Christmas, in Russia, 78-83; in North
  America, 85-91
Church, early Mennonite
  meetinghouses, Amsterdam,
  Danzig, Elbing, North America,
  57-58
    memories of Gnadenfeld, 58

language in Prussia, 34, 57;
  sermons, music and singing in
  Russia, 58;
  pietistic influence on, 58
  importance of German language,
  59
  services in North America, 59, 60-
  61, 80
Civil War, Russia, 175
Cold bedrooms, 160, 161, 162
Cookbooks, old handwritten, 273, 275
Cooking for threshers, 22, 197-200
Coldshack for threshers, 200
Corner room (*Akjstow*) in Mennonite
  house, 10
Courtship and marriage customs
  Vistula Delta, 139-140
  Russia, 140-149
  North America, 152-158
Crimea, 181, 188; see also Annenfeld
Curriculum, *Dorf Schule*, Russia, 39,
  42-43; rural schools, North
  America, 47-48
Czar, birthday of, 45; visits to
  Mennonites, 130

Danzig, 8, 34, 36, 37
Danzig, first Mennonite church, 57
Dining Room (*Atstow*) in Mennonite
  home, 10
Dominion Day, Canada, 129
Dowry, bridal, 139, 149, 156
Drogge, 130
Droschkje, 130
Drying fruit, 175, 246
Dubrovna, 113
Dung cakes for fuel, 24, 25

Easter bread (*Paska*), 114-117, 127
Easter eggs, history of and coloring,
  118-119, 128
Easter and holy week, Russia, 113-
  120; in North America, 125-129
Eastern Orthodox traditions and
  Mennonites, 79, 108-109, 113-118
Education, early Mennonite Russia,
  39-47; in North America, 47-55
Education, higher schools, Russia, 42
Epiphany, 82, 111
Estate manse, Mennonite, Russia, 12
Estate orchards and gardens, Russia,
  236

Fadawoage, 142
Fall season in Mennonite home, 179
Famine, Russia, 120, 161
Faspa, memories of, 63, 64, 66, 68, 71-74
Faspa song, 73-74
Flemish branch, Mennonite church,
  35, 139
Flour, sacks, uses for, 213; storage,
  245, 246
Food preservation, 245-249, 252-254
Frakturmalen und Schönschreiben,

Russia, 42
Fria (bridegroom), 145, 152
Frisian Mennonites, 34; Frisian-style
  house, 18
Front entry (*Faastow*) in Mennonite
  house, 10
Fuel, cheap
  corn cobs, 25, 112, 213,
  cow chips, 25, 213, 222,
  flax, 20, 22,
  grass, 24, 213,
  manioc trunks, Paraguay, 22,
  straw, 24, 213

Gardens, Mennonite
  vegetables and flower, 11, 64, 169,
  170, 232-235,
  Dutch influence on, 11, 232, 237;
  see also orchards and berries
German, Low, see Low German
Gesangbuch mit Noten, 64
Gnadenfeld (village), Russia, 43, 57,
  58, 107-108, 114, 115-116, 125, 140,
  146, 181, 183, 233, 235, 247
Golden era, Russia, 12, 119-120
Grassburner ovens, 17, 22, 170;
  diagram of, 22
Grasshoppers, 176-177, 188, 214
Great room or living (*Grootestow*) in
  Mennonite house, 10, 39, 47, 79,
  141, 142, 145, 226
Grundonnerstagkringel, see Green
  Thursday
Gymnasium, Girls' Russia, 42

Hail storms, 214
Halbstadt (village), 67; business
  school, 42
Hallelujah *Schöner Morgen*, 60,61,64
Handwork, women's, 86, 161, 162, 214
Hanseatic League, 35
Harvest festival, Mennonite, Russia,
  134-135, 183-184
Harvest, wheat, see wheat harvest
  and threshing
Heubuden (village), West Prussia, 139
High schools, Mennonite, Russia, 42
Hochfeld (village), Russia, 245
Hollanderdorfer (Dutch villages),
  Vistula Delta, 14
Holy Saturday, Russia, 114-115
Holy Week in Russia, 113-120; in
  North America, 125-129
Hops for yeast, 238
House floors, 7, 15, 227
House, Mennonite, diagram of, 9
House raising bee, 13-14
Houses, Paraguay, 15

Ice cream, homemade, 136, 174, 199
Ice skating, 161, 162
Independence Day, U.S.A., 135-137
Immigrant houses, 1874-1875, 186
Immigration delegation, 1873, 185

Immigration, Russian Mennonites, 1874, 184-188
Institut fur Niederdeutsche Sprache, 37
Ironing, and flat irons, 24, 223, 224; mangling, 216, 224

Jugendverein, 65

Kafir bread, 21
Kansas state milita, exemption from, 186
Kesterbedersche, Vistula Dela, 140
Kitchen (*Kjaak*) in Mennonite house, 10
Kjast Tauntes, 146, 147
Korochun, Russian agricultural celebration, 108
Krimmer Mennonite Brethren, 67, 185
Kruschkjes, (wild pears), 170
Kuban, 89-90, 111, 116-117, 124, 131, 184, 203, 233, 236
Kutscha, 142

Lard, quantities at butchering, 114
Lepp, Peter, builds threshing machine, 181
Literary programs, school socials, North America, 53-54
Little room (*Kjleenestow*) in Mennonite house, 10, 17
Log houses, Canada, 12
Low German language, history of, 34-37; dictionary for, 37
Lunches, school, North America, 51-52
Lupushorst (village), Vistula Delta, 256
Lutheran pietists and Mennonites, 58
Lutherans and Mennonite village, 58, 141

Madchenschule, Russia, 42, 170
Makhno, Nestor, 237
Manitoba, early Mennonite education, 47-48
Mangling, 216, 224
Marion (Kansas) *Record* and Mennonite gardens, 237
Marriage, see courtship and marriage
Maundy Thursday or Green Thursday, 113
May Day, Russia, 130
Mennonite Agricultural Association (*Mennobschevsto*), Russia, 117, 181
Mennonite Brethren Church, beginning of, 58; in Russia, 115; in Hillsboro, Kansas, 60; in Ingalls, Kansas, 65
Menus, Mennonite, for holidays, harvest and buterching, 256-269; daily menus in Russia, 258-260
Mesthupe, 24
Mexico, Mennonite hospitality in, 268-269
Miagrope (copper cauldron) in Mennonite house, 23; many uses of, 116, 175, 203, 208, 222
Midsummer's Eve, 134
Midwives, 214-215, 230
Missionary festival, Coldowa, 57
Molotschna, 11, 24, 36, 39, 57, 67, 114, 120, 130, 140, 181, 235, 257

Molotschna Low German dialect, 36
Moltschna school memories, 43-44
Moon planting, 238
Morello cherries in Mennonite orchards, 236
Mummers, Russia, 110
Munich, Germany, refugee camp, 150
Music and instruments, early Mennonite church, 58, 60, 61

Nach-Hochzeit (after-wedding reception), Canada, 157
Napoleon's army in Vistula Delta, 202
Netherlands, 34, 35
Newspapers in Mennonite home, 162
Newton, Kansas, 129; and Santa Fe Railroad, 185
New Year celebration in church and home, 104-112
Nikolaipol, Russia, 143
Nokjast (wedding reception), Russia, 146

Orchards, Mennonite, 143, 175, 176, 187, 235-237, 239-241
Organs in eary Mennonite church, 58
Osterwick (*Ofenbank*) in Mennonite house, 10, 17
Ovens, brick and clay, 17-20

Pantry (*Koma*) in Mennonite house, 10, 253
Paraguay, food preparation, 230; house building, 15; making mud bricks, 230; pioneering in, 230; ovens, early, 21-22
Paska (Easter bread), 114,117 , 126, 127
Pentecost, Russia, 124-125; and decorating the barn, 125
Peppermint drops as medicine, 73
Picnics, 44-45, 137
Pietsch, 17-18
Pioneering Mennonite women, Canada, 12, 14, 19; in North America, 12, 161, 176, 177, 188, 213, 222-224, 228, 248
Plautdietsch, see Low German
Polterabend (wedding eve celebration), 144, 155, 156
Pork vs. beef in Mennonite menus, 204
Portselkje, fritters for New Year, baking of, 105, 107; and nummers in Russia, 107; poem for children, Vistula Delta, 107
Prachakuake (beggar's cookies) for star boys, Russia, 111
Prairie, grass, 24, 188, 213; loneliness of, 188, 214; winds, 188, 214, homes on, 12-13;
Prayer, in church, 65; in High German, 36; at meals, 258; at New Year, 108
Prussian Consul, Berdyanski, 184
Pysanky (Russian Easter eggs), 116, 318

Railroad, Santa Fe and Mennonite immigration, 1873-1875, 184, 188
Red Star steamer, 186, 189
Reinland, Manitoba, school curriculum, 29; old village homes today, 14

Revolution, Russian, 46, 49, 80, 111, 120, 144, 160
Rosental (village), 113
Rowhouses, Frisian style Mennonite houses, 8
Russians singing, 115, 116, 174, 183
Russian Orthodox customs and Mennonites, see Eastern Orthodox

St. Johannes' Day, Vistula Delta, 134
St. Martin's Day and Mennonites, 135
Santa Claus, 86, 90
Saturday in the Mennonite home, 182; baking, 227; chores, 226; cleaning, 226-227; family baths, 228; shopping and socializing, 186, 229
School of commerce, Mennonite, Russia, 42
Schools, in Vistula Delta, 39; in Russia, village and high, 39-46; in North America, early rural, 47-55
Seasons of the year in the Mennonite home, 159, 179
Semlin, Serrei or *Saraj*, pioneer dugout house, 11, 214
Servants in Mennonite household, Russia, 10, 12, 81, 82, 109, 116, 117, 118, 124, 170, 174
Seven Sleeper's Day, Vistula Delta, 134
Sewing circle, 60
Sewing for the family, 80, 89, 214
Shivarees, North America, 151
Siberia, 47
Simons, Menno, 35
Sleeping bench (*Schlafbanke*), 10
Smoking pork, 17, 208
Soap, homemade, 225
Sod bricks, making, Paraguay, 15, 230
Sod ovens, Paraguay, 21
Songbook, first German, Vistula Delta, 36
Sowing tradition at Easter, Russia, 118
Spoaheat (hearth) in Mennonite house, 22
Spring cleaning, 169
Star boys, Russia, 78, 111
Steinfeld (village), Russia, 275
Stille Bilder, Christmas program, 46
Stove, Mennonite grassburner, 17; diagram for, 22
Stove(s), wood burning, 23-24; warm piglets, calves, chicks, newborn triplets, 24
Stove, pot-bellied in schools, 48, 50
Sugar cubes and *Faspa* customs, 73, 127, 146, 149
Sugar, scarcity of, 73, 127
Summer kitchen (*Sommakjaak*) in Mennonite house, 17, 22, 147, 175
Summer room (*Sommastow*) in Mennonite house, 10
Sunday, activities, dinners, games and visiting, 63-68; see also *Faspa*

Teacher training, Russia, 39
Thanksgiving celebration (*Ernte Dank Fest*), Russia, 183-184
Threshing, see wheat farming and harvest
Threshing machines, early, 181, 182,

189, 190, 191
Threshing stones, 182, 189
Thunderstorms, 66
Trundle beds, 161
Turkey Red wheat, 12, 181, 187, 188; export from Russia, 181; imports to United States, 1900, 188

Umbitter (matchmaker) Vistula Delta, Russia, 139, 149

Vorsanger (chorister) in Mennonite church, 58

Waffle irons, 17
Wall bed (*Himmelbett*), 8
Washing clothes, 215, 222, 224

Washing dishes, 66, 72, 88, 227
Wedding customs, see courtship and marriage
West Friesland, 35
Wheat and barley blessing, Russia, 108, 109
Wheat farming and harvest, in Russia, 181-184; in North America, 185-200; and 1874 immigrants, 186-187, 188, 189; and women, 197-200
Willow switch tradition, Russia, 117, 118
Windows (*Fenstre*) in Mennonite house, 11
Winter activity, Mennonite home, 160-152
Women, and harvest, 136, 183, 191,

197-200; build ovens, 19-20; stack grain bundles, 199; and hard work, 213-216, 222-224, 226-228, 230
Wood-burning stoves, see stoves
Woodpile, 25
World War I, 120, 237
World War II, 120, 145

Yard (*Hoff*) of Mennonite house, 11

Zagradovka, 110
Zentralschule, Chortitza, 42, 170
Zur Heimat, regarding 1878 Kansas harvest, 189

About the Author

Norma Jost Voth's grandparents were among the original Mennonite settlers who came to Kansas from the Ukraine in 1874. Good Russian Mennonite food has always been at the center of their family celebrations and seasonal activities. Aunts and cousins exchanged recipes and talked food as much as they ate it.

In addition to *Mennonite Foods and Folkways, Volume I*, Norma Voth is the author of five books about holiday baking. She lives with her husband in San Jose, California, where they are active in a ministry to prisoners and their families.